Assurance and Warning

ASSURANCE
ASSURANCE
ASSURANCE
ASSURANCE
AND
WARNING
WARNING
WARNING
WARNING

Gerald L. Borchert

BROADMAN PRESS
Nashville, Tennessee

Unless otherwise noted, Scripture translations are the author's from the Greek. Scripture quotations marked (GNB) are from the *Good News Bible,* the Bible in Today's English Version. Old Testament: Copyright © American Bible Society 1976; New Testament: Copyright © American Bible Society 1966, 1971, 1976. Used by permission. Scripture quotations marked (KJV) are from the King James Version of the Bible. Scripture quotations marked (NIV) are from the HOLY BIBLE *New International Version,* copyright © 1978, New York Bible Society. Used by permission. Scripture quotations marked (RSV) are from the Revised Standard Version of the Bible, copyrighted 1946, 1952, © 1971, 1973.

Library of Congress Cataloging-in-Publication Data

Borchert, Gerald L. 1932-
  Assurance and warning.

  1. Assurance (Theology)—biblical teaching.
2. Warnings—Biblical teaching. I. Title.
BS680.A86B67 1987   225.6   86-30999
ISBN 0-8054-1011-2

To
Mark and Timothy

Preface

The subject of assurance and warning is a theme that has flowed in my spiritual veins ever since I became aware of the Lord Jesus in my life. In my pilgrimage as a Christian, I have tried most of the easy answers to the Christian tension. I have learned as a student, a lawyer, a preacher, a missionary, and a professor that easy answers do not adequately represent the perspective of the Bible. My earnest prayer is that this study will assist Christians to look again to the Bible and to Christ Jesus, our Lord, for an answer to the great tension of security in their lives.

In completing this work, I stand indebted to many people. First, I express my sincere gratitude to several of my colleagues at The Southern Baptist Theological Seminary who encouraged me to undertake this work in the wake of so many concerns in our denomination over the security issue. They pointedly asked me for a balanced biblical study on the subject. I have not sat down at my desk without such a prayer crossing my mind each time I approached this work. I hope their desire is partly fulfilled in this book.

Second, I continue to be very grateful to President Roy L. Honeycutt and Dean G. Willis Bennett for their continuing support of my writing and research projects and to the staff of the typing pool who have seen a great deal of Jerry Borchert. Particularly in this project do I thank Cindy Meredith who transferred my difficult scribbling to the computer keyboard.

I also express my heartfelt gratitude to my dear friends in the administration and faculty at Southwestern Baptist Theological Seminary who graciously welcomed me as a visiting professor for a semester while I wrote one of the chapters of this book.

My sincere prayer is that this study will direct readers to the biblical texts to discover again the tension between the divine and the human elements in salvation. It is also my hope that readers will watch for the marvelous balance that is presented by the biblical writers. My dream is that readers will then use the model of the biblical balance as a pattern for their way of thinking about Christian faith and matters of Christian life.

At this point I should mention for the sake of my readers that I believe it would be very helpful if you would keep a copy of the Bible at your fingertips. I have worked directly from the Greek New Testament, and my translations have been included purposely to help you sense what I believe are the biblical writers' intentions. My goal is that you, the readers, might sense more clearly the meaning of the inspired texts.

A word of special indebtedness belongs to my dear wife, Doris Ann, who as a colleague in the School of Christian Education at Southern is my companion critic. She has endured many of my absences and countless hours of my work on manuscripts. Yet her constant concern for clarity in communication has made this academician very sensitive to readers. I trust her warnings have kept me from engendering a great deal of theological fog into an already cloudy situation.

Finally I am herewith publicly expressing my gratitude to God for our two sons, Mark and Timothy, who have taught me much about the necessity of balancing both assurance and warning in life and who desire that their lives might count for God's kingdom. To them I dedicate this study. They have reminded me time and again of the many Christians in various places who struggle to be authentic Christians in the sight of our Lord.

Contents

1
The Question of Assurance and Warning

Acknowledging the Biblical Tension

The hijacking of planes, terrorist bombings, endless hostage problems, and rampant thievery mark an era in which security has become a major concern for the Western world. Society's uneasiness spills over into the church as Christians struggle for a sense of security in Christ. Easy answers and simple slogans may be happily dispatched to calm the troubled troops, but the uneasiness frequently persists because life does not readily fit into convenient formulas of security.

Dealing with the frustrating tension between the perfection of God and the imperfection of humans is one of the great themes of the Bible. That tension is in no way reduced for us in our lives when we append to our names words like *the Reverend, Doctor,* or *Professor.* Indeed, I remember one incident in my life which made that reality rather clear. During my early tenure as a dean of a theological seminary, I received a letter from someone of another denomination addressed to "The Very Reverend Doctor Gerald L. Borchert." As this fourth generation Baptist pondered that politely addressed "high church" letter, I was struck with a sense of incredible unworthiness in the presence of the only One who is truly "very holy." While we as humans receive many polite titles in the course of our lives, unless we are deluded, we recognize that our human titles of grandeur do not reduce the tension that we feel as sinful mortals in the presence of an impeccable God. Titles do not really bring assurance or security to us.

The tension of our sinfulness is never fully eliminated even when

11

we become Christians. It is present in every Christian's life although we may not admit it. Indeed, even our concerns for assurance and our discussions on security reveal the existence of this tension. Many Christians become extremely anxious when the issue of security is raised, unless they can be given a comforting and assuring word that their thoughts on security are not in fact being examined. We long for assurance, but we do not always look for it in the right places.

Many Christians adopt *convenient formulas* like "once saved, always saved" as a shorthand statement of their concern for assurance, even though it is really not a biblical statement. They may even be supported in their views by a contemporary writer like R. T. Kendall.[1] Slogans, however, need to be employed with great care because they may in fact communicate patterns of thought that are really foreign to the Bible.

For example, in Kendall's attempted defense of this thesis, he has created two distinct categories of Christians in 1 John: those who are merely saved and those who are blessed by the Lord because they have been faithful. Moreover, he has viewed sinning in 1 John as temporary sinning.[2] These categories are impositions on the text. He seems to have little concern about ethics or life patterns and has argued for the protection of the believer "no matter what sin (or absence of Christian obedience)" might have been present.[3] I think he has imposed a very rigid Calvinism on the Bible that would astonish many Calvinists.[4] Kendall seems unable, perhaps because of a mathematical mind-set, to tolerate the tension in the Bible.

The other side, I believe, is equally true. Discussions on apostasy usually trouble believers, and most of them should because of the way they are formulated. The formulations are often as unbiblical as the slogan "once saved, always saved." The term *apostasy* is basically an English construct from the Greek verb *apostēnai* (*aphistēmi*). It is a transliterated word rather than a translation. When scholars transliterate a word like *baptizō* into "baptize" rather than translate it, they may create a whole set of meanings that can be read into the word so that it is used as a technical term. Does "baptize" really mean to sprinkle or pour? The technical term does not answer the question precisely. The question that faces one in interpreting any particular text is to determine whether the technically created term applies to the passage under discussion. For my part, I consider the term *apostasy* to be misleading and not representative of the great biblical tension between assurance and warning.

Selecting an Appropriate Method for Study

Given these problems, a suitable method for studying this tension is needed. Frequently biblical texts have been lifted out of context and used to support either one side of the issue or the other. But without the context to guide the interpretations, the biblical phrases can be made to say whatever we wish them to say. Such a phenomenon is unsatisfactory.

My goal dictates my method. I have made a conscious decision to present the ideas of assurance and warning in the framework of selected New Testament books. I have chosen to discuss three books: an epistle, a Gospel, and a sermon. The form of each book has something to tell us about interpretation, and we need to pay attention to the form of each book. The books also represent three important perspectives. In formulating our ideas on assurance and warning, we need at least these three perspectives.

The first perspective is that of Paul. It seemed most natural in dealing with Paul to choose 1 Corinthians because the issues of Christian living are in the forefront of the epistle. The confidence and warning in this epistle mark it as a model of Paul's understanding on the subject. The Johannine perspective is treated next. I could, of course, have selected to study 1 John because of its strong statements on both assurance and warning. It certainly would have been a shorter and an easier task. But the Gospel of John contains these elements, and more. It identifies the great theological issues with the life of Jesus and thus provides illustrations of the meaning of our theological views. Moreover, the Gospel contains some of the great texts which have been involved in the controversies on the present subject. Finally the perspective of Hebrews is included because the reader would be justly disappointed if I omitted from this study the most debated texts in the New Testament.

The Gospel of John has frequently been pitted against Hebrews in arguments even by new Christians who struggle to understand their faith. Paul has been used by both sides to strengthen the cases being made. The selection, therefore, should prove to be helpful to the reader because it provides a basis for developing a fairly composite view of the Christian perspective on assurance and warning.

Dealing With Matters of Background

As we turn to discuss these three New Testament books, we must remember that they were not written in a vacuum. To understand the books adequately, therefore, means we need to know as much background information about them as possible. To understand the setting helps greatly in sensing the correct meaning of the words which were written. With each book I have summarized very briefly the general issues of introduction. These matters have been placed early in the discussions of each chapter in smaller type to alert the reader that they are background matters which are assumed. If the reader requires further information related to these issues, bibliographical references are available in the notes. Special background matters, such as social conditions which might affect the interpretations of a particular text, are discussed in the immediate context of the text.

One area of background study which requires further comment, however, concerns the Old Testament. The Old Testament, particularly the Greek version (the Septuagint = LXX), was the Bible of the New Testament writers. The Old Testament stories and ideas formed a kind of seedbed out of which much of the church's understanding of Christ and Christian theology has sprung. One cannot understand the New Testament adequately without an appreciation of the faith of Israel. Throughout the interpretations of 1 Corinthians, John, and Hebrews, therefore, a concerted effort has been made to remind the reader of the Old Testament themes and stories that lie behind the texts of the New Testament.

Of particular importance to the topic of assurance and warning stands the formative experience of Israel in the Exodus. It was an event initiated by God; accordingly, the divine perspective permeates the entire episode from the calling of Moses (Ex. 3—4) to the period of plagues (Ex. 7:8 to 12:36), the leading of God by a pillar of smoke or fire (Ex. 13:21-22), and the destruction of Jericho at the entrance into the Promised Land (Josh. 6). But throughout the entire story, there was a very human dimension as well. The weakness of humanity likewise permeates almost every aspect of the story from the excuses of Moses concerning his inability to speak (Ex. 3:11; 4:1,10,13) to the people's failure of obeying God in collecting and keeping manna (Ex. 16:20), their construction of the golden calf (Ex. 32:1-10), their murmurings (Ex. 16:1-12) and rebellions in the wilderness (Ex. 15:24; 16:2; Num. 11:1), their refusal to enter the Promised Land at Kadesh (Num. 13:25 to 14:28), their disobedience at Jericho and the resultant trouble at Ai (Josh. 7).

The story of Israel's faith is a story of weakness and failure, whether it involved a scheming Jacob, a disobedient Saul, an immoral David, a terrified Elijah, or a rebellious Jonah. The story is a tale of woe that involved destruction and exile. Israel was consistent in her pattern, which was highlighted in the later rejection of the Messiah.

But the hero of the Old Testament is not a Moses or a David or a Daniel or even an Abraham. The hero of the Old Testament is God! *God* called Abraham and Moses and Gideon and David and, indeed, the people of Israel. God assured them, in repeated encounters, that He wished them good and not harm. God's constant goal was to be their God and for them to be a faithful people. His pattern in dealing with them was one of continual warning and of periodic judgment.

In spite of the people's failures, however, God sought again and again to renew them to their place of acceptance in His sight. He reminded them repeatedly of their relationship to Him through their worship patterns of sacrifice and their prophets who spoke the word of the Lord. They were a people with whom God had made a *covenant*, and God would not break His covenantal agreements with His people.

But what about God's people? Did they keep the covenant? Were they faithful? Was the covenant only one-sided, or was it two-sided? Did God make the covenant without any concern for the response of His people? Or did He reaffirm His covenant with each new generation? Why was it necessary to address the covenant not only to Abraham but also to Isaac and Jacob and later to Saul and to David and to Solomon?

Perhaps the answers to these questions were most clearly perceived by the great prophet Jeremiah when he pointedly reminded Israel that *all declarations of God with humanity were conditional.* God's judgments of people are conditioned on their lack of repentance while God's blessings of people are conditioned on their consistency of obedience. A change in either one, Jeremiah announced, meant a change in the way God dealt with people (Jer. 18:7-11).

As human beings we are usually not overjoyed with the idea that God pays attention to the way we live. We would just as soon that God would set up some system for our assurance and let us work with it. Systems we can deal with—whether it means walking the aisle to join a church, being baptized, or offering sacrifices according to Israel's pattern. We like systems. But Israel received its answer to easy systems of assurance. The prophets and the psalmists made it indelibly clear. Sacrifice without a humble heart before God and a caring spirit for others was an empty system which was as hollow as the hollow commitments of the worshipers (for example, Amos 5:21-24; Hos. 6:6; Isa. 1:10-17; Mic. 6:6-8; Jer. 7:21-26; and Ps. 51:16-17).

God wanted and still wants obedient lives not just systems for placating His anger. God has always been the forgiving God. The stories of the Old Testament do speak of the anger of God being kindled against Moses (Ex. 4:14) and the people of Israel (for example, Num. 11:1,10; 25:4; Josh. 7:1; Judg. 2:14,20). But the God of the Old Testament was pictured best as One who was slow to get angry and One who if He was angry at His people did not want to stay angry (for example, Ps. 103:8-9; 145:8-9).

The warnings of the Old Testament, therefore, were intended to be redemptive. God's goal was to build a faithful people. He began with Adam and Eve, but they failed. He began again with Noah and his family; however, they failed too. He began yet again with Abraham and his offspring. They also went astray. But in the midst of these failures, God assured His creatures that He would not abandon His human enterprise because of human failure. Even in the pangs of the Exile, God had a message of comfort and hope for His people (Isa. 40:1-11).

While a major contextual study on assurance and warning in the

Old Testament needs yet to be written, the pattern of tension is clear. This pattern I am convinced was genuinely understood by the writers of the New Testament. The tension between God and Israel was the womb from which the New Testament writers birthed their views on assurance and warning.

The inspired writers of the New Testament were schooled in the faith of Israel, even if some of them were not Jews. They knew that God had been working with a people who were rebellious and disobedient. They knew that God had continually sought to restore those people to an authentic relationship with Him, and they knew that the prophets longed for the day of the new heart (for example, Jer. 31:31-34; Ezek. 36:26-27; compare Ps. 51:10).

Facing the Question of Assurance and Warning

The New Testament writers interpreted the new era as beginning with the coming of Jesus. But they also recognized that the church was not born perfect or complete. One only needs to refer to the Corinthian church as proof of the church's sinfulness and imperfection.

The New Testament writers did not hide their heads in the sand and pretend the church was something it was not. They faced the reality of Christian imperfection and provided a word from the Lord to their situations. The word was usually a twofold message: *assurance and warning.*

The writings of the New Testament seek to deal realistically with the tension between God and humanity in the light of Christ's redeeming work. But many questions may arise in the minds of readers. For instance: What is the significance of the coming of Jesus as it applies to the personal relationship of a Christian to God? How did the New Testament writers deal with it? Since we as Christians assert that there has been a shift in the pattern between God's dealings with Israel and with the church, how does that shift affect the way we live? What did the New Testament writers have to say about it? What does it mean for us as Christians both to *look back* to the decisive act of God in Christ's coming to earth and also to *look forward* to Christ's coming in glory? How does this double look touch where we live? What did the New Testament writers have to say about it?

The above questions are only a sampling of the many that probably have come to you at one time or another. You may have others which, before you proceed further in reading, you may wish to write down on a piece of paper and keep before you as you continue with this study. Such questions are not at all illegitimate. Jesus came to deal with the issues of life.

The divinely inspired writers were thoroughly involved in the questions of life. Their writings were not academic exercises. They were concerned about the lives of people. Concern for the questions of life is reason enough to turn to the New Testament and examine the profound interplay of assurance and warning in 1 Corinthians, John, and Hebrews.

Notes

1. See R. T. Kendall, *Once Saved, Always Saved* (Chicago: Moody Press, 1985; originally published by Houghton & Stoddard, 1983.)

2. Ibid., p. 113.

3. Ibid., pp. 41–43.

4. For a perceptive critique by a Calvinist see Iain H. Murray, "Will the Unholy be Saved?" *The Banner of Truth* 246 (1984): 1-15.

2
Assurance and Warning in 1 Corinthians: An Epistolary Style

Whenever Christians consider the subject of salvation, the name of Paul will be found somewhere in the forefront of the study. Certainly the apostle to the Gentiles stands out as one of the most dynamic thinkers in the history of Christendom. Moreover, as I have said to my students for over a quarter of a century, if Protestantism were to choose a patron saint, it would doubtless have to be the passionate Jew from Tarsus.

To imagine any human other than Paul who embodied more the combination of evangelistic zeal for Christ and perceptive thought about the significance of the gospel is difficult. Paul's fervor for the Lord "carried him across an empire in the days when sailing ships were hardly more than modern lifeboats."[1] From the twenty-seven works that encompass our canonical New Testament—the standard of Christianity—thirteen letters start with the name of "Paul."

Luke wrote a great deal about Paul in the Acts of the apostles. There we are told of Paul's remarkable transformation (Acts 9:1-31) and of the fact that he raised a dead man at Troas (Acts 20:9-12). We learn that he healed a possessed woman and was miraculously freed of chains in Philippi (Acts 16:16-28). We find that he was called a "god" at Lystra (Acts 14:12) and that he created an economic crisis and a riot at Ephesus (Acts 19:23-40). We discover that he caused a major Temple incident in Jerusalem (Acts 21:27-36). And if tradition is correct, finally, after many beatings and incarcerations, he reportedly died the death of a martyr in Rome—the center of the empire.[2] By whatever rubric one might use to describe him, Paul was hardly an unexciting, ordinary person.

Moreover, no matter what position you, the reader, may take on introductory matters concerning Paul's Epistles, you would have difficulty denying the fact that sheer intellectual genius stalks many of the pages of those letters. Perhaps an experience from my time in doctoral studies will illustrate what I mean. Ashley Montigue, a scholar scarcely known for his attachment to Christianity, when visiting Princeton, announced to a gathered assembly that he regarded Paul to be every bit as great a thinker as Plato or Aristotle. Even apart from any consideration of inspiration, therefore, I would argue that Paul was an incredible intellect.

But as an inspired servant of God, Paul's letters are more than mere documents of the intellect. They are messages to Christians of the first century which carry a significance far beyond their ancient settings. Their words have something profound to say to us today. To perceive correctly their meanings, however, the historical settings must be clearly understood. Otherwise the reader is liable to misperceive the nature of the inspired messages and miss the point of Paul's tight logic.

Sometimes twentieth-century, Western Christians have difficulty thinking in the categories of persons from the ancient Jewish world like Paul who was trained in the technicalities of rabbinic arguments and who then became a missionary to the Hellenistic world with all of its social and philosophical implications.[3] Western Christians must try to understand ancient people's beliefs and fears in all types of fates, spirits, principalities, powers, and gods who were thought to occupy their bodies and regulate their activities.[4]

Our task of interpretation is perhaps made a little easier by the fact that we have witnessed within the context of our so-called sophisticated era the growth of many spiritist and demonic movements. This development can be closely aligned with the growing insecurity we feel today. We have become frustrated by the haunting realities of nuclear bombs, earthquakes, drug problems, terrorist attacks, and kidnappings. We may have the scientific know-how to land on the moon, but we cannot quite discover the secret of peace and security. I believe Paul's letter to an ancient church may have something to say to us if we will study it carefully.

To obtain the perspective of Paul on the subject of assurance and warning, I have selected the letter of 1 Corinthians for discussion. I believe it possesses most of the qualifications which are necessary to obtain an adequate representation of the way in which Paul's thinking emerged on this subject. His thoughts are clearly contextualized in a genuine church setting. He was not arguing, like we so often do, about the intellectual question of apostasy or security. Paul was dealing with an actual church context where the people's lives were, to say the least, causing him some problems or nightmares. The way he dealt with these people and their problems can be very instructive for us. His ideas and his way of treating the worrysome people of Corinth provide us with some very important lessons on the theme of assurance and warning in Paul.

Introductory Issues

The Pauline Corpus

The Pauline authorship of 1 Corinthians is not doubted among scholars. Even the skeptical F. C. Baur acknowledged that 1 and 2 Corinthians, Galatians, and Romans were genuine.[5]

The Pauline corpus can be conveniently divided into four parts, according to subject matter. The first part contains the soteriological (salvation) letters: 1 and 2 Corinthians, Galatians, and Romans. The Christological letters (about Christ) form the second part: Philippians, Colossians, and Ephesians. Because of temporal attachments, Philemon is usually treated by modern scholars with this group. Third are the eschatological letters (about the coming of Christ and the end of time): 1 and 2 Thessalonians. And fourth are the ecclesiological (pastoral leadership) letters: 1 and 2 Timothy and Titus.

Paul's letters in the New Testament were not organized primarily according to date of writing but according to subject matter. *The collectors of our New Testament did not think chronologically but thematically.*[6] They placed the salvation letters first, the letters about Christ second, the letters about the end of time third, and the letters addressed to persons fourth (notice that the New Testament differs from many contemporary scholars about where Philemon is treated). The early medieval grouping of the Pauline books also included Hebrews which gave the corpus a total of fourteen documents—a very holy number! But for a further discussion of the relationship of Hebrews to the Pauline works see my discussion in Chapter 4 of this book.[7]

Geographical Considerations

When turning to the subject of the destination of 1 Corinthians, almost every Sunday School student is aware that the city of Corinth was the kind of place that caused eyebrows to be raised at its mention.[8] Indeed, the expression "Corinthian Girl" was an ancient cliché for prostitute.[9] Corinth, with its two seaports, was a haven for sailors on shore leave. The city's lack of moral standards was legendary. However, Strabo's well-known quotation to the effect that the temple of Aphrodite had a thousand courtesans or prostitute priestesses to serve the needs of the sailors may have been a convenient overstatement and part of Strabo's intrinsic desire to categorize places.[10]

The fact that the city was at the crossroads of Greece and at the midpoint of the shipping lanes between Asia Minor and Italy is an indication of just how significant and cosmopolitan it was. Lucius Mummius destroyed it in 146 BC because of its leadership role in the Achaean League's war with Rome. But in 44 BC Julius Caesar had it completely rebuilt and bestowed on it "colonial" status because of the site's strategic military and commercial importance. It was a booming success almost as soon as it was refounded. By the time of Paul, Corinth had become the capital of all Achaia (27 BC) and was the fourth largest city in the entire empire after Rome, Alexandria, and Ephesus.[11]

The intermingling of people at Corinth produced an environment of permissiveness. Syncretism in religion was also an accepted routine for the worshipers in this city which was filled with temples.[12] And pride in the well-being of the citizenry of this thriving ancient metropolis was scarcely an unexpected reality. As one reads 1 Corinthians, one cannot help but sense that the church people had drunk very deeply from the nectar of their environment.

Dating and Place of Origin

First Corinthians was probably written during Paul's third missionary journey. He stayed at Ephesus (1 Cor. 16:8) during that period. The time frame for the letter falls between AD 54 and 57, depending on one's chronology for Paul's life.[13] My preference is about the midpoint of that period.

How Many Corinthian Letters?

One of the issues related to this study concerns the number of letters Paul wrote to the church at Corinth. Even a hasty reading of 1 Corinthians indicates that it was not the first letter he had penned to that church. Paul indicated in this epistle that he had already written them an earlier letter in which he specifically informed them to avoid the company of Christians who practiced immorality (1 Cor. 5:9-11). Johannes Weiss and others have suggested that a fragment of that previous letter may be contained in 2 Corinthians 6:14 to 7:1 because those verses seem to break the contextual sequence of 2 Corinthians 6:13 and 7:2.[14] In evaluating this complex theory about all one can say with integrity is that there appears to be a kind of seam in 2 Corinthians at that point. But whether the break in the thought of Paul implies an editorial insert in the document is difficult at this point to determine. It is, from my perspective, even more speculative to attach these verses to a fragment of the earlier letter.

In addition to 1 Corinthians and whatever letter preceded it, Paul apparently made a difficult trip to Corinth (2 Cor. 2:1) in which there must have been a good deal of friction and little joy experienced between Paul and the Corinthians. Then he wrote another letter (2 Cor. 2:4). That letter was severe and would hardly fit the time frame or the context of 1 Corinthians. It probably needs to be regarded as a third letter written after 1 Corinthians and Paul's previously stated intention of visiting them (compare 1 Cor. 16:3-8). Counting 2 Corinthians then, it seems to me that Paul wrote at least four letters to the Corinthians, two of which have been lost or, as some scholars have suggested, were later edited into existing letters.[15]

Integrity of 1 Corinthians

The idea of editing raises the issue of the integrity of these letters. My concern is particularly with 1 Corinthians. Jean Héring and Walter Schmithals are convinced that 1 Corinthians is a composite work, although their reconstructions are quite different.[16] I, for one, am scarcely moved by their arguments.[17]

I would certainly agree that 1 Corinthians may not appear to be organized like a systematic theological textbook. Romans may seem to be more organizationally ordered than 1 Corinthians, but even Romans is not to be understood as a treatment of systematic theology. Paul wrote "occasional" letters.[18] These epistles primarily addressed issues affecting particular churches. For example, in 1 Corinthians Paul tended to jump from problem to problem as the issues related to the Corinthians came to mind. The structure of the letter was, therefore, determined by the issues. The attempts at systematizing the materials and dividing the letter into several separate letters have been, I believe, efforts to impose a foreign structure on the epistle. Its canonical form is quite intelligible as it stands, and it needs to be studied in that format. Indeed, I believe there is a sense of unity in the letter, and its natural flow needs to be perceived.

The Nature and Purpose of 1 Corinthians

Paul obviously had had a considerable amount of communication with respect to the Corinthian situation. Clearly he had received a letter of inquiry from the Corinthians themselves (1 Cor. 7:1), which seemingly raised some very important questions. They had requested Paul's perspective on appropriate sexual patterns, including relations between husbands and wives (7:1 ff.), and the role of men in marrying off their daughters (7:25 ff.). In addition, the Corinthians were apparently concerned about such matters as the legitimacy of eating meats offered to pagan gods (8:1 ff.), the pattern of worship in the church (11:2 ff.), and the place of spiritual gifts (12:1 ff.). These issues would have been enough to spark a reply.

Paul also had received a delegation from Corinth composed of leaders whom he must have regarded very highly because he praised the consistent hard work of Stephanas and people of similar commitment. Paul expressed heartfelt joy at the visit of Stephanus, Fortunatus, and Achaicus because it resulted in a refreshment or a revival of his spirit (16:15-18). One wonders, however, if there were not also a slight hook in Paul's words because those visitors were said to have provided for or filled up the Corinthians's deficiency (husterēma). The sense of Paul's refreshment, Conzelmann has argued, was not the result of financial support because such support would have negated Paul's claim in chapter 9 that he had not made use of his apostolic rights of support (9:15).[19] Nonetheless, while Paul may not have demanded nor sought apostolic rights of support, it seems to me that he wanted the Corinthians to recognize how uplifting in a difficult situation the refreshment of the visitors had been.

But the mention of difficult situations reminds us of the problem with which Paul began his letter. Reports had come from the household of Chloe that the Corinthians were entangled in a web of infighting (1:11). If Paul had no other reason to pen this letter, the problem of division was a sufficient reason to cause his apostolic blood to pump faster and the ink to flow. He knew that the Corinthians were on the verge of major problems because of factionalism and that they needed an authoritative word from their missionary father.

The letter the Corinthians received was probably more than they anticipated because it sketched for them some very needful counsel. The words of counsel moved between offering weak followers a sense of assurance and erring Christians a message of warning. Paul had sensed that something was inherently wrong with the way the Corinthians were practicing their Christianity. Paul did not begin his letter by answering their questions because, I maintain, the questions were symptoms of a more basic problem; he addressed that problem first.

Paul had an amazing ability to identify the heart of a problem and to focus attention on the real issue. I believe Paul's uniquely inspired sense in focusing issues has made 1 Corinthians so valuable for Christians today. We are hardly worried about meat offered to idols, and few women in the West have their heads and faces covered with veils, like I have often encountered in parts of the Muslim world. Yet there is something about 1 Corinthians and the way Paul dealt with the problems of those Christians that touches the core of what it means to be Christian. The warnings are not merely soundings from the past; the assurances are not simply ancient reminiscences. There is a vital interplay between the human and the divine dimensions in this book that mark it as one of the classics of our faith.

The letter was directed to a Christian's relationship with God and how that relationship ought to affect a Christian's relationship with other people. Many scholars have considered 1 Corinthians 13 an insert into the argument. I would hardly deny that chapters 12 and 14 seem to be a continuing argument on the subject of spiritual gifts. But I would strongly affirm that chapter 13 is not an unrelated insert from some reconstructed Hellenistic hymn on love.[20]

Chapter 13 expresses Paul's fundamental concern in this letter. In the matter of spiritual gifts, the failure of the Corinthians became most evident. What the Corinthians considered to be the divine dimension in their lives had in fact been twisted into an expression of the human dimension. The apostle of the cross and resurrection of Jesus could scarcely tolerate such a perversion of the gospel. His message in chapter 13 became the foundation for reckoning the real motive for Christian life. It is, therefore, an important key to understanding assurance and an incisive standard for perceiving warning. It was Paul's double-edged sword which divided between authentic life and pretense among Christians.

Organization of 1 Corinthians

Paul began this letter to the Corinthians with a typical epistolary introduction. He then attacked the Corinthian situation, in chapters 1 through 4, of divisions or factions in the church. He illustrated, in chapters 5 and 6, the plight of the Corinthians with tragic examples of the Corinthian life-style with reference to cases of sexual immorality and litigation. He turned next to the Corinthians' own questions about marriage; meat sacrificed to pagan gods; worship practices, including the roles of men and women; the Communion meal, and spiritual gifts. In this process he tied the examples of their tragic life-style to their own perturbing questions by emphasizing the theme of loving responsible Christian living. He discussed the crucial theological thesis of the resurrection of Jesus which formed a kind of climax to Paul's counsel. He concluded his letter by referring to an offering, notes concerning the missionaries' travel plans, and some significant final words of advice.

The Letter Called 1 Corinthians

A. Assurance and Warning
at the Beginning and End of 1 Corinthians

Can anything important be revealed from the beginning and the end of a letter like 1 Corinthians? In the case of the Gospel of John and the Book of Hebrews the answer is rather obvious. Both of those books have profound prologues which provide keys to interpreting them. They also contain well-conceived conclusions which offer additional clues. But what about a letter like 1 Corinthians?

THE BEGINNING OF 1 CORINTHIANS (1:1-9)

The beginning of 1 Corinthians sets the stage for understanding Paul's presuppositions. The epistle opens with the typical Hellenistic format.[21] In the simplest form the address is "X to Y Greetings." It is very similar to many contemporary office memos except that today the person addressed is usually identified first. But there is more in 1 Corinthians than a simple statement that Paul and Sosthenes were sending a letter to the Corinthians. Paul was an apostle, and his apostleship flowed from the fact that he believed himself to be a person called (*klētos*) through the will (*thelēmatos*) of God (1:1).

Not only was Paul called but also the people of Corinth to whom he addressed the letter were identified as people who were sanctified or made holy (*hēgiasmenois*) in Christ. Indeed, they were "called saints" (1:2). Having taught 1 Corinthians for many years, I have repeatedly asked my students: What was Paul doing? He was about to condemn the Corinthians for inappropriate behavior, including immorality, but he began his letter by calling them holy. Was Paul writing tongue in cheek? I doubt it very much.

To understand this statement by Paul, one must sense that Paul started with the God perspective. He realized that his mission and the very existence of the church at Corinth resulted from a divine calling. Thus, it was not a different Paul here than the Paul of Romans who wrote of the calling God (Rom. 8:28-30) or the electing God (Rom. 9—11). Paul's fundamental thesis was that salvation always begins with God. Paul's theology was not, as Bultmann emphasized, existential and man centered.[22] Paul's theology was Christ centered in the sense of God centered. Although he frequently spoke of living "in Christ," he knew that Christ was in God and that in the end God would be all and in all (1 Cor. 15:28).[23] Whenever Paul mentioned being "in Christ," Christ was the means by which he experienced the assurance of God.[24] Moreover, grace and peace—the Christian greeting[25]—were rooted in both the Father and the Son, not just the Son (1:3). Thanks for the Corinthians, therefore, was directed to God because God initiated the coming of Jesus (1:4).

Most Hellenistic letters followed the salutation with a thanksgiving section.[26] It was a polite way of beginning a written conversation. Seldom would one begin the body of a letter the way Paul began in Galatians 1:6—"I am shocked (*thaumazō*)" In that letter Paul came out of the corner fighting, and he was in no mood to spare the punches.

The Galatians had strayed from the message of salvation (Gal. 3:1-5), and Paul was not prepared to be polite. Galatians, then, is an epistle where from beginning to end Paul was fighting for the integrity of the gospel against false preachers.

But in 1 Corinthians, Paul had a different agenda. The integrity of the Christians themselves was at stake. They needed to recognize the authentic source of their calling. Therefore, in opening the body of the letter, Paul used the typical Hellenistic thanksgiving transition to spell out the foundation or basis of their calling as Christians. In this statement he reminded them that their knowledge of salvation or *gnōsis* was given to them in Christ Jesus. It was not something that they had either deserved or earned. They had become rich (*eploutisthēte*) in Christ as a gift (1 Cor. 1:5), benefitting from grace, and apparently some had even attained wealth and were flaunting it (compare 4:8).

Paul knew how the Corinthians had become Christians. They had been confronted with the truth of Christ by testimony, and that truth had been confirmed in their own lives (1:6). In addition, the spiritual gifts which they possessed in abundance (1:7) and in which they took pride (compare 12:1-31) were in fact gifts which they did not acquire for themselves. Furthermore, their eschatological expectation of salvation which assured them of eternal life to the end (1:7-8) was the result of Christ's resurrection (15:1-57) and of God's faithfulness. It was not achieved through their puny efforts at righteousness. God had called them into community with His Son (1:9), and their perseverance was wrapped up in their relationship to God (1:8).

Those who are familiar with 1 Corinthians will recognize immediately that this thanksgiving statement is not a mere polite transition to the body of the epistle. Instead, it forms a clear summation of the basic concern expressed in the letter. But it is more. It is a revealing statement which locates where the answer to the problems of the Corinthians may be found. Indeed, it stands as a powerful statement of assurance that the answer must be found in Christ Jesus, the Lord.

THE END OF 1 CORINTHIANS (16:1-24)

If the beginning of 1 Corinthians provides a foundation for assurance, the astute reader probably has already asked about the ending. In chapter 16 one encounters an amazing series of statements which forces one to ask some hard questions about the Corinthians.

After challenging the Corinthian Christians to be responsible in giving, Paul discussed the matter of visiting them (16:5-12). First, he mentioned his own situation, and the reader gains the feeling that Paul was very tentative in his intentions. Although his desire was to go to Corinth, he was not prepared to do so at that time. Did he prefer to be in Ephesus, even though he had opponents there (16:8)? Then he told them to expect Timothy. But Paul sternly forewarned them not to mistreat Timothy and to send him on peacefully (16:10-11). Finally Paul noted that he had tried to get Apollos to visit them, but Apollos was just not ready to go (16:12). When I read statements like verses 5 to 12, I get the feeling that Corinth was quite low on the priority list of places the missionaries wanted to visit. Did they expect to be shunned? The church people from the capital city of Achaia (Southern Greece) were apparently a proud, self-centered bunch; all the missionaries seemed to have known it.

How different the situation was in Thessalonica, the capital of Macedonia (Northern Greece). Paul regarded the Christians there as models for all of the believers in Macedonia *and Achaia* (1 Thess. 1:7)—in fact for the whole world (1:8)! Paul's heart seemed to beat passionately for them, and he pictured himself as their nurse (2:7) and father (2:11). Absence from them was hardly tolerable (3:1-5), and he rejoiced in their faithfulness when reports came to him (3:6-10).[27]

About the Corinthians, however, Paul seemed to have had quite a different feeling. He had to tell them to respect their leaders like Stephanas (1 Cor. 16:16). A spirit of independence seemed to prevail at Corinth. They seemed to be going their own way, choosing leaders who promoted rivalries and factions.

In this context, therefore, Paul's words of warning reverberate through time. An eschatological theme to these warnings can be seen in his words of caution to the Corinthians: "be alert," "stand steadfast in the faith," "live courageously," and "become strong" (16:13). Paul concluded his warnings by charging them to remember that everything they were *doing* ought to be done in love (16:14)! Moreover, as he took the pen from his scribe, he added a warning with his own hand that he was calling down a curse (*anathema*) upon anyone who failed to exemplify true love for the Lord (16:21-22).

Just as surely as assurance is the keynote of the opening words of 1 Corinthians, uneasiness and warning is the theme of chapter 16. The Corinthians may have been designated the church (*ekklēsia*) of God, they may have been declared holy in Christ Jesus, and they may have been called saints (1:2), but they were a very human people who desperately needed to be warned about their attitudes and conduct.

Yet Paul did not close this letter on a negative note. He believed in the power of God in spite of the Corinthian situation. Therefore, he summoned them to remember the coming of the Lord with an early Aramaic prayer-confession *Maranatha,* "Our Lord, come!" (16:22). Then he pronounced on them his benediction in the grace of the Lord Jesus (16:23). Finally he added his own commitment of love. Paul was their father in the faith; in spite of their faithlessness, he loved them in Christ and wanted them to know it (16:24).

B. Assurance and Warning
in the Midst of Factions (1 Cor. 1:10 to 4:21)

1. THE PROBLEM OF FACTIONS

Paul confronted the Corinthian problem by drawing attention to a report he had received from those associated with Chloe (1:11). The Corinthian church was troubled with factionalism. Whether the members had actually divided into parties, the Christians had taken to a kind of banner-carrying party spirit or to the choosing of champion's names in order to represent their causes. Their champions were people like Paul and Apollos and Peter (Cephas). Some apparently had the audacity to stick their noses in the air and claim that the champion of their group or view was Christ (1:12). Paul knew that such a spirit of fragmentation could easily destroy the church. Thus he pleaded for unity (1:10).

Paul also realized that mere exhortation to unity would hardly solve such a devastating problem. Therefore, he tackled the root of the Corinthians' disunity. They had forgotten the foundational element of their faith—the self-giving death of Jesus. Accordingly Paul asked them if he had been crucified for them or if they had been baptized in the name of Paul. The answer was obvious. They were merely using the names for their own purposes. They had in fact become proud windbags—Christians who were puffed up by their divisive ideas and by the feeling of power that came from impressing others.

While any attempt to identify these groups is speculation, one can imagine the type of people who were involved. Those who claimed Paul for their petty views were probably the traditionalists who said that they held to the truth as it always had been and who probably stressed typical founder syndrome arguments. The Apollos types were probably impressed with Alexandrian-type erudition and promoted the notion that they were the wisest people. The Cephas personalities were likely the legalists, and the so-called "Christ" types were probably those who saw themselves as spiritually superior. All of them were probably a bunch of "know-it-alls," who thought they had captured the vast universe of God's truth.

2. Paul's Alternative

Paul, however, knew how to put the entire picture into focus. He turned the Corinthians' attention to the cross and reminded them that he would not participate in their self-centered, clever, rhetorical arguments. He was not interested in emptying the gospel of its power by manipulating words (1:17). Instead, he proposed a sublime paradox which clearly defined the basic difference between the two opposing ways in the world: the one, the so-called worldly wise way of self-centered affirmation; the other, the so-called foolish Christian way of self-denial. Moreover Paul flatly warned the Corinthians to remember that the way of the cross may have seemed foolish to those who adopted the ways of the world but that it was foolish only to those who were in jeopardy of perishing. The way of the cross, however, actually brought an assuring sense of power to those who were being saved (1:18).

The wisdom, prestige, and power of the world was then not what it appeared to be. In fact, by employing a rather loose translation of Isaiah 29:14 (LXX), Paul reminded the Corinthians that the wisdom of the world was very transitory. He asked them to compare the divine perspective with their ideal models of human understanding.

From this perspective the wise man (sophist), the legalist (scribe), and the logician (the debater) were all just passing fancies (1:20). Even the best of their wisdom could hardly encapsulate the way of knowing God. Instead, God chose to spread divine wisdom among humanity by a pattern that seemed to lack even mere human sophistication—the foolish means of proclamation or testimony which called for believing (1:21).

Celsus, the well-known opponent of early Christianity, seized the statements in this context to argue that the God of Christians truly lacked nobility (compare 1:26) and that the only people to whom such a Deity would appeal were the "foolish, dishonorable and stupid"—namely, "slaves, women and small children."[28] Celsus, indeed, understood the radical nature of Paul's message and scoffed at it. The power-grabbing Corinthians also undoubtedly understood it and disliked it. Power-hungry Christians usually try to distinguish themselves from the Corinthian deviates, but to observant people the truth is evident.

Relying on earlier commentaries, John Polhill suggested that, for Paul, Christ made somebodies out of nobodies. Some interpreters have rejected such an analysis, but I think that there is an important point to be made here.[29] Paul's description of the early Christians seemed to imply a ragtag band. He argued that God had collected the weak and the foolish and had given them a new life that confounded the strong and wise of the world (1:27). He really made nobodies into somebodies (1:28) and in so doing rendered meaningless self-centered pride and boasting (1:29).

Furthermore Paul used himself as a model of the Christian way by refusing to enter into their petty bickering. He also reminded them that he had not followed the way of the philosophers in presenting the mystery of God through high-sounding syllogisms and clever verbalisms (2:1).[30] In looking for a convincing religious perspective, the Jews had sought signs of God's power and strength and the Greeks had desired the brilliance of convincing wisdom. Both, however, had rejected the logic of the crucified one (1:22). Paul would not deviate from the example of Jesus. Paul's own pattern was to show them his personal weakness and fear while refraining from the use of enticing rhetorical arguments. His reason was that he did not want them to exalt his human wisdom but to see beyond his humanness to the power of God (2:2-5).

If the Corinthians had perceived the power of God and the true nature of the crucifixion, they would have understood the real nature of the world and the inherent failure of the principalities and powers in the world to provide the answers to the issues of life. They would have been able to sense what the spiritual forces who opposed Jesus could not understand—the crucifixion of Jesus would prove to be the Achilles' heel for the forces of evil (2:6-8). God's logic was different than that of the world. And God would prove that even in the weakest infinitesimal part of Him there was more wisdom and strength than the world had ever imagined (1:25).

Paul also wanted the Corinthians to remember that God's power was working in those who loved God (2:9). He supported this claim by a scriptural passage. But he must have been quoting the text from memory because it is similar to the Greek (LXX) of Isaiah 64:4, yet it seems altered to fit the situation.[31] Nevertheless, there is little difficulty in following Paul's thought since he wanted the Corinthians to recognize that the amazing power of God was available to those that genuinely loved the Lord.

3. GOD'S SPIRIT AND THE CORINTHIAN IMMATURITY

By referring to the Spirit (a subject of vital interest to the Corinthians), Paul informed them of two matters concerning the Spirit and in so doing focused their attention on our concern for assurance and warning. He first highlighted the role of the Spirit in the process of revelation, and then he reminded them of the Spirit's incisive perception in all things (2:10).

Knowledge of God and of God's work among Christians has never been merely the result of human observation and intellectual skill. It is the result of the Spirit's work, and it is not programmable by human design but depends upon the working of the divine dimension in the sphere of humanity. Therefore, one must look not to the frail characteristics of humanity but to the consistent characteristics of God in order to perceive the significance of revelation. When one looks to God, one has tremendous reason for assurance concerning God's revelation in Christ.

But what about the Spirit's perceptive ability? Ah, that is an equally important matter. Indeed, in Paul's discussion with the Corinthians and bearing in mind their inconsistent living patterns, it was in fact a crucial factor. Since the Spirit understood the unfathomable reaches of God, there is nothing that the Spirit cannot perceive (2:10). This thesis of the inquiring power of the Spirit became Paul's means for introducing stern warnings to the Corinthians. It also became a derivative foundation for assurance.

Employing the ancient theme of the attraction of similarities (light understood or comprehended by light[32]), Paul differentiated between those who were directed by the spirit of the world and those led by the Spirit of God. Matters pertaining to God, he argued, could only be understood by the Spirit of God and by those who had received God's Spirit. Therefore, they should have been thinking like spiritual (*pneumatikoi*) people (2:11-13). Natural or psychic (*psuchikoi*) persons could hardly think like spiritual ones because they had not received characteristics that pertain to the Spirit (2:14). The Corinthians should clearly have been spiritual and should have evidenced spiritual characteristics in their lives. They, like Paul, had the "mind (*nous*) of Christ" (2:16)—an important theme which Paul developed in texts on renewal (Rom. 12:2) and on humility (Phil. 2:1-11).[33] Unfortunately the Corinthians were not living like spiritual people. Therefore, Paul castigated them as carnal or fleshly (*sarkinoi*). They might well have committed their lives to Christ, but one could hardly tell it. They were living like unregenerated pagans, and Paul did not hesitate telling them so. They were hardly out of the womb, so to speak, yet they were pretending to be mature. They should have been ready for solid food; but like the Christians in Hebrews 5:12-14, they were still in the nursing stage (1 Cor. 3:2).

The basis on which Paul judged the Corinthian Christians was not their impressive words but their unimpressive lives. He focused first on the Corinthians' *contentious spirit*. In self-righteousness they proclaimed themselves to be somebodies and in a factious spirit condemned others (3:4). No matter how important they thought they were, Paul exclaimed that they were nothing but breast-feeding infants in the faith. They were not much different than people of the world.

These words of Paul ought to send a spine-tingling warning up the back of every Christian whose lofty self-righteous words are a judgment upon the way they treat other Christians. The Corinthian problem raises its ugly head in many parts of the church today, as humans pretend to be the measure of God and seek to have everyone else bow to their canon of righteousness.

Paul's warning needs to be heard. Factionalism transfers a Christian's focus from the divine realm to the human. Paul understood this fact and condemned the Corinthians as still being oriented to the flesh (*sarkikos*, 3:3). Their attention was directed to human figureheads like Paul and Apollos, and they failed to recognize the servant nature of each of these personalities (3:5). Paul said that he and Apollos were workers in God's garden. Whether the workers planted or watered was not the issue. God made it possible for the plants to grow, and the Corinthians had missed the point of God's mission (3:6-9).

In case the Corinthians still had difficulty in understanding what he meant, Paul used another illustration. He likened the Corinthian situation to a building and himself to an architectural contractor (*architektōn*). The goal of the builder was to produce a building which would conform to the intentions of God. Paul asserted that he laid the foundation in Jesus Christ (3:11). He had no doubt that he had started the building correctly. Paul's concern was not with the foundation but with the work of the subcontractors. What kind of materials were they using? He knew that the building would be tested (3:13). The fires of hostility, persecution, and even the arena were coming; these pressures would test the essential nature of the Christians at Corinth. Paul wanted his church, his "building," to make it through the testing fire. He realized that the way the Corinthians were conducting themselves was disastrous. Therefore, he sternly warned them that in the day of testing they should expect a tremendous loss if they continued to build with their shabby materials (3:12-13,15).

Instead of destruction, Paul wanted the church to survive in strength. He wanted the Corinthians to receive from God the reward that comes from work that was well done (3:14). But even if they did not build well and even if very little of their construction finally survived, Paul consoled them with the assuring words that God was

faithful and would rescue them out of the devastating testing fire
(3:15). He wanted them to sense that God would care for them in
spite of the fact that their lives were not all God had hoped.

The concerned apostle, however, did not want the Corinthians to
take lightly their security in Christ. Apparently they were skilled at
manipulating words. So, to prevent any misunderstanding of his words
of assurance, Paul added another warning. His assuring words were
not meant to be interpreted as license either to destroy other Christians or to do anything that would injure or destroy themselves. All
Christians are to be viewed as temples of God. Therefore, Paul asserted
anyone who destroys God's temple will have to face the severe, destructive punishment of God (3:16-17).

4. HUMILITY AND THE MISSIONARY MODEL

Having clarified the destructive nature of their factions, Paul returned to reprimanding their foolish attempts at being the dispensers
of wisdom. How empty was their wisdom and boasting with God
(3:19-21). The Lord had given them the missionaries, the world in
which to live, and both a present and a future. They belonged to
Christ, and Christ belonged to God (3:22-23). So where was their
basis for pride? As Christians they had made a fundamental error.
They could talk a good line, but they had placed themselves at the
center of their universe. God belonged at the center! And where
God is the center, there is no room for human boasting and pride.

In support of this theme on humility, Paul used himself and Apollos
as examples. He wanted the Corinthians to picture the missionaries
as underrowers (*hupēretai*) to Christ. This concept of servanthood
comes from the low rank of people who rowed the ancient gallies
that plied the Mediterranean Sea. To be an underrower was to be
an assistant to a laborer. As it pertained to Christ, Paul viewed himself
an underrower (4:1).

As it pertained to them, however, he viewed himself as a steward
(*oikonomos*) or manager of God's mysteries, responsible to God for
the faithful exercise of his duties (4:1-2). Paul did not consider himself
answerable to their petty little criticisms of him (4:3). They had placed
themselves on a par with God in their judging, and he reminded
them very pointedly that God was the Judge. God knew the secret

thoughts of people; at the proper time, He would reveal people's actual purposes in life (4:4-5). God gave the real rewards, not the petty Corinthian critics. The Corinthians had a major lesson to learn about judging and criticizing others. Even for Christians today, that lesson is very hard to learn. We need enough trust in God to allow Him to be the Judge. He is quite capable of doing it! Our problem is that we think He does not act fast enough or that He will not do it the way we want it done. We are probably correct in that evaluation. But that is hardly God's problem. Our judgments are frequently not God's!

The Corinthians' pride had puffed them up like windbags. They needed to begin living according to biblical principles and *not criticize beyond what had been written in Scripture* (4:6). They became the measure of their judgment and not God; they were "fencing" their Bibles much like the Jewish rabbis had fenced the Torah.[34] The rabbis had made law upon law to protect the law. In so doing, they drew further and further from God who gave them the law. Paul had been educated in that way of thinking; but once he discovered Christ, he would permit *nothing* to come between him and the self-giving salvation in Jesus. To understand Christ was to recognize that life was an unearned gift (4:7).

If the Corinthians had understood the crucial nature of their lives in terms of gift, they would have come down from their lofty seats of judgment and would not have reckoned success in terms of this world's blessings. But they were proud of their economic successes and interpreted them as God's hand of blessing (4:8). Paul was not so sure about that evaluation and told them to reflect on how the missionaries were being treated. They were like people who were being exhibited "last of all" (4:9). Those familiar with the Roman games will recognize that this expression refers to those who were sentenced to death in the arenas and were brutally killed either by vicious gladiators or by ferocious animals as the "exciting" conclusion to the sporting events of the day. The missionaries experienced little of this world's successes. They were hungry, thirsty, poorly clothed, persecuted, worked hard, and frequently slandered. They were regarded as the dregs of the world (*perikathama*) and the garbage of humanity (*pe-*

ripsēma). The picture in 1 Corinthians 4:11-13 is hardly one that Madison Avenue would find worthy of promotion unless it was attempting to engender sympathy.

Yet sympathy was precisely what Paul *did not seek* (4:14). He did not want the Corinthians to feel remorse about him. He was perfectly secure in his relationship with the Lord Jesus. Instead, Paul wanted them to recognize him as their spiritual father; he wanted them to copy him, to be imitators (*mimētai*) of him (4:15-16)! Moreover, he was sending Timothy with his letter to be sure that they received this message and understood it. He wanted them to know that he would follow and that they needed to be prepared for his coming. Therefore, he closed this section with a warning. The windbags had better shape up (4:18) because when he came, he would not play games with them. They would have to choose between a whip and his gentleness (4:21). The way the warning ends makes clear what choice Paul preferred. The decision was theirs; Paul was ready to respond with either option.

C. Assurance and Warning
in the Corinthian Tragic Life-style (1 Cor. 5:1 to 6:20).

1. THE PROBLEM OF IMMORALITY (1 COR. 5:1-13)

Paul turned abruptly to a new topic: "I have heard that some horrible immorality is going on in Corinth" (5:1). It was so disgusting to Paul that he was sure pagans would have condemned it. One of the male members of the church had apparently been having sexual relations with his stepmother.[35] What embarrassed Paul even more was that the Christians at Corinth did not seem to be bothered by such incestuous behavior. Their high and mighty sense of freedom was simply astonishing.

When Paul encountered among Christians such a "criminal" state of mind, he set his jaw with firm determination and attacked the whole matter with the ferociousness of a wounded buffalo.[36] The ballooned arrogance of the Corinthians needed to be punctured, and Paul was prepared to do it. He pointedly warned the Corinthians to repent of their unwholesome pride and advised them immediately to excommunicate the immoral man in the name of the Lord Jesus

(5:2-4). Paul had no problem in calling sin *sin* and in summoning the young church to take a firm stand against it.

But Paul's condemnation of sin was hardly intended to be nonredemptive. His stance was aimed at restoration. To exclude a Christian from the community of faith, Paul believed, was to set such a person outside the protective, spiritual power of the church and to open that person to the wily power of Satan. Paul's hope in such a situation was that the excluded sinner would soon sense the effect which the power of the evil one then had on his life and repent (5:5). Paul believed in the power of the spirit world.[37] For him, the gospel was the *power of God* at work (see Rom. 1:16; 1 Cor. 1:18; and 2:4-5). To be removed from that sense of power was to be set adrift in a powerful, hostile world with the name of Christian but without the power in the name. The attacks of Satan and his powers, Paul believed, would soon make evident to the man his loss of the upholding power of Christ in the church.

In addition to the man's problem, however, Paul ordered the Christian community to evaluate itself in the entire situation. The incestuous relationship pointed to a major problem of pollution within the church, and Paul called for a time of cleansing. Employing the Jewish symbolism of preparing for Passover, Paul charged the Corinthians to begin their housecleaning process in order to ensure that no leaven would be found among them (see Ex. 12:15; 13:7; Deut. 13:4). But the leaven about which Paul was speaking did not refer to baking yeast that permeated an entire lump of dough. *Leaven* was a symbol for evil that was infecting the entire community. Paul expected the Corinthians to understand the proverbial statement: "a little leaven leavens the whole batch" (1 Cor. 5:6; see Gal. 5:9).

Apparently the problem of sexual immorality (*porneia*) among the Christians was not being addressed to the Corinthians for the first time because Paul reminded them that he had touched on this matter in his previous letter, which has not survived (1 Cor. 5:9). He also reminded them that when he advised them to shun an immoral person he had not been referring to a non-Christian. His warning was directed to shunning Christians who were living like immoral pagans and who were claiming to be faithful members of Christ's transformed body

(5:10-12). Paul would have hardly pitched his hostile warning against associating with pagans because he let God be the judge of those outside the church (5:13). Moreover, a missionary like Paul would scarcely have ceased relating to pagans since that stance would have meant an end to evangelism. In this respect, it is interesting that Paul did not speak of the incestuous woman. In all likelihood she was not a Christian. If she had lost her husband, she may well have been open to any sort of relationship, including prostitution, in order to keep herself in food and clothing. The man who claimed to be a Christian was Paul's concern. Action needed to be taken against him, but the hope was that such action would work for the man's ultimate salvation (5:5).

The aspect of warning is not difficult to see in this setting of tragic immorality. The interpreter, however, struggles to find the sense of assurance. All sorts of questions arise: Was the immoral man really a Christian? To answer that question is very difficult because on the one hand Paul dealt with him as a person who was within the community of faith, yet on the other hand he consigned the man to the sphere of pagans who were outside the church in the hope that the man might experience the assurance of salvation in the end.

This text reminds us that Christianity is not merely a matter of words. At its core, Christianity is a way of life which must be lived in conformity to the model of Christ. It is easy to say one is a Christian, but living like a Christian in matters of morality, economics, peacefulness, harmony, and in care for others requires a deep commitment. The way we live is a mirror of the way we really believe.

2. THE PROBLEM OF LEGAL DISPUTES (1 COR. 6:1-8)

As a former lawyer I can vouch for the fact that chapter 6 raises some intriguing issues. The basic thesis of verses 1 to 8 is that Paul considered it a tragedy when Christians were unable to settle their differences and needed the help of pagan courts to bring about fair and just solutions. What a sad testimony such squabbling presented to the pagans. The Christians had claimed to be transformed people of love but were, in fact, acting no different than the rest of the world. They were lying, cheating, and misrepresenting the situation just like the pagans were doing. The legal squabbles were the final stage of an unjust and unholy way of life.

How could Paul get cheaters and liars to understand that cheating and lying did not belong in the church? One method was to remind them of their eschatological (future) destiny. Faithful Christians were going to be active in the judgment of the world. Indeed, they were going to assist the Lord in evaluating even the angels (6:3). Were there not persons already in their congregation who were qualified to handle justly and fairly mere earthly squabbles (6:2,5). Were pagans fairer than Christians? Or was that really the issue? Did the Christians actually want a fair solution or did they want whatever they could get by law even though it might not be fair in the eyes of God and the other members of the church?

Throughout history, when Christians have truly desired fairness and equitable justice, they have generally been able to solve their problems without going to court. But when Christians have wanted their pound of flesh, they have not usually been willing to settle issues fairly themselves. In the history of the British and American legal systems, the harsh justice of the King's Bench which made decisions on the basis of strict interpretations of legal formulas was softened by the equitable decisions of the Courts of Chancery (which descended from the church).[38] The combination of both courts especially following the Judicature Act in Britain (1832) determined that decisions ought to be made both at law and in equity.[39]

In looking at the Corinthian situation, Paul was probing Christians for their basic commitment. He knew they were ready to take each other into court at the drop of a hat (6:8). Therefore, he asked them, in effect, Are your lives focused around the way of God or economic security? Paul's assurance was obviously not built on economic stability. He had willingly risked alienation of his Jewish parents and sacrificed his inheritance, as well as his status as an emissary of the high priest (see, for example, Phil. 3:4-8; Acts 26:9-12), in making his commitment to Jesus. He had been beaten and imprisoned, and he undoubtedly realized that he would ultimately give his life for Jesus (see 1 Cor. 4:9-13; Gal. 6:17; Phil. 1:21). Out of this context, Paul asked what may have seemed an extremely foolish question. He cut to the heart of the issue when he asked them if they were willing to suffer the trauma of being defrauded (1 Cor. 6:7).

To someone who has given up everything for Jesus, being defrauded means very little. But for rich or moderately rich persons, being defrauded can easily rob them of the economic security they had planned to enjoy. Power and wealth are sources of woe and blessing. Rich and powerful churches soon discover, like rich and powerful people, the twofold nature of possessions and power.

Perhaps this is the reason Jesus said that it was easier for a camel to pass through the eye of a needle than for a rich person to enter the Kingdom (Matt. 19:23-24). It was not impossible with God, Jesus acknowledged, but it was difficult (19:25). The rich young man realized the pain of foregoing his riches and sadly rejected Jesus (19:22). The idolatry of possessions and power makes it difficult to seek assurance in God alone. Paul knew where assurance was vested, and he warned the Corinthians that their priorities were obviously in the wrong place. That warning stands as a benchmark of commitment even today.

The matter of Christians and the law is complex today. For example, insurance policies are often constructed in such a way that a son may have to sue a father (or vice versa) in order to collect from an accident policy. I can think of a case where a doctor was drunk when he performed surgery on the mother of a Christian young man. The mother died as others had done previously. A suit was necessary to establish the basis for the ultimate removal of the doctor's right to practice medicine. When churches and denominations incorporate, they are legal business entities! But the complexity today of the relationship between Christians and the law does not alter Paul's basic concern for Christians in respect to their commitment. His question to us would be: Is our fundamental commitment to God or to economic advancement and power? The way we answer that question is not determined by our words but by our lives. I have the uneasy feeling that many Christians today would attempt to straddle the fence. Truly, I think that most churches and Christian institutions would do the same.

We Christians must never forget that there is a God around who really knows how we live. Whether we like it or not, we are going to have to face Him and review with Him our manipulative ways. It should be clear that we desperately need the warnings of Paul. Yet I am grateful that while we are basically failures in our commitment to Christ, God uses frail people to do some amazing things. We are not excused for our perverted greed and power grabbing, but we can be thankful for a God with whom nothing is impossible (see Matt. 19:26). Here then are the fundamental ingredients of our study on assurance and warning: (a) a sovereign God in whom we can have great confidence and (b) fallible human beings who fail repeatedly and who need constantly to repent and return to their Savior.

3. The Life-style of the Corinthians and Christian Principles of Liberty (1 Cor. 6:9-20)

Paul Minear correctly observed that in the Corinthian church there was more at work than "stubbornness" and "willful wrongdoing."[40] The Christians had opened themselves to deception, and Paul had to ask them repeatedly if they were ignorant (1 Cor. 5:6; 6:2-3,9,15-16,19). But their problem was more than the mere lack of correct information. Their pride had greatly distorted their reasoning ability; therefore, they had difficulty thinking correctly. The distinctions between goodness and evil had become fuzzy, and Paul's goal was to make indelibly clear the difference between right and wrong.

He began this section by reminding the Corinthian Christians that "unrighteous people absolutely *shall not* inherit the kingdom of God" (6:9). The Corinthians had to understand the basic issue, or they would not understand anything that Paul was saying. So he proceeded to list the evil ways of life that were unacceptable to God. The list was an attempt to include a number of representative categories pertaining to the Corinthian life-style. Of concern were all forms of sexual immorality, such as adultery and all types of sexual perversion including various homosexual relations.[41] Also represented in the list were possessive sins, such as stealing and extortion, because Paul knew that greed was a major problem. Idolatry was listed because of the tendency among people to worship or revere humanly conceived gods. As Paul finished the list, he repeated his warning that such people would not inherit the kingdom of God (6:10).

With this list in mind, Paul reminded the Corinthians that some of them *had been* these types of people but that they had subsequently experienced a change—they had been washed, sanctified, and justified (6:11). As he spoke of their regeneration, however, he was very disturbed by the inconsistency of their living. Therefore, are verses 9 to 11 a statement of assurance or warning? I believe that Paul was expressing his uneasy sense of the tension between the two and was informing the Corinthians that an experience of regeneration without transformation of life was hollow. Paul's double warning that bad life practice would not lead to an inheritance in the kingdom of God was meant to be taken seriously. He believed firmly that genuine Christian regeneration should be evidenced in the activities of life.

On the basis of that thesis, Paul turned to tackle the matter of Christian liberty (vv. 12-20). The importance of Paul's perspective can hardly be overestimated. Yet novice readers of Paul may be hindered from understanding him if they fail to perceive the dialogical nature of Paul's words in this passage. Whether or not Paul was using the diatribe style of presentation employed by the Cynic and Stoic philosophers,[42] the reader must realize that Paul was countering arguments of the Corinthians by using the format of dialogue. Fortunately, to help readers in interpretation, several recent translations have set in quotation marks some statements that seem to be ideas which Paul was quoting from the Corinthian logic.

Paul's view was that a Christian's life should not be centered in the self but in service to God and others. The Corinthians were self-centered (v. 12). Paul agreed with the Corinthians that Christ made believers free. Indeed, Paul taught that life was no longer a matter of rules. But they had learned only half the lesson. All things might be permitted, yet not all things were profitable (6:12). Paul added that, while he was free to do all, he would not allow anything to dominate him. He found in Jesus that mere freedom to do something did not mean that one had to prove his liberty by doing it. That would be slavery and not freedom.

The Corinthians apparently had another catch phrase to justify their immoral sexual activity. Meat was meant to be consumed in the digestive tract, they argued; therefore, the digestive tract ought to be employed for meat. It is not difficult to sense where such logic was headed if one applied it to the sexual organs. Paul's response to such logic was to warn them that they were headed for destruction (6:13). God did not create the body to be misused in immoral passions.

The body was made to serve the Lord and to experience the marvelous power of the resurrection (6:14). To advocate and participate in sexual immorality was a clear sign of spiritual bankruptcy. The Corinthians' arguments were pathetic indications that they were deceived. The sexual act was a sign of unity between a man and a woman. For a Christian who was also linked with Christ to be joined in sexual union with a prostitute was a perversion of Christ. To attempt any justification of such activity on the basis of liberty or the construction of the body was pure nonsense, according to Paul (6:15-17).

Paul's response to this entire train of thought was a command: "Flee immorality!" (*pheugete tēn porneian*). Seldom did Paul warn anyone to flee anything. But here the words almost jump out at the reader (6:18; see also 10:14). This command was meant to be taken as the *sternest possible warning* which Paul could give. Immorality was horribly destructive because it violated a Christians's integrity with God. Christians were a purchased people in whom God's Spirit resided. They were the sanctuaries (*naoi*) of God on earth, and any ancient person knew the seriousness of violating a sanctuary. A sanctuary was a place where God was to be glorified, and Paul expected Christians to use their bodies to glorify God (6:19-20).

Chapters 5 and 6 of 1 Corinthians, thus, detail the head-on confrontation of Paul with the horrible living patterns of the Corinthians. Paul's words pulsate with concern, as though he were attempting to grasp the Corinthians from the jaws of a terrible fate. They had succumbed to deception, and they needed to be warned as forcefully as possible that they were violating not only their own integrity but also their fundamental relationship with God. The warnings are followed by a closing exhortation to glorify God, assuring believers that in spite of their terrible wickedness the redeeming God was waiting for their repentance.

D. Assurance and Warning
Related to the Corinthians' Questions (1 Cor. 7:1 to 14:40).

In this major section of 1 Corinthians, Paul sought to provide answers to a number of questions which at least some of the Corinthians had raised in a letter addressed to him (7:1). Unfortunately, like Paul's

earlier letter to the Corinthians (5:9), this letter to Paul has not survived. Our knowledge of their concerns, therefore, must be reconstructed out of what we can glean from 1 Corinthians. We can be
extremely grateful for their inquiry because it has provided us with
apostolic insight into some very significant issues.

1. MATTERS PERTAINING TO THE MARRIED AND UNMARRIED
(1 Cor. 7:1-40)

The first issue in this section focuses on proper relations and procedures as they pertain to marriage and sexual matters. While it is a
little speculative to attempt a reconstruction of the problem situations
at Corinth, some patterns may be suggested by way of example. To
begin with, in matters related to sex and marriage, Paul's arguments
were formulated out of his eschatological (futuristic) perspectives. Paul
believed that he would live to see the return of Christ, that the time
until the end was short. Therefore, Christians should seek to concentrate on their relationship with Christ rather than on matters associated
with this life. He obviously viewed sex and marriage as belonging to
the category of the present world. While he scarcely thought of sex
and marriage as significant in his own life, he recognized that not all
Christians were put together the same way (7:6,26-28).

At the outset of analyzing this text, the reader should be alerted
to the fact that in 1 Corinthians 7:1 Paul was most probably quoting
something from the Corinthians' own letter to him about not touching
a woman. In this respect, we must remember that he had just finished,
in chapters 5 and 6, dealing with the libertine mentality where everything was permitted. Here he turned to the ascetic mentality where
very little was permitted. The expression "touch a woman" was a
euphemism for sexual relations and not, as some modern translations
have suggested, a way of talking about entering into marriage.[43]

To contextualize the situation then, we should probably imagine
some man in the congregation who had come under conviction with
respect to his life and had resolved out of some form of dedication
to refrain from sexual relations with his wife. Naturally, one can easily
picture the reaction that might have occurred on the part of the wife
if she had not been a party to this decision.[44] Such a tension-filled
situation would certainly have set up a question concerning sexual

patterns in marriage that begged for a comment from the missionary. Paul was ready to respond because he knew that improper ascetic patterns were also harmful to the well-being of the Christian community.

For Paul, sexual intimacy in the proper context was not evil. Indeed, in the husband-wife relationship it was not only permitted but also expected. Moreover, one partner should not make decisions in this matter without consulting the other partner. Marriage means that both partners have agreed in matters of sex that they are no longer single entities but recognize the rights of *each other* over their bodies (7:3-4).

Some people in Corinth must have thought that they could prove their holiness to God by transforming their marriages into a non-marriage state. For Paul, that practice was no way to achieve assurance with the Lord. Accordingly, he warned such pious dreamers that they were in fact opening themselves to the powerful temptations of Satan (7:5). He knew that there were enough dirty (*porneia*) things going on in Corinth already without creating further temptations for Christians. He also understood that these super-spiritual Corinthians had in fact reversed the biblical perspective on marriage by suggesting that it was not good for a husband and wife to cleave to each other and become one flesh (contrast Gen. 2:24).[45]

Paul's task was to help the Corinthians understand the human tension present in this matter. In giving himself to the Lord, Paul found that he did *not* need a wife and sexual intimacy in order to find personal fulfilment. His wish was that everyone would follow his pattern, but he understood that not everyone had the same spiritual giftedness (*charisma*) from God (7:7).

We all like people who are similar to us. The temptation is to play God to others and to try to force them to become like us in their thoughts and actions. Even though Paul was very zealous for his perspectives, he resisted the tendency to play God. Would that Christians today could learn that lesson!

If the reader understands the way Paul dealt with this personal tension, the pattern of Paul's advice in 1 Corinthians 7 should become fairly easy to perceive. For example, married persons can legitimately

agree to refrain from sexual intimacy. Yet abstinence should not be
a matter of philosophical principle (which in fact would impede the
marriage), but it should be a matter of mutual agreement. Moreover,
abstinence should be limited so as not to engender the temptation
to seek sexual fulfillment outside of marriage, and it should be aimed
at spiritual development in prayer (7:5). Paul considered that it would
have been wonderful if unmarried persons and those who had lost
their spouses through death continued in their state of singleness
rather than becoming involved in all the issues of married life. But
if persons were made in such a way that their lives are unsettled
without marriage and human intimacy, then they should marry (7:8-
9). For such persons, marriage is not a poor second choice to celibacy.
It is, as Paul Furnish has reminded us, *"the best"* choice.[46]

With respect to matters of divorce, Paul believed that Jesus had
reaffirmed the permancy of marriage (7:10; see Matt. 19:4-6).[47] Divorce
is something that God does not intend (Mal. 2:13-16). It is an accommodation to human weakness (Matt. 19:7-8). Like Jesus, however, Paul
recognized that divorce was a reality of life. But Paul did not see
divorce as a route to easy remarriage (1 Cor. 7:11). He knew the lax
morals in Corinth, and he rejected them as a pattern for Christian
life. What do you think he would have said about the church of today?
Did he not warn Christians against conforming to the ways of the
world (see Rom. 12:2)? Yet Paul also tried to deal with difficult situations in the spirit of loving concern. Christians ought to try to work
out their marriages. But what about problem, mixed marriages? Paul's
advice to Christians was to try to work them out also. They might
be able to win their unbelieving spouses. But Paul was a realist. He
faced difficult situations without putting on rose-colored glasses, and
he wanted Christians to be realists as well. Therefore, he asked the
Corinthians point blank how they could be sure they would save their
spouses (1 Cor. 7:16). Those words were meant to warn the Corinthians
against assuming unreal expectations.

But what would happen if the marriage did not work out? What
would happen if there was such antagonism to Christ that a divorce
occurred? How Paul dealt with this ethical problem reveals both his
sense of freedom in Christ and his logic as a former rabbi.[48] For

Paul a Christian brother or sister who had done all that was possible to save a marriage to a non-Christian was freed of responsibility if such a divorce occurred. The expression "not bound" (*ou dedoulōntai*) for Paul meant that a Christian in such a case was fully relieved of the restraints of the marriage vows (7:15). Remarriage, therefore, was not forbidden.

Paul, however, wanted Christians to honor their marriage vows; he did not want the Christian partner to be the reason for the dissolution of the marriage. At the same time, he was a realist and knew that not all marriages would work out. As in other matters of biblical theology, therefore, Paul maintained the tension between the standards of Almighty God and the failures of weak humanity. The balance is something that every Christian needs to understand.

Paul's basis for this balance flowed from his confidence in God and his assurance of God's hand in the world. God had called Christians (7:17). They did not call themselves. Therefore, they should sense that God was with them in every situation. It did not matter with God whether one were a slave or a free person, whether one were a circumcised Jew or a uncircumcised Gentile (7:17-22; see Rom. 1:16; 2:11; Gal. 3:28; Col. 3:11; and Eph. 2:14). With God there was no need to feel insecure about one's background. Of course, if one were a slave and could gain freedom, that change would be advantageous (1 Cor. 7:21). But assurance with God could not be gained by external things like circumcision. Therefore, Jews and Gentiles should remain as they were (7:18-20). The same reasoning, Paul argued, applied to marriage and sexual matters. Because they pertain to this realm, neither marriage nor divorce were ultimately determinative. Therefore, because Paul viewed the world as very soon coming to an end (7:26,29-31), he considered that there was no point in changing one's marital status (7:27). But he added that it was not sinful to enter into marriage (7:28).

Paul's primary concern was to turn the attention of the Corinthians away from the world and toward their commitment to the assuring Lord (7:35). Paul had found a personal sense of freedom in serving Christ through singleness. He wished everyone else could experience that same sense of commitment (7:38,40). He pointedly warned them

that marriage carried responsibilities that were not to be shirked
(7:28,33-34). But he assured all of them that, even though he thought
he had the Spirit of God in giving them his advice (7:40), no one
should ever regard marriage as either sinful or illegitimate (7:36). A
person's relationship to God was Paul's chief concern, not marriage
or celibacy. But human relationships quite clearly affected the way
one related to God. Therefore, Paul firmly warned the Corinthians
that marriage for Christians ought only to be contracted in the Lord
(7:39). By this expression, Paul undoubtedly meant that marriage for
Christians should only be *between Christians and under the direction
of the Lord*. Christians owed their first love to God; therefore, the
marriage relationship was subject to their relationship with God.

2. FOOD OFFERED TO IDOLS (1 COR. 8:1 TO 11:1)[49]

The Greek phrase *peri de* ("now concerning") in 1 Corinthians 8:1
signals the transition to a new idea (see 7:1,25; 12:1; 16:1,12). The
Corinthians had raised another question that Paul obviously regarded
as crucial. In chapters 5 and 6, he had made a frontal attack on libertine
morals. By contrast in chapter 7, he had dealt rather temperately
with some ascetic views and the issues of marriage in general. In
this section, he returned to another aspect of the libertine life-style
and once again positioned himself for a frontal attack.

In this critique of the libertine way of life, Paul focused on the
Corinthian concern for food sacrificed to idols (*eidōlothutos*). But he
was interested in a far bigger subject than food. Paul's attention was
directed to the interplay between freedom and syncretism. He used
quotations from the Corinthians' letter or familiar sayings from them.

Paul opened the discussion by citing a commonly accepted thesis
of theirs, namely, that all of them possessed knowledge (8:1). This
comment has led a number of scholars, principally Walter Schmithals,
to speculate that the Corinthians were beset with an early form of
Gnosticism.[50] In response, one can assert that whatever proto-Gnostic
or pre-Gnostic forms there might have been present at Corinth, there
is certainly little evidence in 1 Corinthians for a mythological structure
akin to the Gnostic patterns of the second and third centuries of our
era.[51] While it is evident from the epistle that there was an interest

in ideas such as wisdom, knowledge, and spiritual superiority, I would categorize these Corinthian factionalists as "know-it-alls" rather than as Gnostics.

Paul's response to these know-it-alls was that the parading of knowledge led to self-inflated attitudes, whereas love, the basic quality of Christian life, formed an edifying link with both God and others (8:1-3). True knowledge was rooted in love. If the Corinthians would have perceived this fact, they would also have recognized its implications for the idol meat issue.

Some of the Corinthians apparently participated in cultic meals at pagan temples and felt no qualms of conscience in such involvement (8:10). Their justification was that since they knew an idol did not exist, and since they affirmed their God was the one true God, then their participation in temple meals was hardly illegitimate (8:4). For them fellowshipping with others at a pagan, cultic meal had little or nothing to do with their theology. They prided themselves on their ability to distinguish between the reality of God and the many false gods of the pagans (8:4-6). Their knowledge, they believed, gave them a sense of power and freedom to participate in pagan worship practices without concern.

Yet those who were involved in such practices had forgotten one important aspect of the issue. In replying, Paul employed the strong adversative "but" (*alla*) to remind them that they were living testimonies and were being observed by weak persons who were not strong in the faith. (v. 7)[52] Paul said that the Corinthians' willful use of freedom had become a stumbling block or a means of offense (*proskomma*) to others (8:7-10). Paul did not attack their theological thesis that an idol did not exist. Indeed, he agreed with them. But he condemned them severely for their moral insensitivity. They did not care what other people thought about their lives. As long as they could justify their actions, they felt perfectly legitimate in doing whatever they wanted, even if it helped destroy others (8:10-11)! This is one of the most insidious temptations: prideful self-righteousness and willful disregard for others. The saddest thing is that the self-righteous hardly recognize the illegitimacy of their actions because, I really believe,

Satan has blinded their eyes so that they lose their sensitivity for hurting people. The principle is what counts with them! If in principle they are correct, they can excuse their questionable activity.

But Paul knew that reality was very different. God is not a principle. God is a person. God hurts with the weak and hurting people of this world. That was the reason He sent Jesus to redeem us from the sin, pain, and hurt of the world. Jesus cared for the weak. He pictured Himself as a caring Shepherd who loved the helpless and despised of the world (John 10:1-30; Matt. 9:36; see Ps. 23) and who sought to comfort and gather the confused of the earth (Mark 6:34; see Matt. 23:37). Moreover, the God of the New Testament is likened most frequently to a concerned father, not to an all-knowing despot who does whatever he pleases and has no regard for people. We recognize this caring quality of God when in prayer we address Him as "Our Father" (Matt. 6:1-18).[53] Few people find comfort and solace by addressing God as "Oh, Thou Immutable, Incomprehensible, Inexpressible One." God certainly may be designated by such qualities because *some* aspects of God are transcendent. But fortunately for us, God has made Himself known and has expressed His love most fully in the caring heart of Jesus, our Lord.

In this tension between God's transcendence and imminence is hidden another aspect of the tension between assurance and warning. Some aspects of God we cannot comprehend, but other aspects of God we understand very clearly. Some aspects of assurance are very evident, while others are cloudy and hidden in the hiddeness of God. Some aspects of warning are most clear while other aspects are fuzzy and cause us genuine concern in our logical deductions. *Our task is not to worry about the fuzzy aspects of either assurance or warning. Our task is to appropriate what we do know and live with what we do understand.* Working on what we know and understand will keep us busy. Unfortunately, the Corinthians were sidestepping the moral implications of Christianity. They were using their knowledge to avoid the full implications of living authentically and caring for the confused and weak. Paul warned them point blank that, if by their cavalier attitudes they caused the destruction of another, *they were guilty of sinning against Christ* (8:11-12)!

However one may want to rank that Corinthian sin—if one is accustomed to ranking sins—it was very serious. Paul's major commitment was to live "in Christ." That was the most important relationship in his life and a central idea of Pauline theology. Paul would have done almost anything to keep from sinning against Christ. Therefore, if there were any chance that someone would be scandalized or caused to sin (*skandalizō*) by Paul's eating meat, he would have avoided meat like the plague (8:13). The Corinthians were not quite up to such a commitment. They needed to be warned to correct their wayward steps. Paul, like Jesus, was concerned with the weak who were seeking the Lord. Jesus had told His hearers that to offend or lead astray a seeking child was a sin of such proportions that the scandalizing person might as well have a heavy rock hung around his or her neck and be thrown into the sea (Matt. 18:6). Jesus and Paul were not gentle with know-it-alls who scandalized seekers by their inauthentic lives.

The Pharisees were by purpose committed to the study of Scripture and to piety. When one reads the Gospel stories, however, one has the distinct feeling that the Gospel writers viewed most of the Pharisees Christ encountered as hypocrites (see, for example, Matt. 5:20; 6:2,5,16; note especially 23:13-36). The Corinthian know-it-alls were really not much different in their attitudes. The same applies to know-it-alls of today. Hypocrisy is a waiting bed partner for know-it-alls. The warning is plain.

But the Corinthians were hardly interested in taking instruction from their teacher, Paul. They were far more interested in making him defend himself (1 Cor. 9:3). If one were comparing the situation to our contemporary setting, one might suggest that the Corinthian know-it-alls had viewed themselves as having far surpassed the understanding of their best seminary professor and were forcing him to defend himself. The critics had become far richer than Paul (1 Cor. 4:8) who had made very little profit from his teaching and preaching (1 Cor. 9:12,15; 4:11) even though by all rights he should have been far richer than they were. But Paul's concern was not with achieving financial security, gaining power, and exercising his rights (9:15-16). He was concerned with fulfilling his commission to Christ. To see people come to Christ and grow into maturity with the Lord was the most fulfilling reward he could anticipate (9:17-18). He had become a kind of slave for them in order to win them and share the blessings of the gospel with them (9:19-23).[54]

If there is any quality which will ruin the effectiveness of the Christian church, it is pride or arrogance or a sense of self-inflated importance (see 1 Cor. 4:6,18-19; 8:1). Paul understood the powerful secret of servanthood, and he accepted the term as a designation for himself (see 1 Cor. 4:1; 9:19; Rom. 1:1). Our Lord reminded His disciples that servanthood was the true path to Christian leadership (Matt. 20:27). But like the early disciples, most of us are usually not very excited about servanthood, unless we can see it as a means to power and prestige. Generally we prefer the promotion pattern of the world because most true servants do not have an opportunity to exercise many rights.

Like Paul, many servants often do not experience genuine acceptance until after they are dead. Like prophets, it is often easier to listen to them and honor them when they are not around any more to harass us with their otherworldly perspectives (see Matt. 23:29-36; 5:12). But thank God that He raises His servants to call us out of our easy promotion patterns and remind us that the servant is not greater than his Lord! If the "pious" know-it-alls in Jesus' day called our Lord Beelzebul (Matt. 10:25) and if the Christian know-it-alls maligned Paul in his day (2 Cor. 11:5), we should expect criticism today. In responding to antagonism, we Christians must not sacrifice our integrity for human praise, but we must wait for the affirmation of God (Rom. 2:29; contrast John 12:43).

Paul realized that he was calling the Corinthian Christians to a difficult style of life—a pattern which was hardly popular. He sought to illuminate the serious nature of his advice with an illustration which may have come to mind because the famed Isthmian Games were held near Corinth. The illustration provided not only a forceful message of warning but also an avenue of assurance.

The goal of runners, a wreath (*stephanos*), could only be claimed by the victor (9:24). To win the crown required grueling or agonizing practice (*agonizomai*). Paul was convinced that his exercising in the Christian life was not going to be halfhearted preparation. His goal was living for Christ; therefore, he did everything in his power to subordinate (*doulagōgō*) his body to Christ (9:27). Paul knew that his preaching and his living had to be consistent. By warning himself of the danger of becoming a "castaway" (*adokimos*), he was in fact warning the Corinthians of the danger of "being disqualified" (9:27). Paul took his responsibility of living for Christ very seriously, and he warned the proud Corinthian advocates of freedom to do the same. The stakes were too high to misuse their liberty. The assuring goal was not a mere perishable victor's wreath. It was the indestructible goal of life (9:25).

Readers who have been brought up with simplistic statements of security may be very troubled by Paul's self-warning at this point. Indeed, they may think Paul *sounded less assured* about his destiny than their preachers or Sunday School teachers. Let me suggest that that might well be true, but the reason may be different than one might think. *I believe that many Christians attach their security to simplistic statements about assurance which are very unbiblical. Paul did not find assurance in simplistic statements. He found his assurance in obeying God and in living with Christ.*

Statements do not save us; God does! Moreover, our goal is not to obey rules but to obey God. Security does not come from words or rules or statements—not even statements of faith. Our security comes from a relationship with the living God. We may be able to master words or rules, but we will never master God! Paul knew that his task was to run with God, not just run a race. Moreover, there was *more than just one victor's crown* for this running. Therefore, Paul charged all of the Corinthians (plural) to run in order to achieve their reward (9:24). In running authentically with God, the Corinthians would find their genuine security and assurance.

But chapter 10 makes clear that authentic Christian living was precisely the Corinthians' problem. From Paul's perspective, they were like the fickle people of Israel. Paul, the former rabbi, easily recognized the similarity between the Israelites and the Corinthians; he turned to the troubled Exodus for a full-scale warning. Israel's wilderness experience could be categorized by three words: *liberation, disobedience,* and *destruction.* Paul saw the same pattern emerging among the Corinthians, and he wanted to initiate a rescue operation. As a result, 1 Corinthians 10:1 to 11:1 forms one of the most powerful yet intricate interplays between warning and assurance found anywhere in Paul's writings.

He began by informing the know-it-alls that he did not want them to be ignorant (*agnoein*) concerning the Exodus (10:1). Throughout the epistle, Paul had been calling them to true knowledge (see for example 1:5; 2:2,7; 3:1-3; 4:14; 6:9,15; 7:36; 8:2; 9:24); I suspect that the puffed-up libertines were particularly irritating to him. He had charged them earlier to "flee immorality" (6:18), and now he turned to condemn them for idolatry.

Paul first directed his attention to the liberation phase of the Exodus. He did so by describing the events in a way that the Corinthians would be able to identify themselves in the story. The description is a masterful stroke of ingenuity and inspiration. But the reader is fore-warned that the parallels are not exact and that identifications should not be pressed beyond the symbolic argument.[55]

The liberation from Egypt is pictured as Israel's baptismal experi-ence. The cloud and the march through the sea (10:1-2) are employed as baptismal symbols comparable to Noah's ark in 1 Peter 3:20-21. Paul used the wilderness manna and the water from the rock as symbols for the second Christian ordinance, the Lord's Supper (1 Cor. 10:3-4). Most intriguing in this picture is the moving rock which Paul employed to represent the continuing presence of Christ (10:4).[56] The point of Paul employing symbolic language to describe the Exodus was to make the Corinthians understand that *just like them* Israel had started the Exodus well. The problem with Israel did not rest with God, nor with the way the Exodus began. Paul wanted the Corin-thians to draw a straight line from the Exodus to themselves and con-clude that their problem was also not with God. It was equally not with their baptism or with God's continuing presence symbolized in the supper.

The second stage, the follow through, however, seemed to be defi-cient. Paul was convinced that God was no happier with the trouble-some Christians at Corinth than He had been with the Israelites (1 Cor. 10:5). He announced that he saw in the tragedy of death related to the wilderness a forceful warning for the Corinthians: "Now these events were types [examples] of us in order that we might not desire evil ways like they desired" (10:6).

What then caused the third phase, the downfall, of the Israelites? It was a twofold problem of idolatry and immorality (10:6-7)! Paul thought these disobedient ways produced a head-on confrontation with the lordship of Christ in the life of Christians (10:9).[57] As a result he expected that attachment to these ways would bring death or destruction to the Corinthians as it did to the Israelites (10:10).

The fall of the Israelites in the wilderness was meant to be a stark warning or example (*tupikōs*) for later generations. God would not accept either a mixing of commitment to Him in worship or a diluting of His ethical standards by playing loose with morals (10:11). In addition, the warning in the wilderness story was not to be limited to later Israelites only. It was applicable to Christians as well (10:11). Therefore, Paul sternly warned the Corinthians that, if they thought they were absolutely secure with God (proudly thinking they stood firmly), they needed to take special care not to fall (10:12).

Paul's ultimate purpose in writing these words, however, was not condemnation. His purpose was to initiate a needful reformation. Moreover, if the Corinthians would listen to him, they would readily discover that in the midst of his stern warnings Paul added one of the most unique messages of assurance found anywhere in his letters. Paul did not want the Corinthians to gain the impression that their plight was hopeless or that their temptations were completely overpowering. The perspective of Paul was in fact quite the opposite.

Paul placed this message of assurance in an unusual framework—in the setting of a Corinthian excuse. The Corinthians had used temptation as an excuse for falling. Paul asserted that everyone was tempted and that the Corinthians needed to recognize that God was faithful in the midst of temptation to provide the means for avoiding enticement and for resisting the ways of error (10:13). The Corinthians offered excuses, but Paul countered with assurance. Excuses would not work with Paul because he knew that reliance on God would result in victory over temptation.

Instead of yielding to temptation, Paul told the Corinthians to "flee idolatry!" (10:14). As indicated earlier, Paul hardly ever told any Christian to flee anything. He was convinced that the mighty power of God was available in the lives of Christians enabling them to stand firm in the face of opposition. But in the case of immorality (6:18) and idolatry (10:14), the situation was different. These were not opponents; these were sins which needed to be totally avoided because they come between Christians and their Lord.

Paul had given his rationale for fleeing immorality. Here he provided his rationale against idolatry. The Corinthians had argued previously (8:4-6) that idols had no existence. With that thesis Paul had agreed. But that thesis did not end the matter with Paul. The Corinthians had assumed that if an idol had no existence, they could partake of both the Lord's Supper and pagan cultic meals without any concern for their spiritual well-being (10:15-19). Addressing them rather tongue in cheek as wise persons (*phronimois*), Paul informed them that they had made a calculated error (10:15).

The Corinthians had made a mistake common to humanity. They had categorized something and assumed they understood it. The term *eidōlothuton* in 8:1 and 10:19 translated "food offered to idols" was an outsider's categorization. No worshiping pagan would have used the designation *idol* because that term was a slur. The pagans used another term *hierothuton*, "something offered in sacrifice" (see 10:28). While the critics of the pagans may not have taken their activity seriously, the pagans did. Therefore, Paul informed the Corinthians that they had to deal with this fact seriously.

In this respect they had two matters to consider. The first was to face the reality of the pagan activity and to recognize that it involved worship. If it were worship not directed to God, Paul concluded that it must have been inspired by demons (10:20). If it were inspired by demons, the Corinthians were compromising with the devil by participating in cultic services (8:10; 10:21). If they participated in such cultic services, they were in no better position than the Israelites of the wilderness because eating the sacrifices made them a participant at the altar (10:18). If, therefore, they were participants at a demonic altar, they needed to remember one of the refrains of the wilderness experience: God was jealous of His people's worship (see, for example, Ex. 5:20; 34:14; Deut. 4:24; 5:9; 6:15). Paul understood the zeal of

God for His people; therefore, he pointedly warned the Corinthians not to confront the zeal of the Lord because they did not have the least chance of standing up to His incredible power (1 Cor. 10:22).

The Corinthians failed to recognize that compromise brought them into direct conflict not only with others but also with Christ. Participation in the Lord's Supper implies a commitment to Christ as Lord of one's life. Paul's warning against compromise, therefore, is not out-of-date, even though a Christian may seldom be tempted to participate in a pagan cultic meal. Many other forms of compromise are demonic and challenge the lordship of Christ. These challenges to our relationship with Christ must be seen for what they are, and we are warned not to misunderstand how they affect that relationship.

The second matter which Paul addressed in this discussion on participation concerned dining in pagan homes and eating food offered for sale in pagan markets. Paul made a slight shift in his focus. First, he reasserted his formula for critiquing Corinthian libertinism: while all things are permissible, they are not all helpful nor edifying (10:23; see also 6:12). Then he shifted the direction of his thought to underline the fact that helpfulness and permissibleness in some matters are quite complementary and not always mutually exclusive. For Paul life was far more than a series of principles; life involved complex relationships.

In the realm of human living, Paul's concern was to exemplify both the freedom and the love of Christ. Relationships were more important than the intricate rules from his past. Of particular importance to the former rabbi had been the strict Jewish food laws. But when he became a Christian, his attachment to legalism ended and a sense of freedom emerged in relation to those food laws. For example, as a Christian, he could buy food in a market without asking any questions concerning how it had been processed—whether it had been prepared in accordance with kosher regulations or as part of a pagan religious ceremony. God had made the food, and religious processing did not affect its giftedness from God (10:25-26).

Furthermore, Paul could eat meals in unbeliever's homes. There was no need to inquire of the unbeliever as to the source of the food. The Christian was at perfect liberty to eat without qualms of conscience (10:27). But that situation was totally changed if the unbeliever made an issue of the fact that the food had been offered in sacrifice (10:28). In such a case, the unbeliever regarded an ordinary meal as a worship experience of another deity. That declaration did not change the quality of the food, but it did alter the relationship between the Christian and the unbeliever. Therefore, out of respect for the unbeliever's commitments (even though they might be totally erroneous), Paul indicated that Christian love would suggest that the Christian would not participate in the meal (10:29). As Harold Songer has well written of this difficult text: "Paul is saying he exercises freedom in choosing not to eat and that he does this out of respect for the conscience of the other person. His conscience is not under the rule of another's weakness, but another's weakness inspires him to exercise freedom in love."[58]

The Christian is called to a life of glorifying God (10:31) and of living in peaceful relationships with other people (10:32). When living in harmony with others, one does not seek personal advantage for oneself but provides the kind of context for others which enables them to experience the saving power of Christ (10:33). Paul's entire life was wrapped in mission. His pervading desire was that these self-centered Corinthians would discover the self-giving nature of mission. That would turn them away from the confining horizons of their own lives and focus their visions on expanding vistas. Such vistas emerge when lives are given in service to God.

To be an imitator of Christ was Paul's personal goal and to call the Corinthians to follow his pattern was his purpose for this letter (1 Cor. 11:1; 4:16-17; also see Phil. 3:17; 1 Thess. 1:6; Eph. 5:1). In the imitation of Christ, Paul knew there was true assurance. But in following their own ways, the Corinthians needed to understand there was great danger of destruction. Paul could not abandon his troublesome children to failure. Therefore, he was impelled to warn them of the trouble they faced if they persisted on the highway to destruction (1 Cor. 10:9-12).

3. WORSHIP PROBLEMS IN THE CORINTHIAN CHURCH (1 COR. 11:2 TO 14:39)

The four chapters included in this section form a Pauline critique of the Corinthian worship practices. They are significant because they provide an unusual window into the practices of one of the early churches. To understand the arguments takes great care in order not to misread the implications of Paul's analyses. Indeed, the more we discover about the social environments of the early churches, the more revealing become Paul's instructions. To explain adequately these chapters would require a full-scale book, but my goal here is to show how Paul's critique of church practices illuminates our understanding of his perspectives on assurance and warning.

  a. Veils and Confusion in Christian Worship (1 Cor. 11:2-16). Typical of the chapters in this section is the debate that surrounds this segment. Unfortunately, there is a great deal of misunderstanding involved in the exposition of this text. Jerome Murphy-O'Connor was undoubtedly correct when he wrote that there has been a "widespread conviction" with respect to these verses: "The point at issue concerned women alone. Acceptance of this consensus inevitably colors the exegesis of the passage, to the point where some commentators refuse to take seriously the reference to men."[59]

  The text refers to both men and women and not just to women. It *assumes* that both men and women were praying and prophesying (11:4-5). The praying and prophesying (proclaiming) were regarded as taking place in the public church context. Now public praying and prophesying per se by either men or women did not concern Paul. These matters, of course, in the past may have been and in the present may continue to be interpreters problems; but they were *not Paul's problem*. When studying a text like this one, we need to be very clear on what issue was being discussed. Only then can we be certain of moving closer to a fair understanding of the text.

  The issue involved wearing veils. Paul was countering some reality in the church. While specific numismatic (coins) or sculptural records indicating that men wore veils in worship have not been uncovered at Corinth, quite a number of Roman coins, freezes, and iconographic records indicate that veils were worn by Roman worshipers, *including the emperors!*[60] Indeed, in a legend about Aeneas' arrival in Italy portrays him as praying with a veil so that his enemy would not find him in worship. The veil was, thus, regarded by Romans as appropriate dress for men in worship settings.[61] It would be hard to deny Roman influence in Corinth—the Roman capital of Achaia! Why then could not converts from paganism consider it in order to wear veils in worship?

What is the focus of this passage? I believe the answer is that Paul was seeking to bring some order to a chaotic worship situation (11:16). While the former Jewish rabbi proclaimed freedom in Christ, he obviously had a low level of tolerance for disorderly conduct in worship. *Indeed, counteracting confusion and disorder in the church was the point of each problem passage in this section.* Paul challenged what he considered to be inappropriate men's and women's dress patterns in worship. Some Christian men were apparently following the Roman imperial style; and as Plutarch argued, such a worship pattern was despised even by the Greeks.[62] On the other hand, some women had apparently accepted Paul's commitment to freedom and had seen in his theological elimination of sexual distinctions no need to wear veils (see Gal. 3:28). The result from Paul's perspective was a confusion in roles, so he sternly warned the Corinthians about the frustrations they had created.

The church, *like other groups in the society*, of that time was viewed as a type of an *oikos* (a house); whether it was a Jewish house or a Greek house, an appropriate societal structure was implied. It ran from God (or gods) to man to woman.[63] Dress in that world often reflected the societal structure.[64] Therefore, for a man and a woman to switch dress patterns created for Paul an abominable confusion. But confusion was typical of the Romans who did not always appreciate the finer points of either the Greek or Jewish ways. To bring an end to confusion was Paul's point. Confusion hindered his work of building strong churches. Therefore, he firmly warned the Corinthians to get their dress code in order and not to balk at established traditions of his churches (1 Cor. 11:2,16).

The societal structures of the Hellenistic world are not the structures of the contemporary world. Western women certainly do not wear the veils of Paul's time. Moreover, even if women wear hats today, we should understand that they are not quite comparable to ancient veils. Clearly, it is out of place to resurrect ancient cultural patterns and apply them to a contemporary world.

Yet the culture of Paul's time was not the crucial element of the Christian message. It was the setting into which the gospel was born. Our task as Christians of the twentieth century is to learn how Paul dealt with confusion and conflict in order that the prayer and prophesying of *both men and women* might continue without hindrance in the present church. Paul's warnings can be valuable lessons for the church of today, if we make a concerted effort to understand his concern and apply his point to our very different cultural setting. If we fail to do so, we may soon discover that the church speaks only to its own subculture and faces an increasingly difficult problem of delivering its message to the contemporary culture as a whole.

A church on mission cannot afford to misunderstand the problems created by the clash of cultures. Any effective missionary knows the difference between suffering for Christ and suffering because one does not understand the problems created by the clash of cultures. I believe Paul understood this difference very well and would never sacrifice the gospel either for cultural novelty or for cultural confusion. He would also not sacrifice the gospel's freedom for cultural security. The *gospel, not culture,* was important to Paul. I have the distinct feeling that some Christians today are like the Corinthians—more attached to their cultural biases than to the gospel. If Paul were in our midst, I am convinced he would thunder a warning: *Security is not to be found in culture, but in Christ alone!*

b. *Community Meals and Schisms at the Lord's Supper (1 Cor. 11:17-34).* Paul recognized the strategic nature of meals in the life of a community. He knew the power of nonverbal communication. Paul knew that the Corinthians had used the church supper as a means of distinguishing social status among Christians.[65] A meal could become a symbol of schism (*schisma*), and Paul asserted that he "partly" believed that such was true in Corinth (11:18). This statement represents a unique tongue-in-cheek expression for Paul because he was really not the kind of a person who partly believed anything. Indeed, he made it absolutely clear that he was totally opposed to the Corinthian's conduct (11:22).

The community meal was the setting for the celebration of the Lord's Supper (11:20), but they had destroyed the community sense of that meal by their practices. To put the idea in a contemporary setting, the rich in whose homes the meals were held would schedule their carry-in dinners before the poor could finish work. They would assemble and overindulge in their rich food and drink before the others could arrive with their ordinary food and drink. The result was an embarrassment and a devastation of the community. Paul did not mince words in his criticism of such actions (11:19-22). As he wrote of the tradition that stood behind the Lord's Supper in the broken bread which symbolized our Lord's body and the new covenent cup which symbolized Christ's blood, Paul called them to remember Jesus (11:23-25). Notice then what was particularly on Paul's mind in verse 26 because it gave a focus to all that he said.[66]

Paul reminded the proud, self-centered, divisive Corinthians that the Lord's Supper proclaimed the *Lord's death!* The supper was itself *a nonverbal sermon* affirming a style of life which was diametrically opposed to that of the Corinthians. It reflected a consistent perspective with the way Paul began his letter when he emphasized the cross of Christ (1:17-18; 2:1-5). The self-giving death of Jesus was the focus of the supper-sermon. But the supper was also an eschatological (futuristic) nonverbal event which was meant to remind the Corinthians (and us also) that Christ would surely return (11:26). Christians live between the two most important points of history. The supper, therefore, stands as a great twofold word of assurance and warning. It looks forward to the coming of Christ in power, and it assuringly proclaims that our future rests not in our own weakness but in the strength of our Lord. It also looks back to Christ's incarnation (life in the flesh) and stoutly warns us that triumphalism must not be the way of the church.

Paul pointedly warned the Corinthians that whoever consumed the Lord's Supper "unworthily"—"without discerning the Lord's body"— consumed damnation (11:27-29). What do you think that warning meant, dear Christian friends? Do you think that Paul was warning the Corinthian know-it-alls about the structure of the church or some theological, ethical, or political technicality so they could be more *technically* correct? Oh, I am certain that Paul would not want the technical matters neglected, but these matters were hardly his major concern. Relationships were falling apart. Like Jesus' condemnation of the hypocritical scribes and Pharisees (see Matt. 23:23), Paul warned the Corinthians to reexamine their way of dealing with the weightier matters of relationships. The technicalities could be postponed until his visit, but relationships needed to be dealt with immediately (1 Cor. 11:34). Paul's warning is just as relevant today as when he first dictated it. But I wonder, do you think we Christians of this era are any more prepared to hear that warning than the ancient Corinthians?

c. *Confusion and the Gifts of the Spirit (1 Cor. 12:1 to 14:40).* Beginning with chapter 12, Paul reached a crucial aspect of his analysis concerning confusion in Corinthian worship practices. The mere length of the discussion is an indication of how problematic the issue probably was. Not only had the Corinthians failed to discern the body of the Lord in the Lord's Supper but they had also failed to discern that the church itself was a body. They were acting as though what one member did had absolutely no effect on the rest of the church. Their independent spirit ran quite contrary to Paul's understanding of the church (1 Cor. 12:12-26).

In confronting their problem Paul addressed this proud group of "superior" people with a familiar refrain, namely, he did not want them to be ignorant (12:1). Then he pointed out that they had not come very far from their pagan past when they were falsely directed (*apagomenoi*) by dumb idols (12:2).[67] In their pride they had made distinctions between church members, and Paul reminded them very forcefully that the world was really divided into *only two groups:* those who cursed Jesus and those who called Him Lord (12:3). Moreover, the Spirit of God never made the mistake of confusing the two like the Corinthian categorizers had done.

Not everyone needed to be molded in the same fashion, according to Paul, because the Spirit provided spiritual gifts (*charismata;* 12:4). Human will did not determine the distribution of gifts, but the Spirit (12:11) gave each person gifts to fulfill God's purposes (12:5-7). Human beings, however, tended to want everyone to be constructed in a similar way with similar attributes. But the Spirit did not endow everyone with the same gifts just as the human body was not all constructed of similar parts (12:12).

Christians come together from various backgrounds, and no part of Christ's body is justified in saying that another part does not fit the church (12:13-21). Instead of excluding parts, the church needs to learn how to think unitedly, cooperatively, and supportively in order that there might not be any schism (*schisma*) in the body (12:22-25). The church needs to understand itself like a symphony where all parts work together. If one part suffers, it affects the entire group (12:26). Clearly, the independent spirit that castigates and separates is diametrically opposed to Paul.

The Corinthians' problem was that they had focused on one particular spiritual gift as a sign of their spirituality. They had elevated to primacy the gift of tongues speaking (*glossolalia*, a term derived from the Greek *glōssais lalein*). Like many spiritualist groups throughout the history of Christianity,[68] these spiritualists had selected the strange, exciting phenomenon of tongues babbling as the key to acceptable spirituality. In so doing, they had chosen what seemed to have been in Paul's mind the least of the gifts (12:10,28) and raised it to the rank of extreme importance. Paul's task, therefore, was to set such tongues speaking in the proper perspective.

Paul was quite aware that the mysterious elements of religion appealed to people. He undoubtedly knew that there were similar phenomena in pagan cults like Dionysus where alcoholic inspiration was used to promote unintelligible speech.[69] Moreover, he must have realized that in famous oracles like nearby Delphi, the inhaling of gaseous vapors escaping from the earth would render cult servants light-headed. The strange speech which resulted was interpreted by the priest of the shrine as a message from the gods.[70] For a Christian to measure spirituality by such ecstatic speaking explains why Paul regarded the Corinthians as having progressed little from paganism in this area of life (12:2).

Nevertheless, Paul recognized a spiritual dimension of the Christian life. He indicated quite clearly that he spoke in tongues more than all of them (14:18), but at the same time he indicated that tongues speaking really ranked very low on his scale of priorities in comparison to prophesying—namely five to ten thousand (14:19). I suspect that most Christians have wished that Paul asserted one thing or the other, *not both!* Yet I believe this is the point that distinguishes Paul from many contemporary Christians. Paul really lived with an amazing sense of freedom that was carefully controlled by his relationship to Christ, his concern for love, and his call to ministry. The goal of reaching the world for Christ with the loving message of the gospel was always foremost in Paul's thought. In criticizing the Corinthian spiritualists, this perspective is very evident.

In the middle of discussing the divisive issue of tongues speaking, Paul warned the Corinthians that the fundamental nature of Christianity was not spelled out in terms of tongues speaking or other mysterious powers (13:1-2). He also made it plain that the key to Christianity is not to be found primarily through knowledge, faith, or self-sacrifice (13:2-3). The heart of Christianity is love which positively involved life patterns like: suffering willingly, acting kindly, believing graciously, rejoicing truthfully, and hoping continuously (13:4-7). But it also means abandoning boasting and arrogance, removing oneself from the center of attention, and giving up calculating the problems of others (13:4-7)!

Love is not what one says; love is *what one does.*[71] It is a way of life that outlasts temporary experiences like tongues and imperfect calculations of knowledge like theology (13:8-9). It is the quality in humans which is most eternal (13:13), and it severely judges our religious piosity and our churchly successes.

Love was the goal to which Paul called every Christian in the context of problems like those related to spiritual gifts (14:1). The Christian must be concerned about the communication of the gospel and the growth of Christians. Tongues speaking was an experience oriented to the self's encounter with God, but prophesying (proclamation) was oriented to others (14:2-4). Paul's concern was to help the Corinthians avoid confusion in the church. Personal experiences with God naturally had a place in the lives of Christians, but tongues speaking in public was clearly the kind of experience that could cause confusion. The results of tongues speaking reminded him of a confused orchestra (14:7) or a confused army (14:8) or a confused discussion between people speaking different languages (14:9-11). Tongues speaking, he thought, was a kind of prayer experience in which the mouth was in

high gear while the mind was in neutral. Paul wanted his mind to
be in high gear along with his mouth (14:14-17). His goal was that
others might join him in prayer and proclamation and grow in Christ.

Paul understood tongues speaking to be a strange religious phenomenon which could be recognized by nonbelievers as an indication of
a supernatural presence in the church (14:22). But the problem was
what the sign communicated to outsiders. If tongues speaking broke
out in the worship service, unbelievers would not be helped but might
think that the Christian assembly had gone crazy (14:23), like the
drunken worshipers of Dionysus.

Paul warned the Corinthians that worship services were to be con-
ducted with strict attention to order, to be acceptable with social
decorum (14:26). If tongues speaking was part of the service, it was
definitely to be limited (14:27) to avoid giving the impression of pande-
monium in the church (14:23). Emphasis was to be placed on interpretation rather than tongues speaking; if adequate interpretation were
unavailable, tongues-speakers were warned to remain silent (14:28).
Paul's basic thesis was that God is orderly. Assurance for life came
from an orderly God, not from a God of confusion (14:33). Paul sought
to avoid or exclude those elements in public worship that created
confusion. He affirmed those elements that contributed to peace and
harmony because they contributed to the worship of Christians and
to the understanding of outsiders.

People who read these verses today should remember that orderliness was viewed by the Greeks as the highest of virtues.[72] Disorder
and confusion were barbaric and out of place in the best of Greek
society. Obviously Paul was conscious of where he was. His goal was
to win the Greeks to Christ. That which stood in the way of communi-
cating the gospel needed to be confronted.

Confusion in the church was an unacceptable pattern for Paul. He
challenged confusion in matters of dress (11:2-16), in community meals
involving the Lord's Supper (11:17-33), and in uncontrolled babbling
(12:1 to 14:32). In the latter case, he warned the Corinthians that
uncontrolled spiritual activity was illegitimate because the use of spiritual gifts was subject to the user just like the spirit of the prophet
was answerable to the prophet (14:32). No one was to employ the

Spirit as an excuse for the improper use of spiritual gifts. The Corinthians were called to orderly worship.

d. *Women Speaking and Confusion in Meetings* (*1 Cor. 14:33b-36*). In the context of orderliness, one of the most sharply debated texts of 1 Corinthians appears. That text involves the silence of women (14:34-35). Some scholars have found the text to be so obnoxious that they have assumed it was added by a later scribe to support a theory of male supremacy in the church.[73] Other people have been angered over the changing status of women; in a spirit of retrenchment, they have used the text as a sledge hammer to crush women's right of speech in the church. In this brief discussion, it is impossible to comment on all of the theological, political, and social aspects involved in these verses.[74]

Nevertheless, certain aspects of the problem can be mentioned briefly. First, I find little reason for rejecting Pauline authorship of these verses since those arguments deal primarily with subjective theology and not with issues of objective transmission. I believe the statement *goes back to Paul*. Second, an adequate interpretation of the text requires the interpreter to take for granted that Paul already recognized that women prayed and prophesied publicaly in the church (11:5).

To use this text as a general condemnation of women's public roles in the church is not acceptable on the basis that the same letter argues against such a conclusion. To argue in this manner one either has to say that one of the texts in 1 Corinthians does not come from Paul or else that Paul was confused in his view on women. I firmly reject both views.

The issue that faces us involves what was going on in the Corinthian church. The suggestions are numerous, and many of them involve interesting hypotheses that are supported by strong sociological and cultural patterns. One possibility is that the seating of men and women at worship was separate, similar to some ancient synagogues. Paul could then have been seeking to avoid confusion that may have resulted when some women were unable to understand the progression of the service or were trying from the rear to control the order of worship. Private conversations during worship in the synagogues and, by inheritance, in the early church were probably frequent. Quietness, then, was not the order of the day in worship.

Another possibility arises from the nature of the house churches themselves and the fact that husband-and-wife disputes may have threatened to explode into an entire church problem. If this were the case, Paul could have been calling the Christians to cease such confusing discussions in the church worship and get such matters settled at home. Paul would undoubtedly have held the man responsible for his wife's behavior and informed the wife to ask her husband about his judgment.

A third possibility involves the very structure of the discussion itself. The concept of speaking in chapters 13 and 14 focuses on immature speaking, which caused confusion or engendered conflict. There was no question in Paul's mind that whatever speaking was taking place in respect to the women was causing confusion in the church. Whether the women were speaking in tongues or otherwise causing confusion, Paul dealt with them severly because the church was obviously being upset by their activity. The result was that he silenced them and called them to an accounting with their husbands.

A fourth possibility, and perhaps the most intriguing, arises from our new sociological studies. Could the concern here have been with church business procedures? If the issue involved business, one could rather readily understand the possibility of confusion. While theologically women were regarded by Paul as equal to men before God (Gal. 3:28), in that society women were subject to their fathers or husbands.[75] Were these women trying to exercise rights in the church that were not recognized in society? If they were, it might surely explain why Paul thought that the issue deserved to be added to this section that concerned confusion in church practices. It would also explain why the women were told to "ask their husbands at home" concerning the matters discussed (1 Cor. 14:35). To apply this statement to Christian public proclamation and prayer, however, contradicts the earlier perspective in 11:5. But sociologically it makes some sense if Paul were talking about the issue of business in the early church.

We do not know all the implications of Paul's warning, but we must be very careful when making a stark evaluation of a woman's relationship to God or a woman's responsibility for spreading the gospel. If women were not to be involved in spreading the gospel, Priscilla would hardly have been a teacher of Apollos and a fellow worker of Paul (Rom. 16:3; 1 Cor. 16:19; Acts 18:26); June would have hardly been an apostle (Rom. 16:7); and Phoebe, hardly a deacon (Rom. 16:1).[76]

We may make all kinds of distinctions to support our preunderstandings of matters like the women's issue in the church, but Christians have grown most in their understanding of God and of the world when they have been willing to subject their preunderstandings to new light. I am continuing to grow in my understanding of Paul, as I have been studying the social and cultural world to which he was sent as a missionary. This emerging field of research is very enlightening. In this respect, I firmly disagree with those women in the liberation movement who despise Paul for being anti-female.[77] But I, likewise, disagree with those men who proclaim Paul as pro-male.[78] Paul was neither! He was pro-God! Paul's goal was to win the world to freedom in Christ. In the process, he did not want the gospel hindered by confusing society with unnecessary novelty in the church.

But what about the issue of women and their activities today? Can women hold property? Are they able to vote? Can they become senators and governors? Is it out of place in our society for them to conduct business? Can they become legal experts and judges? Then let us ask: Is there any difference between women in our society and the first century? Indeed, more to the point: Is it viewed as a confusing pattern for women to participate today in our church business meetings? Remember that not too long ago they were disfranchised even in our churches. Today are they able to speak to issues? Do we recognize their vote? Is their vote recognized in our national church conventions?

Here, then, is the crucial issue: Do women participate in matters of business in our society and in the church? The way one answers that question may be very critical for the way one relates to Paul. In Paul's day women were not allowed to participate. However, in religious matters, Paul judged them as fully competent before God.[79] In our day we may at times tend to reverse that pattern. In contemporary society, women vote and hold office, but we may try to keep women out of church leadership. In a hundred years, I am convinced people will wonder what all the present fuss was about. It will be like the issues of slavery and women's franchise. But in the meantime, I wonder what the great apostle would really say to us today if he could visit our contemporary churches? What kind of an impression are we giving to outsiders?

e. Conclusion. Paul was not a revolutionary in the sense of over-throwing the structures of society. He had little political power, so he could hardly abolish slavery. But he knew that the gospel would change the way people viewed world structures if Christians would treat slaves as brothers (Philem. 16). He recognized the role of women and their freedom in Christ, but he did not want their newfound freedom to destroy the stability of the church. Therefore, he sternly warned them to follow the social customs (1 Cor. 14:35-36). Similarly, he wanted the Corinthians to enjoy the assurance of spiritual freedom and he warned their opponents not to deny them their freedom (14:39). But he also warned the Corinthian who spoke in tongues not to destroy the harmony of the church by the disorderly use of their freedom (14:40).

The presence of Christ in the life of a Christian provides a marvelous sense of assurance that enables a Christian to live a new life of freedom in the Spirit. But freedom is a gift, and the Christian is forewarned that freedom must be accompanied by a sense of responsibility for one's calling in Christ and by a burden always to act lovingly toward others. This section of 1 Corinthians provides a vivid record of the fact that the divisions and imperfections of the church's life can be devastating hindrances to the proclamation of the gospel. They must be addressed just as much as matters of doctrine if the church is to achieve authenticity.

E. Assurance and Warning.
in the Proclamation of the Resurrection (1 Cor. 15:1-58).

Paul reached a magnificent climax in this section of his powerful letter. It is without doubt one of the most strategic chapters in the entire New Testament because it deals so perceptively with the central affirmation of Christianity. The resurrection of Jesus is the cornerstone of the Christian's assurance, and Paul warned Christians that denial of the resurrection left them totally without foundation for their faith. In all of the Pauline writings, there are probably no more strategic words than these: "If Christ has not been raised, then empty (*kenon*) is our proclamation and empty is your faith!" (15:14).

For the Corinthian know-it-alls, Paul pointedly opened this discussion by informing them that they should "know" (*gnōrizō*) that the gospel he preached was not something he invented or formulated. The gospel was given to him. He was part of the delivery system (*paralambanō*) and not the creator of the gospel (15:1). Paul's task, therefore, was to transfer (*paradidōmi*) to them the gospel without change (15:3) because the gospel was their basis for assurance of salvation (15:2). The expressions here and in 11:23 represent terminology related to the transmission of tradition. "They are meant to assure readers that what follows is authentic tradition."[80]

While Paul was very conscious of his unworthiness before God because he had earlier persecuted the church, the appearance of the risen Christ assured him that he was numbered among the apostles (15:9-10). Paul's response to God's graciousness was a commitment to Christ of such proportions that he believed that with God's help he outworked all of the other witnesses of Christ. But his tremendous sense of assurance and personal feeling of satisfaction was not self-centered. Instead, it was rooted in a conviction that he was part of a divine mission in which he was joined with the others in the proclamation (*kērussomen*, v. 11) of the Christian message or kerygma concerning the death, burial, resurrection, and appearing (15:3-8) of Jesus Christ, who was the focus of the Corinthian's believing (15:11).[81]

Paul was greatly concerned because the Corinthians had been reconstructing Christian theology, trying to conform it to a Greek understanding of the immortality of the soul.[82] In so doing they were actually denying the significance of the resurrection. Their folk theology was probably like a great deal of the folk theology in our churches that emphasizes the immortality of people's souls and fails to understand that such theology usually conflicts with the Christian view of resurrection.[83]

The folk theology of the Corinthians denied resurrection. But Paul—

the preacher of the resurrection—was not about to compromise this core element of the Christian faith. He warned them that, if they downplayed resurrection, their theology attacked the resurrection of Christ. Consequently the church's faith and proclamation were at stake (15:13-14). By holding such a view, they implied that Paul was a liar, that they were still sinners, that the dead in Christ were deceived, and that all Christians were miserable, powerless fools (15:15-19).

But they were absolutely wrong because Christ had in fact been raised! Christ's resurrection was, thus, the sign that the descendants of Adam could experience the great destiny of the resurrection if they were joined to Christ (15:20-22). They could also be assured that, because they belonged to Christ, they would have a part in the kingdom of God. Moreover, after death all God's enemies, including the final enemy (death itself) would be destroyed and they would witness the full implications of the lordship of God over all (15:23-28).

In spite of the fact that the Corinthians argued against the resurrection, they were apparently participating in strange baptismal practices involving the dead. The significant matter for Paul was that the Corinthians did not realize how inconsistent they were.[84] If they really considered resurrection to be unthinkable, why were they so concerned about the dead? Their actions were futile (15:29).

Moreover, Paul asked them: If resurrection were impossible, why would he subject himself to persecution and violent attacks? Why should he not rather live for the moment and indulge himself (15:31-32)? Ah, that idea fit the Corinthian libertine thinking perfectly! They had constructed a theology to fit their life-style—namely, eat and drink because there was no tomorrow, only death! But Paul would not let them get away with such rationalizations for their horrible morals. He quickly called them to task and warned them to come to their senses and to quit sinning. They were keeping bad company, and their lives were shameful.[85] Indeed, they were abysmally ignorant of God (15:34).

Nevertheless, in case some really believed their foolish theology (15:36), Paul informed them that their view of the resurrection was gross. The body that would be raised was not like the physical body on earth. Employing illustrations dealing with seed, animal life, and stars, Paul argued that the resurrection body would be a transformed body (15:36-44). It would be modeled not on the creation of Adam but on the image of Christ (15:45-49). The eternal kingdom of God, therefore, was not populated by mortals made of dust but by those who experienced immortal transformation (15:50).

This transformation would affect both those who were dead and those who were still alive at the time when the final trumpet would sound.[86] The change would occur in an apocalyptic second (*atomon*), in a moment which Paul likened to the "blinking of an eye." It would introduce victory for the Christian, a victory which would mean the collapse of death—the last enemy (see 1 Cor. 15:26; Rev. 20:14-15). In this announcement of the termination of death, Paul used two Old Testament texts (Isa. 25:8 and Hos. 13:14) with some modifications to produce a kind of a taunt song against death (1 Cor. 15:54-55). He highlighted the special significance of this important victory in the history of humanity's quest for assurance in salvation. Death, the terminator of human life, ultimately would itself be terminated.

Paul's mention of "sting" in this taunt song reminded him that the stinger of humanity was sin (15:56). Using arguments similar to Romans 5 and 7, he informed the Corinthians that the power (*dunamis*) of sin lay in the law. Some scholars have found little reason for the introduction of the law into this context and accordingly have judged it to be a gloss added by a later scribe who was familiar with Paul's thoughts.[87] Yet it is quite reasonable that the apostle for whom victory from legalistic bondage was so transforming and who penned the strategic arguments of Romans and Galatians could see in the reference to victory here a transcendent representation of the victory he had personally experienced in becoming a Christian.

The thanksgiving statement that follows is not merely a theological summation to a doctrinal argument concerning the resurrection (v. 57). The resurrection was never simply a theological proposition for Paul. It was not just some pie-in-the-sky answer to death. The resurrection of Jesus was the personal, powerful assurance that victory in life was possible in Christ. This thanksgiving statement, therefore, was Paul's confession of assurance that God gives Christians victory in this life through the living Christ.

Paul was not the kind of preacher who could conclude such a magnificent thought without a word of counsel or warning. If dynamic victory were possible in this life, the Christian's only option was to pursue it. Paul united all his thoughts in what may be his finest exhortation, reflecting both a guarded sense of concern and a great sense of confidence. The efforts of a Christian to live an authentic life would never be empty (*kenos*), like the misconceived theology of the Corinthians. God would see to it that authentic Christian effort would count. The Christian's task was to be faithful in a living commitment to the living Lord (15:58). What a finish to a superb climactic chapter!

Conclusion

The Letter of 1 Corinthians is a model for Christian criticism. The problems in the church were horrendous. The problems involved hateful bickering, incredible immorality, grasping court suits, unwise ascetic piety, blatant syncretism, confusing worship practices, and deviant theology. The church was a terrible hodgepoge of unchristian patterns. Yet Paul did not regard the situation as hopeless. He positioned himself positively in the midst of this crisis situation because he possessed both a superb understanding of the loving God who made Himself known in Christ Jesus and a realistic view of tragic humanity that seeks constantly to be its own master.

Paul's striking ability to deal with the tension between the power of God and the weakness of humans marks him as one of the outstanding figures in the history of Christianity. Because he perceived so clearly this divine-human tension, he was able to balance the relationship between assurance and warning with great finesse. The Letter of 1 Corinthians itself, therefore, forms an ideal example of the concerns which have prompted the writing of the present study.

In this letter Paul repeatedly criticized the proud Corinthian schismatics with great severity and continually warned them that, although they thought they were wise, they actually lacked an understanding of God. He frequently admonished them to turn from their ignorant ways and to flee from their disgusting immorality and pathetic idolatry. The warnings flow with such constancy that the reader might at first glance think that the letter was merely a long harangue against Corinthians rebels. But such a conclusion is very one-sided and superficial.

In spite of all the warnings, the letter pulsates with a tremendous substructure of assurance. Paul began the letter with a genuine sense of thanksgiving for the Corinthians as a people of God. While he warned them of their foolish factions and elevated views of their own knowledge, he nonetheless seemed confident that he could teach them, as a loving parent in Christ, to control their arrogance. While there were horrible problems of immorality and greed among them, he was sure that the church could learn to respond with a spirit of discipline in Christ. While they were involved in syncretistic idolatrous practices, he was positive that they could accept his warning and begin to imitate his disciplined life. While they were troubled by confusing worship practices, Paul was certain that loving order could be restored and that fragmentation could be avoided. While they had developed deviant theological views that supported their loose living, he was convinced that if they heard his heartbeat they would realize they were foolish and would recognize the tremendous power of God available to them in transforming their lives and assuring them of a great destiny with Christ.

Although Paul was sincerely troubled by the way the Corinthians practiced their Christianity, he did not give up on them because of his great confidence in the Lord. The Corinthians had some very good leaders in spite of all their problems. They could build a strong church, if they understood the true meaning of love in Christ Jesus. If they failed to love the Lord, however, Paul was realistic enough to announce his sternest warning—a horrible curse on them (*anathema*). Yet cursing was not the goal of the letter. Proclaiming love in Christ Jesus was. And Paul's proclamation was not merely a matter of words because he clearly believed and firmly prayed that the Lord whom he proclaimed would soon come in power (*maranatha,* 16:22).

At the very end of this great letter, Paul reminded his readers that, when he viewed the church, he had to live with an uneasy tension between serious warning and overwhelming assurance. The church was not a game in life or a private kingdom for Christians to use, and Paul knew it. But Christ was absolutely faithful, and Paul also knew that. To live with this tension between warning and assurance is the Christian heritage from Paul.

Notes

1. Gerald L. Borchert, *The Dynamics of Pauline Evangelism* (Forest Park, Ill.: Roger Williams Press, 1969), p. 1. See also Gerald L. Borchert, *The Dynamics of Evangelism* (Waco: Word Books, 1976), p. 93.

2. For an excellent analysis of Paul and Rome see Brown's discussion in Raymond E. Brown and John P. Meier, *Antioch and Rome* (New York: Paulist Press, 1983), pp. 97-98.

3. For general discussions on Paul's background and its effect on his ministry see, for example, F. F. Bruce, *Paul, Apostle of the Heart Set Free* (Grand Rapids: Wm. B. Eerdmans, 1977); W. Knox, *St. Paul* (New York: Appleton, 1932) which is a summary of his two larger works on *St. Paul and the Church of Jerusalem* and *St. Paul and the Church of the Gentiles;* and G. Ricciotti, *Paul the Apostle,* trans. A. Zizzmia (Milwaukee: Bruce, 1953).

4. See for example G. B. Caird, *Principalities and Powers* (Oxford: Clarendon Press, 1965) and Heinrich Schlier, *Principalities Powers in the New Testament* (New York: Herder-Herder, 1961).

5. F. C. Baur's important works *The Church History of the First Three Centuries,* 2 vols., 3rd ed., trans. A. Menzies (London: Williams and Norgate, 1878-1879) and *Paul the Apostle of Jesus Christ, His Life and Work, His Epistles and His Doctrine,* 2 vols., 2nd ed., trans. A. Menzies (London: Williams and Norgate, 1875-1876). For a brief introduction to Baur see his article "Hebraists, Hellenists and Catholics" available in the collection by Wayne Meeks, *The Writings of Paul* (New York: Norton, 1972), pp. 277-288.

6. See Gerald L. Borchert, *Discovering Thessalonians* (New York: Guideposts, 1986), Introduction.

7. See also Gerald L. Borchert, "A Superior Book: Hebrews," *Review and Expositor* 82 (1985):319-328.

8. For discussions of Corinth see, for example, James L. Blevins, "Introduction to 1 Corinthians," *Review and Expositor* 80 (1983): 315-317 and Jack Finegan, "Corinth," *Interpreter's Dictionary of the Bible* (Nashville: Abingdon Press, 1962) 1:682-683.

9. See for example Plato, *Republic,* 404d. See the comments of Jerome Murphy-O'Connor, *St. Paul's Corinth* (Wilmington Glazier, 1983), p. 56.

10. Strabo, *Geographia,* 8.378. For an evaluation of Strabo see Hans Conzelmann, *1 Corinthians,* Hermeneia, trans. J. W. Leitch (Philadelphia: Fortress Press, 1975), p. 12.

11. See C. K. Barrett, *A Commentary on the First Epistle to the Corinthians* (New York: Harper & Row, 1968), pp. 1-3.

12. J. A. Callaway, "Corinth," *Review and Expositor* 57 (1960): 384-385.

13. For various views on the chronology of Paul see, for example: J. Gunther, *Paul: Messenger and Exile* (Valley Forge: Judson Press, 1972); R. Jewett,

A Chronology of Paul's Life (Philadelphia: Fortress Press, 1979); D. Moody, "A New Chronology for the New Testament," *Review and Expositor* 78(1981): 211-231; G. Ludemann, *Paul, Apostle to the Gentiles* (Philadelphia: Fortress Press, 1984).

14. Johannes Weiss, *The History of Primitive Christianity*, trans. F. C. Grant (New York: Harper & Brothers, 1959) 1:324-325.

15. See, for example, the discussion of D. Guthrie, *New Testament Introduction*, 3rd ed. (Downers Grove: Inter-varsity Press, 1970), pp. 439-441 and W. G. Kümmel, *Introduction to the New Testament*, trans. H. Kee (Nashville: Abingdon Press, 1975), pp. 275-279, 287-293.

16. See Jean Héring, *The First Epistle of Saint Paul to the Corinthians*, trans. A. W. Heathcote and P. J. Allcock (London: Epworth Press, 1962), pp. xii-xiv and Walter Schmithals, *Gnosticism in Corinth*, trans. J. Steely (Nashville: Abingdon Press, 1971), pp. 87-96.

17. See for example Barrett, p. 15.

18. See for example J. Christiaan Beker, *Paul the Apostle: The Triumph of God in Life and Thought* (Philadelphia: Fortress Press, 1980), pp. 23-25.

19. Conzelmann, p. 299.

20. Ibid., pp. 217-220.

21. For discussion on the form of the Greek letter see W. Doty, *Letters in Primitive Christianity*, ed. D. Via, Jr., Guides to Biblical Scholarship: N. T. Series (Philadelphia: Fortress Press, 1973) and F. Exler, *The Form of the Ancient Greek Letter: A Study in Greek Epistolography* (Washington: Catholic University Press, 1923).

22. For Bultmann's view of Paul's theology see R. Bultmann, *Theology of the New Testament*, vol. 1, trans. K. Grobel (New York: Charles Scribner's Sons, 1955); R. Bultmann, *The Old and the New Man in the Letters of Paul*, trans. K. Crim (Richmond: John Knox Press, 1967); R. Bultmann, *Faith and Understanding*, vol. 1, trans. L. P. Smith (New York: Harper & Row, 1966).

23. See G. Borchert, "The Resurrection: 1 Corinthians 15," *Review and Expositor* 80 (1983): 408.

24. For a discussion of "in Christ" and Pauline mysticism see L. Cerfaux, *The Spiritual Journey of Saint Paul*, trans. J. Guiness (New York: Sheed & Ward, 1968); A. Schweitzer, *The Mysticism of Paul the Apostle*, trans. W. Montgomery (London: A. C. Black, 1931); G. Verity, *Life in Christ* (Greenwich: Seabury Press, 1954); A. Wikenhauser, *Pauline Mysticism* (Edinburgh: Nelson Press, 1960). Also see F. F. Bruce, "Was Paul a Mystic?" *Reformed Theological Review* (1975), pp. 66-75.

25. For a discussion of the Christian greeting and its relationship to Greek (*chairein*) and Hebrew (*shalom*) greetings see Borchert, *Discovering Thessalonians*, Chapter 1. Almost any major commentary should discuss the issue. See, for example, Conzelmann, pp. 23-24 and Barrett, pp. 34-35.

26. For a discussion of the thanksgiving sections in Greek letters see P. O'Brien, *Introductory Thanksgivings in the Letters of Paul*, Novum Testamentum Supplement 49 (Leiden: E. J. Brill, 1977) and P. Schubert, *Form and Function of the Pauline Thanksgivings* (Berlin: Töpelmann, 1939). See also J. Sanders, "The Transition From Opening Epistolary Thanksgiving to Body in the Letters of the Pauline Corpus," *Journal of Biblical Literature* 81 (1962): 348-362.

27. The Thessalonian letters are great books in which to obtain a picture of the caring Paul for his children in the faith. See Borchert, *Discovering Thessalonians*.

28. See Origen's apology, *Contra Celsum* 3.44.

29. John Polhill, "The Wisdom of God and Factionalism: 1 Corinthians 1-4," *Review and Expositor* 80(1983): 330. For the contrary position see Karl Donfried, "The Sociohistorical Setting of 1 Corinthians," an unpublished lecture delivered to Studiorum Novi Testamenti Societas, 1986.

30. For a discussion of the relative weight of "mystery" (*mustērion*) see Bruce M. Metzger, *A Textual Commentary on the Greek New Testament* (London: United Bible Societies, 1971), p. 545. In contrast to the RSV reading of "testimony" here, I prefer with Metzger to read "mystery" which seems to be supported by the original hands of the third century Chester Beatty Papyrus (P[46]) and the fourth century Sinaiticus (Aleph) as over against the fourth century Codex Vaticanus (B) and the sixth century Claromontanus (D). The Alexandrian reading, I believe, is superior to the Western text.

31. The quotation as it stands is really not to be found in any Old Testament text. Nor is it known in the other Jewish writings. For a helpful discussion of the problem please see Conzelmann, pp. 63-64.

32. See for example Erwin R. Goodenough, *By Light, Light: The Mystic Gospel of Hellenistic Judaism* (New Haven: Yale University Press, 1935).

33. For a discussion on the Romans text see C. K. Barrett, *A Commentary on the Epistle to the Romans* (New York: Harper & Row, 1958), pp. 230-233.

For the classic treatment on the emptying (*kenōsis*) passage of Philippians see Ralph Martin, *Carmen Christi: Philippians ii.5-11 in Recent Interpretation and in the Setting of Early Christian Worship* (Cambridge: University Press, 1967). See also Frank Stagg, "Philippians," *The Broadman Bible Commentary*, ed. C. Allen (Nashville: Broadman Press, 1971) 2:195-197 and Gerald Hawthorne, *Philippians*, Word Biblical Commentary (Waco: Word Books, 1983) 43:71-96.

34. Fencing the Torah is an expression used for the development of traditions, first oral and then written which guided the Jews in obedience of laws. The development of tradition was emphasized in the schools such as the Sadducees, Pharisees, and Essenes prior to the time of Christ and was

accelerated in later centuries by the Pharisaic survivors. The Mishnah and Talmud are results of the development of tradition.

35. The expression "his father's wife" in 1 Corinthians 5:1 most probably indicated that the woman was not the man's mother but was another wife of his father. For the distinction between expressions of a mother and a stepmother see Leviticus 18:7-8. There is no indication here of whether the man's father was dead, feeble, or otherwise incapacitated.

36. Ray Summers has well noted that such an incestuous relationship was regarded as illegal "even under the guise of marriage" in Roman, Greek, and Jewish legal systems. See R. Summers, "First Corinthians: An Exposition," *Review and Expositor* 57 (1960): 403. See also Conzelmann, p. 96.

37. For references to principalities and powers in the Pauline context see note 4 in this chapter. For a discussion of the satanic in Paul see J. Kallas, *The Satanward View: A Study in Pauline Theology* (Philadelphia: Westminster Press, 1966).

38. For a brief history of the development of equity see Theodore F. T. Plucknett, *A Concise History of the Common Law*, 4th ed. (London: Butterworth & Co., 1948), pp. 647-656.

39. The streamlining of the court systems particularly in Great Britain was greatly enhanced by a series of Judicature Acts which dated from 1813 through 1881 that reformed the enormous load of the Chancery in 1831-1832 and resulted in an amalgamation with King's Bench in 1881. See Plucknett, pp. 199-207.

40. Paul Minear, "Christ and the Congregation: 1 Corinthians 5—6," *Review and Expositor* 80 (1983): 344-345.

41. It has been intriguing to observe translations of 1 Corinthians 6:9 where there are two Greek words for homosexual deviants. The KJV and other earlier translations were generally too polite to use the terms. The RSV in its early rendering combined the terms and read "homosexuals." The most recent RSV rendering has "sexual perverts." The two Greek words really mean both the effeminate and masculine partners of homosexual relations.

42. Rudolf Bultmann in his early research argued that Paul was influenced by the Cynic and Stoic Diatribe. See: *Der Stil der paulinischen Predigt und die kynisch-stoische Diatribe* (Göttingen: Vandenhoeck & Ruprecht, 1910). Recently, the issue has received further study by S. Stowers, *The Diatribe and Paul's Letter to the Romans*, SBL Dissertations 57 (Chico, Calif.: Scholars Press, 1981). The question rages whether Paul actually used the format of the Diatriabe or just dialogical patterns of discussion.

43. The translations of the GNB and NIV at 1 Corinthians 7:1 concerning marriage are not the best. To "touch a woman" means having sexual relations with her. See Gordon Fee, "1 Corinthians 7:1 in the NIV," *Journal of the Evangelical Theological Society* 23 (1980): 307-314 and David Garland, "The

Christian's Posture Toward Marriage and Celibacy: 1 Corinthians 7," *Review and Expositor* 80 (1983): 351-352.

44. Paul's background in Judaism would have alerted him to the fact that it was the prerogative of men to make most of the decisions in the marriage relationship at that time. The significance of Paul's discussion in this chapter lies in the importance of mutuality in decision making within the marriage patterns.

45. See John C. Hurd, Jr., *The Origin of 1 Corinthians* (London: SPCK, 1965), especially at pp. 165-169 for an excellent discussion.

46. Victor Paul Furnish, *The Moral Teaching of Paul* (Nashville: Abingdon Press, 1979), p. 39.

47. For a discussion of the translation problems in 1 Corinthians 7:10-11 see D. Garland, p. 355. The explanation of "the Lord" in 1 Corinthians 7:10 seems to imply that the teaching went back either to the historical Jesus' words or to the resurrected Lord's instructions.

48. See the discussion in J. Drane, *Paul: Libertine or Legalist? A Study in the Theology of the Major Pauline Epistles* (London: SPCK, 1975). See also J. Drane, "Tradition, Law and Ethics in Pauline Theology," *Novum Testamentum* 16 (1974): 167-178.

49. For a full discussion of the matters related to idol meats see the dissertation of my former student William H. Lawson, "First Corinthians 9:24 to 10:22 in its Contextual Framework," a dissertation presented to the faculty of The Southern Baptist Theological Seminary, Louisville, 1984.

50. See, for example, Schmithals.

51. For a discussion of Gnostic structures see G. Borchert, "Insights into the Gnostic Threat to Christianity as Gained through the Gospel of Philip" in *New Dimensions in New Testament Study,* ed. R. Longemecker and M. Tenney (Grand Rapids: Zondervan, 1974), pp. 79-93. For helpful introductions to the subject, Robert Grant, *Gnosticism and Early Christianity,* 2nd ed. (New York: Harper Bros., 1966); Hans Jonas, *The Gnostic Religion,* 2nd ed. (Boston: Beacon Press, 1963); Edwin Yamauchi, *Pre-Christian Gnosticism: A Survey of the Proposed Evidences,* rev. ed. (Grand Rapids: Baker Books, 1984).

52. For a discussion of the strong and the weak in 1 Corinthians see Gerd Theissen, *The Social Setting of Pauline Christianity,* ed. and trans. J. Schütz (Philadelphia: Fortress Press, 1982), pp. 121-143.

53. For a discussion on the significance of calling God Father please see G. Borchert, "The Lord of Form and Freedom: A New Testament Perspective on Worship," *Review and Expositor* 80 (1983): 15-16 especially.

54. For an excellent statement of Paul's accommodation as a slave in order to win Jews, those under the law (proselytes?), those outside the law and the weak, see Harold Songer, "Problems Arising from the Worship of Idols: 1 Corinthians 8:1-11:1," *Review and Expositor* 80 (1983): 368.

55. See ibid, p. 370.

56. For a fuller discussion of the rock as a symbol for preexistent wisdom, see Conzelmann, pp. 166-167. The idea of a moving rock as used in this sense, however, is unusual.

57. There is a variant in the Greek manuscripts at 1 Corinthians 10:9. The most likely reading from my analysis is "Christ" because of the support of P^{46}. Some other early uncials read "Lord" instead. From my perspective, Paul here was strengthening his case for the linkage between judgment in the wilderness setting and judgment in the New Testament era. The rules of textual analysis would, I consider, therefore favor the rendering of the KJV over the RSV at this point.

58. The text of 1 Corinthians 10:28-29 has been the subject of much discussion. See, for example Barrett, *First Corinthians,* p. 242 and Conzelmann, pp. 177-178. Songer, p. 373.

59. Jerome Murphy-O'Conner, "Sex and Logic in 1 Corinthians 11:2-16," *Catholic Biblical Quarterly* 42 (1980): 483.

60. I am indebted to Richard Oster for information contained in a helpful paper entitled "Cultural Background to 1 Corinthians 11:4," an unpublished lecture delivered to *Studiorum Novi Testamenti Societas,* 1986.

For further information see I. S. Ryberg, *Rites of the State Religion in Roman Art,* Memoirs of the American Academy in Rome 22 (Rome: American Academy, 1955), pp. 38-63, 96, 109-114, 156-158.

61. See Dionysius of Halicarnassus 12.16.2-3.

62. Plutarch, *Quaest Rom.* 266d. See also Dionysius of Halicarnassus, *Antiq. Rom.* 12.16.3. See also Oster, pp. 5, 15-18,21 for a discussion of the clash of cultures. See K. J. Marquardt, *Römische Staatsverwaltung. Das Sacralwesen,* 2nd ed. (Leipzig: Verlag von S. Hirzel, 1885) 3:186-187.

63. For excellent discussions on the church as an *oikos* (house) see John H. Elliot, *A House for the Homeless: A Sociological Exegesis of 1 Peter, Its Situation and Strategy* (Philadelphia: Fortress Press, 1981), pp. 21-49 and Wayne Meeks, *The First Urban Christians: The Social World of the Apostle Paul* (New Haven: Yale University Press, 1983), pp. 75-77.

64. The Romans were especially known for attachment to dress as a means of identification but so, too, were the Greeks. See for example Harrianne Mills, "Greek Clothing Regulations: Sacred and Profane," *Zeitschrift für Papyrologie und Epigraphik* 55 (1984): 255-263. See also Margarete Bieber, *Entwicklungsgeschichte der greichischen Tracht,* 2nd ed. (Berlin: Verlag G. Mann, 1967), especially at pp. 40-42.

65. See Theissen, pp. 145-174.

66. For a helpful discussion of this perspective see Beverly R. Gaventa, " 'You Proclaim the Lord's Death': 1 Corinthians 11:26 and Paul's Understanding of Worship," *Review and Expositor* 80 (1983): 377-387.

67. For a discussion see Conzelmann, pp. 205-206.

68. The tension has been present throughout Christian history from the Corinthians to Tertullian and the Montanists to the Medieval ecstatics to the more recent Pentecostal churches and the contemporary Charismatic Movement.

69. For a description of the festivals of Dionysus see Oskar Seyffert, *Dictionary of Classical Antiquities*, rev. H. Nettleship and J. Sandys (New York: Meridian Books, 1957), pp. 189-194.

70. For a discussion of the Greek oracles see ibid., pp. 434-436.

71. See J. W. MacGorman, "Glossolalic Error and Its Correction: 1 Corinthians 12-14," *Review and Expositor* 80 (1983): 395.

72. The concept of order or harmony was inherent within Heraclitus's concept of *logos*, but the Pythagoreans gave force to the idea of "harmony" and in reality designated harmony as virtue. See Wilhelm Windelband, *A History of Philosophy* (New York: Harper & Bros., 1958) 1:63.

73. See for example Conzelmann, p. 246.

74. For a much fuller discussion of the issues involved in these verses see the dissertation of one of my former students, Sunday Olusola Aworindle, "First Corinthians 14:33b-36 in its Literary and Socio-historical Contexts," a dissertation presented to the faculty of The Southern Baptist Theological Seminary, 1985. The reader will find that my solution differs from that of my former student.

75. For a discussion on women in the Greco-Roman context see Meeks, pp. 23-25. See also David L. Balch, *Let Wives be Submissive: The Domestic Code in 1 Peter*, SBL Monographs 26 (Chico, Calif.: Scholars Press, 1981).

76. While many English translations assume that *Iounian* in Romans 16:7 is a masculine name, that rendering is an unproven assumption for a *first declension* Greek noun! Moreover, "kinspersons" is just as correct a rendering for *suggeneis* as the RSV's "kinsmen." The use of "men" in that same verse is a term which is not in the Greek and has been added by the translators for clarification. I have translated the word *Iounian* here as "June" because I think it is the most probable rendering. The issue of how theology affects our translations, at the very least, needs to be recognized.

The rendering of Phoebe as "deaconess" rather than as deacon in the RSV and other versions needs to be faced even more squarely because of the distinctions in the contemporary church which are read back into the early church. If the English term *deaconess* meant in the minds of the people a genuine, fully qualified, female deacon, then the rendering would be acceptable. But I doubt that most church people would so read it. I think in this respect it is well to remember that Phoebe was a deacon in Cenchreae which we should also remember was the seaport city of Corinth!

Now I am not trying here to deal with all of the issues in the New Testament respecting women. That would be far too complex for this present study.

My concern is to be as fair as possible with the situation in Corinth. Someone should do the *theological and sociological* studies related to Ephesus and elsewhere. They might be revealing.

77. See for example Elizabeth Schüssler Fiorenza, *In Memory of Her: A Feminist Theological Reconstruction of Christian Origins* (New York: Cross-road, 1984), especially Chapters 5 to 7.

78. See Grant Osborne's study of perspectives, "Hermeneutics and Women in the Church," *Journal of the Evangelical Theological Society* 20 (1977): 337-352.

79. Cults like Isis were beginning to suggest a change in the cultural pattern, but women still had difficulty in matters of legal equality. See Meeks, p. 25. For a discussion of women's growing legal rights see Ramsay MacMullen "Women in Public in the Roman Empire," *Historia* 29 (1980): 208-218.

80. See Borchert, "The Resurrection," p. 401. See also Oscar Cullmann, *The Early Church*, ed. A. Higgins (Philadelphia: Westminster Press, 1956), pp. 55 *ff.* and W. D. Davies, *Paul and Rabbinic Judaism*, pp. 248-249.

81. For a discussion of Paul's kerygma here see Borchert, "The Resurrection," pp. 402-406.

82. See Bruce, *1 and 2 Corinthians*, p. 144.

83. See Oscar Cullmann, *Immortality of the Soul or Resurrection of the Dead?* (New York: Macmillan, 1958).

84. See Borchert, "The Resurrection," p. 409.

85. See ibid., p. 410. The quotation from Menander's lost comedy *Thais* does not necessarily indicate that Paul knew Menander. The quotation by that time may have been proverbial. See Barrett, *First Corinthians*, p. 367.

86. For a discussion of trumpet see Barrett, *First Corinthians*, p. 381.

87. See Conzelmann, *1 Corinthians*, p. 293, n42.

3

Assurance and Warning in John: A Gospel Style

The Fourth Gospel is one of the most beloved literary works in Christianity. It captivates its readers and sears their memories with unforgettable stories that set theological discussions of Christian faith and life into memorable dynamic contexts. This Gospel contains some of the best known and most often quoted verses in the entire Bible. While its vocabulary is simple and repetitive, the structural development and interweaving of thematic motifs or themes combine to make it one of the most intriguing documents of Christianity. This Gospel gives "the sensitive reader the feeling of being encompassed by the work of an awe-inspiring artist in much the same way one is awed by the intricate complexity of a sophisticated symphony."[1]

The poetic simplicity of this Gospel makes it quite easy to memorize, but its complex perfectionistic theology makes it somewhat difficult for contemporary readers either to understand readily or to adopt comfortably as a way of life.[2] This Gospel provides a model of Christian integrity that illuminates our half-hearted commitments and judges our self-centered ways of life. Clement of Alexandria well categorized this book when he referred to it as a "spiritual gospel."[3] It is, indeed, an inspired book which has been "inspirited" by the Spirit of God.

The Johannine Gospel, however, has also been at the center of controversies related to assurance and warning. Many like Augustus Strong have used texts from the parable of the shepherd (John 10:27-29) and from the prayer of Jesus (17:11-12) as stack poles around which to develop their views of perseverance and security.[4] Others like Dale Moody have sought to employ verses from the parable of the vine and the vinedresser (15:2,6-7) to argue for apostasy.[5] Since this Gospel has been employed to support such alternatives, it needs to be included in this discussion.

Such divisions over the Johannine perspective are not basically the result of varying views of biblical authority. For example, two of my New Testament associates from the Tyndale Fellowship (Britain)/Institute of Biblical Research (North America), Donald A. Carson and I. Howard Marshall, are both committed to a very high view of Scripture, but the results of their studies of John have led them to just as diverse theological opinions as the systematic theologians Moody and Strong.[6] In contrast to all of these treatments, which I believe extract texts from their contexts and attempt to systematize them, I will review the divine and human dimensions presented in the Gospel and identify the teaching on assurance and warning as it unfolds. Perhaps in so doing, readers will gain a better handle on the debate and be able to judge the merits of the arguments for themselves.

The Problems of Authorship, Dating, and Setting

Readers interested in pursuing the issue further should consult works by scholars such as Raymond Brown, George Beasley-Murray, William Hull, Leon Morris, Rudolf Schackenburg, Stephen Smalley, or George Turner and Julius Mantey.[7] Introductions by Donald Guthrie and W. G. Kümmel will also be helpful.[8]

Dating

Concerning dating, I find little reason to reject the traditional date of the mid-nineties for the writing of the Gospel. The early dates proposed by W. F. Albright and by J. A. T. Robinson, I believe, lack substance whereas the second century date of some German writers I consider to be far too late and built upon speculative theological ties with patterns such as Gnosticism.[9]

Authorship

The authorship question may be a little more difficult to decide. However, it does not really make a vast difference whether the writer was the beloved disciple of tradition or a Johannine school (such as proposed by Alan Culpepper and others[10]) which assembled reflections from their great teacher. It is clear from John 21:24 that a school or a church had an important hand in publishing the Gospel. That verse certainly was not written by the beloved disciple. The theory of Floyd Filson, however, that Lazarus wrote the Gospel is clever but totally speculative.[11] Moreover, the idea of C. H. Dodd that the Gospel and 1 John were from quite different hands is not convincing.[12]

Integrity

Another introductory matter that probably needs some comment concerns the order of the Gospel stories (theories of displacement) and the process of editing the Gospel (theories of reconstruction). Reconstruction theories of writers like G. H. C. MacGregor and A. W. Morton which result in a cut-and-paste document and displacement theories which attempt to re-edit the document on the basis of the geographical locations of the stories usually miss the finely turned theological organization of this amazing Gospel.[13] Even when the computer is summoned to support such investigations by those like Morton, the results are merely accelerated human calculations and are only as dependable as the programmer's insights. If studies fail to deal with the theology of the Gospel, I think they are hapless examples of deficient scholarship.[14]

Geographical Considerations

Finally, concerning the geographical setting of the Gospel, I find no adequate reason to abandon the traditional site of Ephesus as the place of origin for the work. For the purposes of this study, however, a site outside the Palestinian context where Christianity was making an impact on the Gentile world would be sufficient to underline John's concern for the entire world (3:16) as well as what must have been for him a genuine sadness that Jesus was rejected by His own people and His own homeland (1:11).

The Jewish rejection of Jesus must have weighed heavily upon John because the portrait of the Jews in this Gospel is exceedingly negative. Most likely the negative reaction to the Jews was not merely based on hostility to Jesus but also on the Christians' experiences with Jews. The *Birkath ha Minim* (the Jewish curse on the Christians as heretics), which was added to the synagogue prayers (the Eighteen Benedictions) in the last part of the first century, is a clear indication of how the Jews regarded the early Christians.[15] A number of early Christians undoubtedly sought to retain a relationship with the Jewish synagogue, while at the same time they attended the Christian community. Some of these believers were likely "closet" Christians who tried to avoid persecution. Other believers were probably more vocal and experienced Jewish hostility like that described in Acts. Some of the persecution they experienced in their cities and regions was doubtlessly instigated by hostile Jews. The curse of the Christians and the formulations of Judaism, which have often been associated with the name of Jamnia (the theory that the Jewish rabbis met in council and restructured Judaism after the fall of Jerusalem), were probably some of the important factors leading to the formal separation of Christians from Jews.[16]

The strained relationship between Jews and Christians seems to be mirrored in the Gospel of John and needs to be remembered as part of the background in discussing the motifs of assurance and warning in the Johannine literature. By alluding to this background I make no attempt to suggest that the conflict itself gave rise to the fundamental theological affirmations in John or to the lordship titles for Jesus, as has sometimes been asserted.[17] But background experiences must have played a part in the selection of materials that were included by biblical writers in their works.

The Nature and Purpose of John

The Nature of the Gospel

This work called John is a Gospel (*euaggelion*). A Christian Gospel is not merely a biography of a great hero called Jesus.[18] The Greek term for *gospel* originally meant the bringing of a good message, and the messenger usually expected a reward for bringing that message. Few runners in the ancient world wanted to carry bad news for fear that the recipient, such as a king, might penalize them by taking their lives. Therefore, bad news bringers often failed to arrive when dispatched. The news and the messenger were thus inextricably linked together. This fact should not be lost when thinking about the meaning of a Gospel.[19]

The term *gospel* appears primarily in the Pauline Letters, and this fact has led some to suggest that Paul was the one responsible for its becoming entrenched in the Christian vocabulary.[20] The meaning of the term is undoubtedly related to the Hebrew *besorah* (good news), and its use in the church was probably in some way dependent upon the Old Testament idea of God's messenger bringing God's message.[21] In the New Testament, the term undoubtedly implied more—namely, the content of the good news or message of God's salvation which came through Jesus Christ. It was also used by Christians as a way of referring both to the power of God and to the "sum total of Christian faith and life."[22]

The linkage of the message with the message carrier was preserved by Paul as he spoke of "my gospel" (Rom. 2:16; 16:25). This expression contrasts with Paul's frequent references to "the gospel of Christ" or "the gospel of God" (for example, Rom. 1:1; 1:16; 15:16-19). The latter expressions involve the content of the gospel and refer to the divine author of the good news of salvation. The former expression, "my gospel," implies that the messenger had an inspired role in the formulation of the good news. This former meaning became associated with the genre (category) of literature known as Gospels. In other words, John's Gospel is John's formulated statement about salvation; his particular formulation focuses on events dealing with Jesus' incarnation, death, and resurrection.

This literary form is perhaps best likened to a "testimony" about Jesus. Its form was something quite new in the history of literature. It was probably developed by Mark, though some scholars continue to argue that Matthew was the first Gospel writer.[23] While the New Testament contains four such documents, three of them (Matthew, Mark, and Luke) are similar in format and are often called the Synoptic Gospels. The Gospel of John has quite a different format. Yet both types of Gospels are inspired testimony documents about Jesus.

In the second century, Tatian thought he could solve the tensions between the four Gospels by combining all four documents into his single harmonized *Diatessaron*.[24] Tatian carefully worked the stories of the three Synoptics into the time frame of the Johannine Gospel. Thus, he eliminated the tensions in the Gospels. But in so doing, he misunderstood what the Gospels were all about. He certainly did not perceive the nature of the marvelous thematic testimony called the Gospel of John. Tatian's primary concern was to get rid of the problems in the Gospels. Thank God, the early church rejected Tatian's harmony as a substitute for the four Gospels! But the temptation of harmonization has not totally passed. We are often more interested in the order of the events of Jesus' life than in the inspired testimony given about the meaning of those events.

If the church had accepted Tatian, we (in the name of conservative uniformity) would have lost the great testimonies of four persons who were touched specially by God, as each gave us his particular portrait of Jesus.[25] Each portrait is unique. Each begins differently. Each ends differently. And each emphasizes different aspects of our Lord. Now the skills of contemporary preachers and teachers are most evident when, with the help of the Holy Spirit, they are able to show others how the picture of each writer bears witness to the wonder of Jesus' words and works.

The Purpose of the Gospel

The purpose statement in the Gospel of John clearly states the Johannine perspective: "Many other signs did Jesus which are not recorded in this book; but these are recorded that you might believe Jesus is the Christ, the Son of God, and believing you might have life in His name" (20:30-31). This purpose statement is, first, a pointer to some of the most basic themes in the Gospel, namely: signs, believing, life, and sonship. It is also a summary of what the Gospel writer expected should happen if people took his message seriously. The purpose, then, is concerned with life transformation—a transformation which results in a life of discipleship. One of the most important lessons to learn from John is that the themes are not merely related to intellectual transformation but to the transformation of one's total way of being. Therefore, *nothing less than personal commitment to Jesus* which issues in *authentic changed living* is adequate for understanding the goal of this Gospel!

With such a perspective in mind, the reader also must remember that this Gospel was written after all the other Gospels were circulating. There is more at work in John, therefore, than the mere presentation of the stories of Jesus. Through these stories, by the inspiration of God, John became more than a simple storyteller. He became a superb communicator to his community of how the Christian church ought to follow its Lord and Master. In receiving the message of John, we must watch carefully for the interplay of the divine and the human dimensions and be prepared to apply both the messages of God's assuring power *and* the Lord's firm warnings personally to our lives.

This aspect of personal application raises one other matter. In contrast to some other New Testament documents which emphasize the

concept of collectivity, Brown has indicated that the Johannine works
are distinguished by an "emphasis on *the relation of the individual
Christian to Jesus Christ.*"[26] By emphasizing the individual believer,
there is an obvious de-emphasis upon corporate church concerns,
such as baptism and the Lord's Supper. If one looks for a dominical
ordinance (a church activity commanded by our Lord) in the Gospel
of John, one quickly discovers that it has to be in the foot-washing
episode (13:14-15,34-35). Such a fact may raise problems for some.
Why foot washing? Why not baptism and the Lord's Supper? The
answer is not that John was unaware of baptism or the Lord's Supper,
as the discussions in John 3 and 6 will certainly indicate. The answer
is that these activities were not John's primary focus of concern. His
concern was with a Christian's personal relationship to Jesus and how
that relationship evidences itself in the life of a believer. If, therefore,
personal relationship is important, the reader is alerted to watch for
how significant both personal assurance and personal warning are in
this Gospel.

The Organization of John

This Gospel breaks beautifully into two sections. In the first section,
frequently called the Book of Signs (1:19 to 12:50), the emphasis is
on who Jesus is and how a relationship is established with Him. In
the teaching portions of this section, ideas of believing and knowing
God's Son are primarily in focus. In the second section, frequently
called the Book of Glory (13:1 *ff.*), the emphasis is on the implications
of being a Christian and how the Christian life is maintained and
developed. In this section the motif of love becomes extremely important. The way a Christian lives in a hostile world without the compan-
ionship of the historical Jesus emerges as a key issue. In this latter
section the teaching of the Paraclete (*paraklētos*, the companion Spirit)
becomes important.

Both sections are tied together beautifully by a profound Prologue
(1:1-18) and by the pithy Conclusion (20:30-31) already introduced
above. So neatly organized have these twenty chapters been and so
natural is the first conclusion to the Gospel that Alfred Loisy exclaimed,
"*Le livre est fini, tres bien fini*" ("The book is complete, quite com-

plete!").[27] Such a conclusion *does not mean* that chapter 21 is an unrelated appendix from a different source.[28]

To illustrate the relationship of chapter 21 to the remainder of the book, one needs only to look at the picture of Peter. Peter had been consistently played down in his relationship to the beloved disciple in the earlier chapters. For example, Peter was not the one lying closest to Jesus at the meal (13:23-24; see 21:20) or that the beloved disciple outran Peter to the tomb and believed first (20:3-8). So in chapter 21, the beloved disciple recognized the risen Jesus first and told Peter (21:7). Then, Peter was humbled in his commissioning (21:17-18) as he had been humbled at the foot washing (13:9-10). Moreover, Peter's life was not to last long (21:18-19), but that of the beloved disciple was likely to last much longer (21:22-23). In evaluating this chapter, Brown correctly suggested that the beloved disciple served in John as a genuine ideal of Christian discipleship.[29] I would add that here the *beloved disciple was the symbol* of the one who evidenced assurance in his discipleship, whereas *Peter was the symbol* of one who needed to be warned periodically by Jesus to live up to an authentic life of discipleship.

The Gospel Called John

A. Assurance and Warning
at the Beginning and the End of John

I have told my students to read the beginning and the end of a Gospel very carefully and they might learn something about what is in the middle. I believe that case is true of the Fourth Gospel. We will begin by looking at the Prologue. For the ending we will look at a portion of chapter 20, rather than looking further at the postscript (John 21). While some aspects of the postscript have already been discussed, its function will be reviewed more in detail later. With respect to John 20, the important summary purpose statement has already been discussed. Our attention here will be focused briefly on the concluding narrative that is a two-part appearance story to the disciples and Thomas.

THE PROLOGUE

The Gospel opens with a profound Prologue (1:1-18) that sets the tone for reading the Gospel. Scholars have directed much attention to discovering the crucial ideas and patterns in these verses. Brown has argued that the prologue is a hymn, J. T. Sanders that it is poetry, and C. K. Barrett that it is poetic prose.[30] Some have posited that the key is in John 1:14; others, that it is in 1:16. Culpepper has thought that he found a chiastic structure with the center being "he gave power to become children of God" (1:12).[31] While Culpepper's suggested "X" parallelisms may require the refining of some minor rough edges, his structure is very intriguing for our study here.

To summarize, I would say that the Prologue begins and ends with the God who reached out to the world in His Word (*logos*, 1:1) or in His only Son (*monogenēs*, 1:18). That Son came into the world as light or glory (1:9,14) but was not accepted by His own people. Indeed, He could not be accepted because humans were born of blood and flesh and human will (1:11,13). But God sent a witness, John (who is not to be identified as the divine messenger, 1:6-8,15), in order that we might better understand what God was doing in Christ. Therefore, to as many as received Him or believed in His name (1:12*a* and 12*c* in Greek), He gave the power to become the children of God (1:12*b*).

The Prologue is incredible in its balance. It begins and ends with the initiative of God. It reaches the turnaround point, I believe, in God's gift of power to become His children. Its author highlighted the typical human pattern of rejecting God's messenger, but he also recognized that some humans would receive and believe. It is an amazing piece of literature in theology because it is really *neither a one-sided statement of election nor of free will*. It contains instead a powerful message of assurance concerning God's role in salvation to those who need it as well as a forceful implied warning to those who reject God's messenger.

THE ENDING

At the opposite end of the book I believe there is a sequel—a unique two-part story concerning the disciples and Thomas. Much attention has been given by scholars to this story, especially to the mention of the Holy Spirit here and the relationship of this story to

Pentecost in Luke/Acts. For our particular purposes, however, the
story is interesting because it is a twofold Christophany (appearance
of the risen Jesus). Both sections contain the typical statement of
"peace" (20:19-21,26) or "Do not fear" which is familiar from the Old
Testament when either God or an angel put in a terrifying appearance
to mere mortals and is recognized (see, for instance, Gideon in Judg.
6:22-23; Zechariah in Luke 1:13; the powerful implication of who Jesus
is in Mark 6:50).

Both parts of the story are important in gaining the implications of
the message. In the first part Jesus breathed on the disciples and
commissioned them (John 20:22-23). In the second part Thomas is
shown the marks of Jesus, which he had earlier stated would be necessary for him to view before he would believe (20:25). When Jesus
insisted that Thomas take note of these marks, Thomas gave Christianity's great confession concerning Jesus: "My Lord and my God!" (20:28).
That confession became the springboard for an important conclusion
to the story which involved both a question and an assertion. The
question acknowledged Thomas's pattern of believing, but the assertion commended another pattern. Thomas had believed because he
saw firsthand. Those who came after do not have firsthand evidence
like Thomas, but nevertheless have been called to believe (20:29).
Thomas did not accept the witness of his fellow disciples; he required
confirmation. In the future, such proof would not be possible. In a
nutshell, then, Thomas's testimony was not condemned, but his demand for firsthand proof was.

When this two-part story is read together as it should be, it provides
the reader with a magnificently balanced presentation. It represents
the two parts of the salvation equation: God who undoubtedly acts
first and humans who respond. Both are necessary. It would be inadequate exegesis, therefore, to bifurcate the story as some Calvinists
or Arminians might like to do. There is here to be found, I believe,
a substructural sense both of assurance and of warning. Assurance
and confidence are certainly suggested because the God who acts in
Jesus both gave the Spirit and commissioned the disciples. The presence of God in our lives and the call to service are both strong elements
of the assuring power of God in our lives. But a question or concern

is also present here because the God who acted in Jesus also confronted Thomas with the test of his basis for genuine believing. Thomas—and so too the church—was firmly warned that Christianity is not simply founded upon external or objectively verifiable phenomena. The church is not a mere human construct; it is instead a living group of people who bear witness to a living God in their lives.

Both at the beginning and at the end of the Gospel, the Johannine perspective is not to be found in a simplistic choice of either divine action or human response. The Johannine answer suggests an authentic role for both. To people who are weak and long for a sense of God's assuring power, the Lord, according to John, steps forward and acts in the world. To authentic believers God has assuringly promised authority (*exousia*) to become his sons and daughters (1:12). But in the emphasis on divine action, John hardly submerged the human will. Human beings have a choice. But they have been sternly warned that the way they decide about their lives has eternal repercussions (1:11). Thomas in this Gospel represents the person who has to make a decision (21:24-28; see 11:16; 14:5). In a sense he represents all of us who long to follow Jesus but anxiously want the security of making the best decisions. To perceive the balance between the divine and the human in John is, I believe, extremely important to an adequate perception of assurance and warning in this Gospel.

B. Assurance and Warning
in the Book of Signs (John 1:19 to 12:50)

The first major section of the Fourth Gospel has been called by various names, but perhaps the most satisfactory title is the Book of Signs. This title is employed to assist in understanding its organization. This major section I subdivide conveniently into three parts for the purpose of discussion: (1) the introductory cameos of witness (1:19-51); (2) the stories of the Cana Circle (2:1 to 4:54); and (3) the Festival Cycle (5:1 to 12:50).

1. JOHN THE BAPTIST AND THREE CAMEOS OF WITNESS (JOHN 1:19-51)

With the close of the Prologue and the clear identification of John as a witness and not as light, the Baptizer is introduced in the context of his ministry. For those who struggle with a Tatian-type mind-set, several facts should be highlighted so that the intention in this Gospel may be clear. First, this Gospel emphasizes the Baptizer as a witness and not as judge (see Matt. 3:7-10). The task of judgment is reserved for Jesus. Second, John's baptizing served merely as means of introducing Jesus and as a contrast to Jesus' baptizing with the Holy Spirit (John 1:26,33). Unless one knows the Synpotics, one would never know from this Gospel that Jesus was baptized by John. It is almost as though that fact has been played down in the Gospel. Finally, the Gospel writer made a point twice of saying that John did *not know* Jesus as the Messiah (1:31,33) until the Holy Spirit revealed it to him.

While these ideas may cause some difficulty for beginning readers, they fit perfectly the Johannine motifs of witness and knowing. *Knowing* for John was not primarily a matter of intellectual information. It was a matter of relationship derived from encounter. Genesis 4:1 contains a helpful illustration of some implications of "knowing" in the Bible.[32] In Genesis 4:1 Adam knew his wife and she gave birth to a son. No one would argue that such knowledge was merely intellectual information! In John's day a "heretical" pattern that emphasized special information or knowledge (*gnōsis*) was developing in the early church. In confronting such a tendency, John completely avoided all use of the nouns for knowledge (*gnōsis*) and for faith (*pistis*). Instead, he used the verbs for knowing and believing. He seems to have wanted everyone to understand very clearly that it is not *what* you know but *who* you know that is absolutely crucial to life. To be a true witness in the Johannine sense, therefore, presupposes knowing *the who* and not merely *the what* of Jesus!

With this perspective in mind, the first cameo (1:29-34) becomes quite clear. The Baptizer had learned the *who*—"This is the one concerning *whom* I said" (1:30; see 3:26). Therefore, he was able to testify both "Behold, the Lamb of God" and "This is the Son of God" (1:29,34)! To understand the Fourth Gospel correctly, one must realize that the episode of the Baptizer's doubt in prison is *not used* in this Gospel (see Matt. 11:2-6; Luke 7:18-23). John the Baptist in this Gospel is a model witness. Some of John's disciples were not sure about Jesus, but such was not said of the Baptizer (John 3:25-30)!

In the second cameo (1:35-42), the Baptizer reportedly repeated his testimony. This testimony led two of his disciples to follow Jesus. After Jesus questioned them concerning their interest, He invited them to "come and see." Andrew, however, first "found" his brother and announced, "We have found the Messiah" (v. 41). When Simon came, Jesus named him Cephas or Peter. It is pointless to argue whether or not Peter originally had two names, one Aramaic and one Greek.[33] The point of the story is that, even though the disciples thought they were the prime movers in *finding* Jesus, there was another side to the issue which they needed to discover.

That side became more obvious in the third cameo (1:45-51). Here Jesus reversed the pattern of the previous picture. He went to Galilee, *found* Philip, and said, "Follow me" (v. 43). But Philip returned to the previous perspective, found Nathaniel, and said, "We have found" the one predicted by Moses and the prophets. Nathaniel had studied his religious lessons well and had developed his neat categories. Jesus of Nazareth did not fit them. Rather than argue, however, Philip used the words of Jesus in the second cameo, "Come and see" (v. 46). Now the reader of the Gospel has been readied for the conclusion to all the cameos and for the announcement of a great Johannine perspective.

As Nathaniel came to Jesus, Jesus designated him as "truly an Israelite in whom there is no guile" (v. 47). The word play is obvious; Jacob, the supplanter, had been filled with guile. At the river Jabbok, however, Jacob was given the new name of Israel (Gen. 32:28). Nathaniel, thus, is introduced as an ideal descendant of Jacob/Israel. But Nathaniel was not quite ready for such a categorization, and he questioned Jesus' basis for knowledge. To which query Jesus replied with a categorization of his own. Nathaniel, Jesus said without seeing him, was a man under the fig tree. Nathaniel quickly caught the implications of that category. He realized that Jesus knew he was an authentic expectant Israelite; therefore, Nathaniel repeated the witness of John the Baptist that this teacher (rabbi) was truly the Son of God. But he added that Jesus must be the long awaited King of Israel! Now such designations did not fall haphazardly on Jesus from the pen of this Gospel writer. He knew what he was doing.

Yet Nathaniel had one more lesson to learn. Nathaniel might have been an authentic Israelite; but for John, Jesus was true Israel come in the flesh. Unlike Jacob/Israel, Jesus was the true means, staircase, or ladder to heaven! Anyone familiar with this Gospel knows that Jesus as the means to God became the major focus of the great "I am" sayings of John. The introduction is, thus, complete.

The implications of these cameos are extremely important for our understanding of Christian theology. We *cannot* climb the staircase or ladder to heaven, as the song about Jacob's ladder suggests. Christian theology affirms the exact opposite, namely, that Jesus descended the staircase from heaven! In all three cameos, there is a recognition of the human will and of the human dimension in salvation. The focus of attention, however, moved inevitably from human activity to the action of God in Jesus. The Baptizer was a witness, but he was an ignorant crying voice in the wilderness until he knew the Son. The disciples sought and found the Messiah, but they always found more than they ever anticipated. This Gospel suggests an element of mystery about Jesus that gives the reader a strange sense of confidence and assurance that the issues of life are not merely left in human hands. In the Gospel of John, humans are not in control. That lesson is hard to learn, but it is a lesson that readers of this Gospel should sense acutely.

2. The Cana Circle and the Introduction of Signs (John 2:1 to 4:54)

The five pericopes or teaching units which I combine into this subsection and entitle the Cana Circle begin in Galilee and move the reader to see expanded horizons from Cana to Jerusalem to Judea to Samaria and back to Cana of Galilee. Some readers might be intrigued with the order, and their minds might fly to the order in Acts 1:8, especially if one recalled that Galilee is sometimes linked with the region of the Gentiles (see for example Isa. 9:1 and Matt. 4:15). Whatever may be the possible link with the Lucan order, John's order becomes an inclusive circle that begins with the first sign (2:1-11) and ends with the second sign (4:46-54). The central core of teaching in this Cana Circle occurs in the third story, and the climax of this section appears to be reached in the fourth story. The fifth pericope is a rather brief reflective emphasis of the first story, but it contains a crucial point for the Gospel.

a. The Wedding Story (John 2:1-12). The first pericope introduces three major Johannine motifs: the ideas of hour, sign, and glory. The first motif of hour is woven into the basic substructure of the entire Gospel and moves Jesus and the reader forward with a sense of impending destiny. Throughout this Gospel, Jesus is called upon to follow consistently the Father's will. Jesus' acceptance of God's will is the crux of His life, even at the crises in the garden (18:1-11).

In this wedding story, the mother of Jesus is pictured as attempting to run Jesus' life. Jesus recognized immediately the implications of such an attempt and with a warning query asked His mother, "How are we really related, woman?" (2:4). When some people read this verse (which by the way is difficult to translate because it involves a kind of Greek shorthand), they may be troubled by what appears to be unkindness on the part of Jesus. Was not Jesus the ideal caring Son? The answer is definitely yes. Even at the end Jesus cared for His mother (19:26-27). But such a question really misses the point of this story. The point here is not unlike the emphasis made in the Lucan story of the boy Jesus who responded to His worried mother. There Jesus questioned her about her lack of awareness that He should be involved in matters pertaining to *His* Father (Luke 2:49). In this wedding story John took pains to clarify the fact that Jesus was not motivated by human relationships, even a relationship which involved a fine Jewish mother who by tradition ought to have had the privilege of making certain demands of her Son. But Jesus recognized that roles were becoming mixed in His mother's mind, and He called her to task.

Jesus' primary responsibility was to God His Father, not to Mary His earthly mother. Apparently, she understood His warning immediately and accordingly instructed the servants to *obey Him* directly and do what He told them to do. She could *not* dictate to Him because she could not really act as a *mediator* for Him. The warning was important both for Jesus and His mother. *She* was not to run His life, and *He* was not to allow such an attempt. The primary relationship to the Father was at stake for Jesus.

The second motif in this story involves the Johannine idea of signs. The first twelve chapters of this Gospel are laced with a series of seven signs. The translation of the Greek *sēmeion* as "miracles" in the King James Version of the Bible at John 2:11 and elsewhere is unfortunate and can only lead the unwary reader into confusion. For John a sign is *not* a mere miracle or some magic performed by Jesus. The signs of John are not strictly parallel to the Synoptic wonders, although the feeding of the five thousand is contained in all four Gospels. A sign in John points beyond itself to who Jesus is and the reason for His coming to earth.

The present wedding story was called by John the *archē*, the beginning and perhaps the key to the signs (2:11). Of course, *archē* also means first in a list, but this strangely simple story must not be underestimated in its significance. Moreover, in interpreting this story one must not become enmeshed in secondary issues, such as whether or not Jesus could make alcohol. Nor is the point of the story that Jesus sanctified marriage, as some wedding ceremonies suggest. That is bad proof texting. John himself told us what is the importance of the story: Jesus revealed His glory and His disciples believed in Him. These motifs of hour, sign, and glory became pointers to the time of the crucifixion in which the self-giving nature of Jesus, as the divine Messenger from God, was to be underscored for all the world to see.

The Johannine balance is present in this story. The powerful activity of Jesus led the disciples to believe. But the story also warned that Jesus would not be used, even by His mother. As she instructed the servants, she herself had come to learn a lesson that we all must learn: "Do whatever *He* tells you to do" (2:5). He is the Director of life.

  b. The Temple Event (John 2:13-25). The second story in the Cana Circle expanded the implications of the wedding sign. Here again it is easy to become diverted from the main point John was making by trying to argue for two·cleansings of the Temple. John was a literary and theological genius; the sooner we learn not to make him a wooden newspaper reporter, the sooner we may have an opportunity to grasp the wonderfully inspired message which he has for us. There are not two cleansings in the Gospel of John, nor in any other Gospel! We need desperately to recognize the inspiration of a great literary artist who used the crucial event in the other Gospels to show us the end from the beginning. Did the writer already know the end? Of course, he did! That is what makes this Gospel story so powerful. He knew how the Jews rejected Jesus; he knew that many, both Jews and Gentiles, continued to do so.

John took the crisis event in the Synoptics and linked it with the *archē* of the signs. The result is that John's Gospel shows us judgment from the beginning. The hostile Jews who were using the Temple (*hierōn*, 2:14) for their own economic ends demanded a sign but, in contrast to the helpless folk at the wedding feast, Jesus gave no sign to the misusers of God's house—no sign except the severe warning of His death and resurrection (2:19-20). The selfish interest of those religious people in sanctuary (*naos*, 2:20) buildings and in money led them to miss the real point of the Temple (*hieron*, 2:15-17). Therefore, they were willing to destroy the true sanctuary (*naos*, 2:19) of God—Jesus—in their zeal to defend their faith and reach their personal goals. What a warning for today! But God in Christ would still have the final word. The religious schemers were doomed from the beginning. The disciples bore witness to that fact after the resurrection (2:22).

The conclusion (2:23-25) to this chapter requires a word of comment. Its profundity is in no way to be measured by its length. John noted that many believed (*pisteuō*) when they saw the signs (pl.).[34] But John added the real point: Jesus did not entrust (*pisteuō*) Himself to them because He understood what humanity was like, and He did not need cheap testimonies of faith.

Jesus gave a clear warning to everyone that He was not fooled by human believing. He understood the frailty of humanity, and He was not diverted either by vocal testimonies about Him or by pious attempts at believing. These verses are a warning to Christians and a call to humility before God and integrity before others. John seems to have highlighted the intense sense of the temptation with respect to religious pride which infects humans. This warning ought to be considered carefully by every Christian. Pious words can be cheap camouflages for hostile and unrepentant attitudes.

c. The Nicodemus Story and Some Theological Reflections (John 3:1-36). The last verses of chapter 2 serve as a perfect transition to the next pericope, the third segment of the Cana Circle. Nicodemus, the well-intentioned seeker, began his conversation by announcing *his knowledge* about Jesus. He knew Jesus was a God-sent teacher. While we as humans might be grateful and would relish such a fine introduction, Jesus is portrayed by John as displaying little interest in such niceties. Instead, He responded to Nicodemus with the first of his three "truly" statements in this context, "Unless one is born anew [or from above, *anōthen*], it will be impossible for that one to see the kingdom of God" (3:3). This statement was of such theological magnitude that Nicodemus was rendereed intellectually and philosophically helpless. As a result, he showed who he really was—an uninformed seeker. His twofold pathetic question "How?" (*pōs*, vv. 4,9) indicates just how confused he had become about the ultimate realities of life. As a teacher, the security of his neatly constructed system was rendered meaningless by the three powerful "truly" statements of Jesus (3:3,5-8,11-15).

Nicodemus's problem was that he thought he knew the patterns and rules of God. *He assumed that earthly logic could be exported to heaven.* He had a big lesson to learn! This problem still plagues Christians. Our security does not come from our theological constructs or our systems of rules and regulations. The so-called rich young ruler of the Synoptics tried this pattern and failed miserably, especially when he was given just one more rule.[35] Our security must come, not from rules or principles but from being born anew! Such birth does not leave us theologically or philosophically helpless, but it reminds us that this type of knowing is not placed easily into the computer-type banks of our human mental systems. Computers just do not work on new birth. The difference between earthly and heavenly realities is something we will never be able fully to program on a microchip. Yet we must never forget the incredible difference.

With this perspective in mind, we turn to the theological reflections in this chapter. In verses 14 and 15 one encounters a familiar type of Johannine linkage. Here a statement concerning the Son of man's action (that is, being lifted up) is joined with a statement that *everyone* who believes has "life eternal" (*zōēn aiōnion*). The balance between

God and humanity is once again evident. Here life is modified with the adjective "eternal."[36] These verses signal the beginning of some very serious theological thinking.

The term *eternal* for John probably carried a time sense. But one problem that we face is that of relating earthly time to heaven. The Bible does *not* say, In the beginning there was God and time. Time is an element of creation. And as Professor Emile Cailliet used to say, humans must take great care lest they "colonize the reality with the intelligible."[37] He meant that we humans have an inbred tendency to apply the aspects of our world (the intelligible) to God and His divine realm (reality). We have grave problems escaping our time-space limitations in thinking. So we try to apply them to God. But we cannot make God in our image—not even in the image of the way we think.

When turning to verses 16-18, one finds a great summary of core theological affirmations about salvation. One also discovers a battleground of theology. The familiar John 3:16 can be read by both Calvinists and Arminians to suit their theological biases. When the Calvinist repeats this verse, *God* is emphasized; when the Arminian recites this verse, *whosoever* is emphasized. But the Johannine answer is a balance between both God and humanity, with the initiative coming from God and the response, from humanity. When taken out of context, verse 17 about the noncondemnation of the world is a marvelous text for the universalist position; verse 18, with its emphasis on "already," may serve as an important text for the existentialist and realized eschatological position.

The exponents of this latter position generally view John as all but having eliminated the future perspective of the Bible in an emphasis on the presence of eternity.[38] John did emphasize the "already" aspect of the Christian hope in the first major section of his book, but he did not eliminate the "not yet" in the second major section. The first half of the Gospel is concerned with the process of coming to Christ, whereas in the second half the concern is for the Christian disciple facing life in a hostile world.

In summarizing verses 16-18, they may be said to provide a three-point explanation concerning the illustration of Jesus as the "lifted up" one through whom the believer finds life (3:14-15). Therefore, verse 17 is the *purpose* statement of God's intention. Verse 16 is the *means* statement that contains both the divine and human elements in the equation. And verse 18 is the *warning* statement that makes clear that salvation is not and never will be a game for God. It cost God too much to play around with salvation.

With respect to these core verses, one additional matter needs to be settled. Because condemnation is viewed as an "already" existing phenomenon, one has to understand the postresurrection perspective of the Gospel. The Gospel writer was looking back at the events in the life of Jesus from the vantage point of the resurrection. The resurrection made a tremendous difference in the way John looked at Jesus! After the resurrection, the meaning of Jesus' coming was clear. After the resurrection, the nature of God's salvation could never be seen the same way again. After the resurrection, response to Jesus became critical. And after the resurrection, judgment became far more decisive for humanity. In summary, after the resurrection there was a marvelous sense of assurance; there was also an urgent sense of warning.

When turning to John 3:19-36 the writer expanded on the implications of the previous three verses and the earlier discussion with Nicodemus in terms of themes introduced in the Prologue. In verses 19-21, the alternatives to life in Christ are clarified by reference to light and darkness and by linking the two ways of living to the deeds or actions of life. Here again a sense of balance is evident; John considered that Christianity was not merely a matter of beliefs but also a matter of observable deeds. Many Christians who magnify belief at the expense of deeds and who claim to be Pauline and thus biblical not only misunderstand Paul but also run afoul of Hebrews and John. For those who think salvation is only a matter of comfortable mental assent, this chapter of John stands as an uncomfortable warning.

Moreover, because of the crucial nature of his Gospel perspective, John called again on the Baptizer to witness from Judea concerning the implications of the coming of Jesus (3:25-36). For the Baptizer there was no question that Jesus was the God-sent, gifted One from heaven. Jesus' origin was from above, and those who would receive this testimony would also receive the Spirit, the seal and assurance of God's truth concerning His Son whom God made His representative on earth in all things. Moreover, linked to the Baptizer's witness concerning Jesus is a powerful summary statement: (1) belief is the basis for eternal life, (2) disobedience is the test of nonlife, and (3) the wrath of God is a present judgment upon disobedience. This message is, therefore, one of incredible balance. There is a tremendous sense of God's hand in the salvation process, but there is also a powerful sense of judgment for disobedience. The elements of assurance and warning are clearly evident in the conclusion of one of the most profound chapters in the Bible.

d. *The Samaritan Woman* (*John 4:1-42*). This fourth story in the Cana Circle provides a wonderful model for witnessing.[39] It also provides a superb model of the divine-human relationship. The woman, who by Jewish standards was little more than the scum of the earth, was trying to run her own life and was making a mess of it.[40] Into the context of her tragic life, Jesus entered with a unique and gentle sensitivity that led the woman beyond any relationship she probably thought was ever possible. She had already tried five husbands and, at that point, was beyond the need for such formalities. Jesus did not violate her selfhood in leading her to understanding. He began with the point where she was (a drawer of water) and led her to confront her selfhood. Her responses were tangential attempts at avoiding true encounter (Does a Jew ask a woman of Samaria? . . . I have no husband. . . . I perceive you are a prophet . . . Tell me which is the right place to worship . . . That may be the case, but I know the Messiah is coming, and *He* will show us). Nevertheless, the ingredients were there that made for encounter. After having realized that Jesus knew all about her fragmented life, she asked the *men* (not "people" as in the RSV) who had probably been part of her fragmentation, "Is this man not the Christ?" The answer was evident. Thus, because of the woman, the half-breed Samaritans (despised by the Jews) were led to believe in Jesus and to make one of the most important confessions in the entire Gospel of John: "This one truly is the Savior of the world" (4:42)!

However, a dark side to the story is revealed as well. The disciples who were closest to Jesus had major difficulties with their prejudicial hang-ups. While they did not come out publicly and ask what right the woman had to talk with Jesus, John let us know what they thought (4:27). Moreover, while Jesus was dealing with ultimate realities, the disciples had great difficulty in getting beyond the mundane interests of food (4:31-34). To the disciples Jesus sounded a warning word of instruction: "Lift up your eyes and look"! They had failed to see God's intention of salvation in the world (4:35-38). In this respect, they represent the many blind, comfortable Christians who are disturbed by the intrusion of outsiders into their neatly packaged Christian circles. They are the type who would be confirmed in their exclusiveness by emphatically setting walls around who belongs in their fellowship and by adopting only those church growth principles which lead to protectionism.[41] Protectionism is hardly a Christian virtue, and Jesus sternly warned the disciples to lift up their eyes.

The story of the Samaritan woman fits fully into the balanced picture of John. The openhearted Lord welcomed the hurting people of the world and assured them of His concern and acceptance. Jesus even stayed with the half-breed Samaritans (4:40-41)—a monstrous thought to the Jews! What a picture of an accepting Lord. Yet for the self-righteous intimates in that little band of disciples, Jesus had a different response—a very stern warning. Self-righteousness is a blinding infection that needs treatment, and Jesus did not fail to exercise His authority in the face of such blindness.

e. The Healing of the Official's Son (John 4:43-54). The fifth and final segment of the Cana Circle brings us back to the town where Jesus performed the *archē* of signs. A father pleaded for Jesus to heal his sick son.[42] John focused again on the issue of believing and its relationship to Jesus' signs. In the first Cana story, the sign pointed to Jesus' glory and led the disciples to believe (2:11). In the second sign story (by the way, only these two signs of John are numbered), there is a major shift in emphasis. According to the purpose statement of the Gospel, the recording of the signs was aimed at leading the reader to believe and gain life (20:31). But it becomes increasingly obvious to the observant reader that the overall goal of John was to help the reader move beyond the need for signs because the way for future believers to enter into life was to believe without seeing either Jesus or His signs, as Jesus instructed Thomas (20:29).

In this second sign story, Jesus confronted the father (a royal officer, perhaps a Gentile) with a warning and asserted, "Unless you behold signs and wonders you will not believe" (4:48). But the man's response to the command of Jesus revealed the kind of model which John sought to find in all Christians. After Jesus said, "Go, your son lives," the man believed and started home. On his way he was confirmed in his believing by servants who came to report the good news of his son's recovery.

The Cana Circle is, thus, complete. It began with signs to engender faith in Jesus. It then turned to Jesus' refusal of signs to those who were hostile to Him at the Temple. Instead, the circle included the ultimate warning sign of judgment. It turned next in the Nicodemus story to what is really the obverse of that judgment sign of the death of Jesus, namely, a marvelous assurance in the "lifted up" One who lovingly provided the new birth to those who believe. But John recorded Jesus' warning that those who disobey that judgment had already been executed. The Cana Circle turned again to show the nonrestrictive nature of the Gospel, as John chose to focus on what to the Jewish mind was the lowest type of a person imaginable, a questionable half-breed Samaritan woman! And Jesus used this person to lead many to confess that He is the Savior of the world. The final turn brought the Cana Circle to its starting point. But in this healing event, there was a subtle shift in emphasis which helps remind us that believing is not to focus on signs but on Jesus, the Son of God. In such believing there is satisfying assurance. Without it, there is great danger concerning, which the reader needs to be forewarned.

3. THE FESTIVAL CYCLE: SIGNS AND STORIES OF DIVISION (JOHN 5:1 TO 11:57)

While I have grave doubts accepting the thesis of Aileen Guilding that the entire Gospel of John is a kind of lectionary-oriented book which was organized according to the Jewish festivals, I am nevertheless quite convinced that this part of the Gospel is definitely festival oriented.[43] I combine five units in this section which I call the Festival Cycle, beginning with an unnamed feast (chapter 5). But the issues first treated are concerned with a sabbath healing. The second segment (chapter 6) revolves around Passover and is initiated by two signs. The large third central segment (chapter 7—9) is signaled by the approach of the Feast of Tabernacles and is concluded with the healing of a blind man. Chapter 10, the fourth segment, is related to the festival of Hanukkah or Dedication and contains the parable of the shepherd. The fifth segment (chapter 11) deals with the raising of Lazarus and signals the coming of Passover. The sixth and final segment (chapter 12) enunciates Jesus' submission to God in readiness for death as He established a self-giving pattern for believers in the new Passover.

a. *An Unnamed Feast* (*John 5:1-47*). John began this Festival Cycle with the simple statement, "There was a feast of the Jews" (5:1). The focus immediately turned to a sick man. We are not quite sure what the man's incapacity was, but the importance of the story lies not in the nature of his illness. Jesus centered instead on the sick man's *will* when he asked, "Do you wish to become healthy?" (5:6). The answer ought to have been obvious, but the man had been seriously incapacitated for thirty-eight years and had been tediously waiting in the porch with the other rejects of society for some kind of a miracle to happen. Imagine the stench of that place that was next to what passed for Jerusalem's slaughter house and was just below the Temple where the blood from the sacrifices was washed down. What would your reaction have been if you had been waiting for thirty-eight years in such a place?

The man had understandably lost hope. His response to Jesus was that he could never win the race to the pool when an alleged miraculous troubling of the water took place. Neither Jesus nor the Gospel writer felt it necessary to enter into a theological discussion on the truth or error of the miracle the man was expecting.[44] Without argument Jesus merely said, "Get up, pick up your sleeping bag and be on your way" (5:8). The result was a miraculous instantaneous healing.

But there was also a dark side to the event, and John introduced it with the stark words: "That day it was *Shabbat!*" Those words signaled the division in perspective which the entire Festival Cycle was developed to reveal. There is no doubt that sabbath was regarded as extremely important in the Torah traditions (for example, Deut. 5:12; Gen. 2:2-3; Ex. 20:8). Some Jews even regarded God as subject to and bound by sabbath. Such, however, was not the God of Jesus.[45] The battle lines were drawn, and there was little room for fence sitters.

In this story the issue is legalism versus the dynamic activity of

God. God is not a *deus absconditus* (a god who creates, gives his rules, and then leaves the scene). God is a worker who is concerned about His creation (5:17). The implication is clearly that the Jewish legalists had misunderstood the nature of both God and the sabbath. Therefore, when the working Jesus linked Himself with His Father God, the theological implications for these legalists became intolerable. Their conclusion that Jesus had to be *killed* was reached quickly (5:18). Notice once again that the end is here evident at what seems to be the beginning of Jesus' ministry.

According to John's understanding of Jesus, the attempts of some present-day Jewish and Christian scholars to reportray Jesus as an acceptable Jewish rabbi and to blame Paul and his Diaspora Hellenistic background for the inception of Christianity is a classic attempt to rewriting history.[46] The perspectives of Jesus and those of the first-century Jewish legalists could not help but collide. It must also be firmly asserted, however, that such a statement does not mean that twentieth-century Jewish nonlegalists are more responsible for the death of Jesus than twentieth-century Christian legalists.

In the context of this legalistic hostility, John once again pointed to the dimensions of the divine and the human and to the concerns of assurance and warning. Jesus readily accepted the legalist evaluation that He was claiming to be divine, yet He carefully maintained that He was not self-oriented but was obedient to the Father (5:19). He argued that failure to honor the Son was the equivalent of dishonoring the Father (5:23). Moreover, while He claimed to have the right of judgment, He firmly asserted that such a right was a gift from the Father (5:22) and that He did nothing on his own (5:30). The reason Jesus said that He had been given this right of judgment needs to be clearly understood and never forgotten. The reason is because He did *not seek His own will* but the will of the One who sent Him (5:30)! While theologians love to speculate in the realm of divine ontology (the nature of God's being), the biblical texts spend far more time in the mundane realities of life. Perhaps a crucial issue for theology today concerns the fact that it is far easier for us to speculate about God than to live in the realities of the world.

In reflecting on these realities, the consistency of the Son gave assurance to those who are hearing and believing (present tense) that they have (present tense) life eternal and that they have passed (perfect tense) out of the realm of death and into the realm of life (5:24)—the tenses are important. What a marvelous sense of assurance is available to those who believe while living in a hostile world. Our temptation as Christians, however, is to leave the realm of living and begin to speculate about our ontology (our being). We need to remind ourselves that for John there were two very different ways of living in the world— one that listens to God and one that does not! Jesus said that these two ways of living have two very different ends—one a resurrection to life and the other to judgment (5:29). We spin our theological wheels to use a text like this one to speculate on the essence and nature of the resurrection(s). The point is that an important warning was being given to the Jews—and by implication to everyone. Those who hear and heed *will live* (5:25)!

The Jewish legalists, however, did not listen. They did not accept the testimony of the Baptizer (5:33), and they refused to recognize Jesus' works (5:36). They could not understand the Father's witness because they did not have a relationship with Him (5:37-38). They missed the point of the Scriptures because they were not oriented to God but to human rules and interpretations (5:39-44). *Their rules and interpretations had in fact become their gods.* As a result, Jesus said that He did not need to be their prosecutor. The Scriptures which they promoted would actually bring them to trial (5:45-47). Let no one think that this warning applied merely to the religious legalists of Jesus' day! It is as appropriate today as ever, and we all need to note how easy it is to replace Jesus with our lifeless ideas about God and His will.

b. The Bread from Heaven and Passover (John 6:1-71). The second segment (chapter 6) of the Festival Cycle has been introduced by the stories of the feeding of the five thousand and of Jesus' walking on the water. These two accounts were already set side by side in Mark (6:30-52) and Matthew (14:13-32). But here there is a difference. John placed these stories in a Passover context. The combination of the two accounts obviously reminded him of two great events in the Exodus: God's control of the sea (Ex. 14:13-30) and God's gift of food

(Ex. 16:4-12). The dialogue which followed undoubtedly has the Exodus events in the background of thought.

The exchange between the Jews and Jesus began in 6:26 with another of the familiar "truly" statements. Jesus said, "You seek me, not because you see [understand] signs, but because you ate of the bread-loaves and were filled." This text provides a key to understanding the correct meaning of signs in John. Unfortunately, the translation of "miracles" rather than "signs" (*sēmeion*) confuses the issue. In reality, the people did see the miracles. Indeed, they had one of the miracles in their stomachs! But even though they saw the miracles, they did not recognize the signs.

The recognition of the sign is the message of chapter 6. The Jews were dying, Jesus argued, because they had concentrated on the wrong things (6:27). Like the Jews in the second segment of the Cana Circle (the temple cleansing), they had once again been asking for signs to support Jesus' claims (6:30). But they really did not want to believe Jesus, and, therefore, they missed the signs. Their problem, Jesus indicated in another "truly" statement, was that they had misconceived who the author of the manna sign was. It was not Moses; it was Jesus' Father who both has given (perfect tense) the manna bread and is giving (present tense) this true bread (6:31-32). That the Jews desired manna which comes from God continually is clear from their request: give (aorist tense) us this bread (6:34). Notice the tenses of the verbs in these verses. Bread (food) they would accept, but they continually refused to recognize Jesus as the true bread (sustaining life) from heaven because of their categorization of Jesus as the son of Joseph rather than the Son of God (6:42).

This dialogue between Jesus and the Jews has some very important theological implications. In the first place, Jesus' message reveals a tremendous sense of the God dimension. According to John, Jesus realized that everything the Father gave to Him would come to Him; He assured the hearers that He would not cast out the ones who came to Him (6:37). Moreover, in restating Jesus' dependence on and submission to the will of God, John recorded the assurance that Jesus would *not lose or destroy* what had been given to Him but that He would raise it on the last day (6:38-39).

While our assurance flows from the submission and obedience of Jesus to the Father, John seemed to be concerned that his readers understand that Jesus was not some haphazard whim in the mind of God. The Word that became flesh in the Prologue was also God (1:1, "*theos*"). In this Festival Cycle, John came very close to giving us ontological statements about Jesus, but they are typically Hebraic and are pictorial descriptions rather than syllogistic definitions.

Anyone who has studied this Gospel knows that John contains a fascinating series of "I am" (*egō eimi*) sayings. The Baptizer had said, "I am not [*egō ouk eimi*] the Christ" in response to the questions of the investigating committee (1:20). But in this Exodus setting which reminds us of Moses, Jesus identified Himself in coming to the boat as *egō eimi* ("I am," 6:20). This statement became the springboard for introducing John's unique "I am" series. Of course, John's mind must have gone back to the burning bush event on Mount Horeb when God said "I am" (Ex. 3:14)! Any other suggestion would be meaningless. For John, the "I am" self-revelations of Jesus identified Him with the self-revealing, companion God of the Exodus. What better way to start this "I am" series than for Jesus to identify himself with the continuing manna, the Bread of life (6:35,41,48,51)? The assurance of the companion God in Jesus is the wonderful inheritance of the Christian.

These marvelous assurance statements in John, however, have been balanced by some intriguing statements which move our minds from the God dimension to the human dimension. John reintroduced Jesus and the concept of the will of God in terms of the expression "everyone who sees . . . and believes" (6:40). Such people, the Gospel writer asserted, have eternal life and Jesus will raise them on the last day (6:40).

With this statement of the human dimension, John introduced the murmuring of the Jews (6:41). Anyone who knows the Exodus story knows how important a role murmuring played. Murmuring was associated with the judgment of the wilderness wanderings and the death of the people in the wilderness. Accordingly Jesus warned His hearers with another "truly" statement: They were facing a situation like their fathers faced when they ate the manna bread in the wilderness and died (6:49). Yet Jesus added the assuring note, "if anyone eats of this bread [Jesus], that person shall live forever" (6:51).

But Jesus did not leave His hearers in a soothing state of nondecision because, at the same time that He introduced assurance, he also added the upsetting statements concerning eating his flesh.[47] The reaction was immediate. The Jews thought that Jesus was promoting some kind of cannibalism. Students of early Christian history know that such a charge was also laid on the Christians by Romans and others when they heard about the Christian celebration of the Lord's Supper.[48] The idea of eating the flesh and drinking the blood of the Son of man was certainly a difficult idea for the Jews to accept. But the Gospel writer added that it was also difficult for many of the disciples to understand (6:60). As a result John noted that many of the disciples went away (apēlthon) and no longer walked with or followed Jesus (6:66). Indeed, Jesus even asked the inner group of disciples if they also wanted to go away (6:67). The confessional response of Peter—"You have the words of life eternal"—is balanced by the Judas illustration in which Jesus said, "Did I not choose twelve, and out of you [pl.] one is a devil!" (6:68-71).

The point and counterpoint of this story is extremely important to notice. Some interpreters emphasize Jesus' foreknowledge—that He understood the patterns of people, that He knew from the first those who did not believe, and that He knew the one who would betray Him (6:64-65). Other interpreters emphasize that the choosing is not at all determinative, otherwise the question of Jesus concerning the possible departure of His disciples would merely be a stage play (6:67).[49]

The resolution, I suggest, is to be found in the fact that the Johannine Gospel has a built-in tension between the human and the divine dimensions. This tension is precisely why John found the story of the Exodus to be such a significant motif. If we choose between the dimensions of God and man and thus reduce the tension, we may be satisfied by our theological conclusions; but such a choice does not mean that we have understood the profundity of the Gospel of John. This Passover segment of the Festival Cycle, I submit, ends with the unresolved tension of the Exodus! Do not reduce the tension of this story! John wanted each reader to ask the question of whether he or she would continue to be faithful or would go away!

c. Tabernacles and the Blind Man (John 7:1 to 9:41). The third segment of the Festival Cycle is concerned with the popular fall Feast of Tabernacles (Booths) and involves chapters 7, 8, and 9. If a messiah needed to reveal himself, Tabernacles and the month of Tishri was the time to do it. But just as Jesus did not allow His mother to run His life in the first Cana story, so here He did not become a pawn in the hands of His brothers in their desire to have Him prove His messiahship (7:3-6). The brothers were interested in having Jesus display Himself to the people and in timing His display for the greatest reaction. Jesus would, indeed, be displayed ("lifted up," 8:28), and He was likewise interested in timing. But His interest in time was two sided—both His time and theirs. The time of Jesus' hour was the turning point of history, a time which was directed by the Father (7:6; 8:28). The brothers' time, however, was an ever-present existential moment of making a decision about Jesus (7:6). Their time, like ours, is "now."

John's Tabernacle sequence employs the theme of trying to decide about Jesus in order to highlight the division of opinion which was among the people. The scene at the feast opened with the Jews who were looking for Jesus and were silently wondering whether He were an authentic God-sent person or a clever deceiver (7:11-13). Jesus' appearance and teaching at the festival pushed them to face the question of how one of the *am ha aretz* (people of the land) could have such learning (7:14-15). This question forced them to focus on the issue of authority. Was He aligned with Moses and God, or was He a demon (7:16-20)? His deed of healing was wonderful. But was not healing on the sabbath a contradiction? Then Jesus reminded them that, although they followed Moses, they yet circumcised on the sabbath (7:22). Thus, the question was raised: Was there really consistency in the Torah? The follow-up question was: Could Jesus possibly be Christ? The response was a question: How could He be? No one knew the origin of Christ! Surely they knew the origin of Jesus. Then Jesus asked them if they really knew his origin (7:28). The answer, John suggested, is that their ideas concerning the Messiah were simply confused speculations. The result of the dialogue was a division. Some tried to arrest him, and some believed in him (7:30-31, 43-52).

This confused division elicited from Jesus another *egō eimi* saying: "I am the light of the world" (8:12). As the pillar of light put an end to confusion in the darkness of the wilderness, so Jesus could have ended their confusion about Himself and His origin. But the Jews refused to accept Jesus' witness because they did not know the Father (8:13-19). Their refusal, therefore, led Jesus to enunciate both a strong word of warning to the hostile unbelieving Jews and a calming statement of assurance for obedient believers.

The warning to the Jews was radical. When Jesus departed (died), they would seek Him; but they would die in their sin (8:21). The reason for their death was that they were from below. Jesus, the "I am," was from above (8:23). Was their death then predetermined? It may seem so at first glance, especially if one's mind set with respect to ontological thinking is deterministic. But the addition by John of Jesus' statement "unless you believe that 'I am,' you will die in your sins" reintroduced the human element (8:24). The issue concerns the people and their response. When Jesus spoke, the elements were there for division and many believed (8:30).

But even to the believers (8:30-31), Jesus sounded a mixed note of warning and assurance when He indicated that the condition of being true disciples is "if you [pl.] abide in my word" (8:31). Notice that *abiding is the condition* for authentic discipleship. The famous verse about knowing the truth must be interpreted neither as a proof text for intellectual endeavor, such as is suggested by its use on the seals of some educational institutions, nor as a means of disparaging education, as is done in some other circles. Verse 32 is dependent on verse 31; together they mean that, *if* we *abide* or continue to live in Christ's pattern, not only we will have the assurance of being His disciples but also will know firsthand the liberating power of the truth of the Lord's personhood. Liberation apart from Jesus was still to be viewed as slavery because everyone who sins is a slave (8:34). Christian liberation movements need to remember that liberty is not real liberty unless it comes in Christ.

Moreover, sonship or daughterhood with God was not a matter of human inheritance or family line. The issue is not whether a person's family tree may have included Abraham, Luther, Calvin, Bunyan, John XXIII, M. L. King, Jr., a fine preacher uncle, or anyone else (8:37-44; see 1:12-13). Sonship or daughterhood was defined in this Gospel by loving Jesus (8:42), by believing in Him (8:45-46), and by keeping (obeying) His word (8:51-52). In these matters, the Jewish opponents failed. They did not *do* what Abraham would have done (8:39)! Therefore, they were not true heirs of Abraham. They were, in fact, heirs of the devil (8:44). No Christian should read these words without self-reflection and prayer. Perhaps clarity of assurance would be more satisfyingly achieved if Christians would heed the implied warning given to the Jews to *do* the will of God.

The healing of the blind man (ch. 9) is one of John's foremost illustrative signs. The story opens with the question of theodicy (the problem of evil and suffering). The disciples did not blame God for the man's blindness. They asked: Was it this man or his parents that sinned (9:2)? The disciples wanted to establish blame and proposed a simple syllogistic answer to the problem. But Jesus did not permit the disciples' syllogism to work. The question of who sinned was not God's question because it did not encapsulate the truth of pain and suffering. Jesus' concern was *not* with the *who* of blame but with the state of a person and how, for God's glory, the man could be helped (9:3).

Instead of a syllogism, Jesus offered a proclamation of hope. He reannounced that He was the "light of the world" (9:5; see 8:12). He was like the God of the wilderness who tabernacled (see 1:14) among the people and led them with a pillar of light as they wandered in the desert at night and as they lived in tents or booths. He was the God who brought them the assurance of hope (the Promised Land), a hope which time and again He renewed as He miraculously delivered them in the face of impossible odds. Jesus was prepared to do what humans thought was virtually impossible. He made a man see who was born blind by plastering his eyes with mud composed of clay and his spit and by sending him to wash in the pool of Siloam (8:6-7). It was an unheard of event!

Humanity has difficulty with such inexplicable events. People, therefore, usually try by many means to find an explanation that suits their presuppositions. The blind man had been miraculously healed, but that healing did not fit the Jewish legalists' superficial formulas. They had two big problems with the healing: it took place on the sabbath; it was done by Jesus, who for them was a sinner. As in chapter 5, the sabbath healing was a major stumbling block. How could a man have been sent by God who violated sabbath rules? He had to be a sinner. Yet how could a sinner have done such an incredible act? The man's opinion that Jesus was a prophet obviously was of no value to the leaders because they thought he had been a sinful blind man. Therefore, they turned to the man's parents. They knew that the parents at least attended the synagogue! Yet these parents did not prove to be much help. They did not want to be excommunicated, so they merely stated the obvious: the man was their son, and he had been blind from birth. Like all people who fear that becoming involved might cost them too much, the man's parents judiciously referred the investigators back to their son (9:21).

In the second round of investigation the leaders informed the healed man that he should view Jesus as a sinner (9:24). But the man did not adopt their presupposition. He merely dealt with the facts. "One thing I know," he said, "being blind, now I see!" (9:25). Nor did another reexamination help. He merely turned their intense concern into an impertinent question: "Why . . . do you also wish to become his disciples?" (9:27). The instant flight of these so-called learned ones to the fortress of tradition and their obvious lack of knowledge concerning Jesus overwhelmed the poor man.

At this point the man who was healed proposed his own syllogism which is negative in form but incredibly profound in its implications: God does *not* heed people as they sin; *never* since the world began had anyone performed such an act; and if Jesus were *not* from God, He could do *nothing* (9:31-33). This beggar had discovered in the life of Jesus a major key to both assurance and warning. The learned legalists could hardly miss the implications of the beggar's (9:8) testimony. He had shown the religious leaders that what one *does* has implications for what one *is*. The man was, thus, very dangerous because *his thesis about doing was more realistic than their logic of being*. They were legalists, but he was a recipient of authentic power.

Divine power confronting words linked to mere human power presented a problem. The only thing left for the Jewish leaders was to categorize the poor man with a stigmatizing name, "sinner," and get rid of him from the context of their thought (9:34). How many Christians think that calling others a name and excluding them from their fellowship takes care of opposition!

But Jesus did not leave the man without assuring hope. The Lord's approach, however, was rather unique. He came emphasizing the human dimension by asking, "Do you believe in the Son of man?" (9:35). The man's earnest desire was to know who that one was so that he might believe. When the man discovered that it was Jesus, He immediately confessed divinity, "I believe, Lord!" (9:38).

The story concludes with a poignant statement of assurance and warning framed in a judgment context. "For the purpose of judgment," Jesus said, "I entered the world in order that the blind might see and the ones who [think they] see might be [judged] blind" (9:39). The weak received assurance! But for the legalists, Jesus made it absolutely clear what He meant. Because they continued to assert their knowledge ("We see") when in fact they were ignorant about the true ways of God, Jesus allowed their sin to work its way ("their sin continues"—not "guilt," 9:41, RSV). The so-called righteous received the stern warning of Christ not to rely on their rules and self-proclaimed traditions about the Bible and the will of God. Thus ended the Tabernacle/wilderness segment of the Festival Cycle with a clear perception that God had acted in Jesus but with a positioning so that human response was set in the forefront of our thinking.

d. The Shepherd and Dedication (John 10:1-42). The divine aspect was brought to center stage in chapter 10 which deals with the festival of Hanukkah or Dedication. The message was set in the context of the very familiar *mashal* (parable or allegory) of the good shepherd.[50] In this incisive chapter, the theme of division (10:19) has been escalated and the argument really has become a commentary on the false shepherds of Ezekiel 34.

John opened this pericope with a stinging "truly" statement by Jesus that clearly marked the difference between the authentic shepherd and the others who sought to deal with the sheep—pilfering thieves, unconcerned strangers, uncommitted hired servants, or plundering wolves. The presence of each of these in the sheepfold meant to a greater or lesser degree the same for the sheep. They engendered in the sheep insecurity and lack of assurance. The authentic shepherd, however, brought a sense of peace, serenity, and assurance to the sheep because they knew him and heeded his voice (10:3-4,14). They trusted him and followed him in a way they would never have done with strangers. Strangers would confuse the sheep (10:5), and hired servants would flee in crisis (10:12-13); but the Good Shepherd was concerned for the welfare of the sheep, and He laid down His life for them (10:11,15). What a model for any leader!

The Shepherd's death, however, was not to be viewed as the conclusion to this *mashal*. Readers of this Gospel knew that there was a different finish to the story because Jesus has been raised from the dead. Moreover, the death and resurrection of Jesus were not understood as some happenstances of history. The power of God was at work in Jesus. Divine power and divine will permitted Jesus' death and subsequently provided for His resurrection. The good news, therefore, was not merely a story of human acts. Humans did not simply take Jesus' life (*He laid it down* or permitted them to kill Him.). Similarly humans could not stop the resurrection power (10:17-18)! God was in control. But such a message was bound to be a problem for human beings who thought they could control Jesus. Division was, therefore, inevitable (10:19-21).

John had an amazing ability to focus the readers' attention. He introduced the great festival of Hanukkah, which commemorates the victorious experience of Judas Maccabeus in the rededication of the Temple after its profaning by the Syrian madman King Antiochus IV (v. 22).[51] Yet John turned the celebration on its head. The Feast of Dedication was the Jewish festival of joy, but John added, "It was winter." We should not miss such Johannine notations. They are not merely time and temperature statements. They are filled with emotion, and they are theological signals for the careful reader. For Jesus and for the world, the winter was arriving. The hostility was coming to a climax. "Tell us plainly, if you are Christ," the Jews said (10:24). Such was exactly what Jesus had been doing, but they refused to accept either Him or His witnesses.

As a result of dealing with their continual hostility and disbelief, Jesus enunciated the basic categorization of two types of people: sheep and nonsheep. The opponents were not believing people, "for" (*hoti*) *they were not His sheep* (10:26). Now great care must be exercised here by interpreters lest the *hoti* is read as introducing a determinative cause. It is clear that the opponents were unbelieving, nonsheep, but one must be cautious not to build the superstructure of a highly negative determinism (*reprobation*[52]) on arguments such as this slippery *hoti*. A little knowledge of Greek can be very dangerous. Nowhere else to this point in John has there been the faintest hint of a doctrine in which God predetermines those who are lost. Without a doubt there is a correlation between unbelief and the nonsheep category. Such a correlation, however, ought to be understood as *the forceful warning* of judgment that Jesus intended it to be. But the text must not be pressed beyond its clear logic to a shaky theory of reprobation.

The underlying purpose of this good shepherd *mashal* goes well beyond judgment and warning. It was also intended to be understood as a statement on assurance for those who are sheep. In periods of hostility and persecution, Christians need to be assured that their stability does not depend on their own resources. Jesus addressed this question of assurance (vv. 27-30). One needs to note, however, the two-sided sense of these verses.

It is interesting, first, to discover that the discussion concerning the sheep begins in verse 27 with the human dimension of the salvation experience. This verse is a clear and simple statement that Jesus' sheep "hear," "know," and "follow" Him. It is parallel to other statements already noted and, thus, conforms to the overall purpose statement of the gospel (20:31).

Second, as a contrast verses 28-30 speak of the divine dimension of the salvation experience. The act of God gave the gift of life eternal. This gift of life has been fully assured, and one does not need to be concerned about its termination point (10:28). Life and death are opposite categories, and Christians ought to stop worrying about death. Indeed, *they ought to stop worrying about their persecutors!* Now here is where the idea of "plucking" (KJV) or "snatching" (RSV), which has been the subject of much debate, was brought into focus. The Greek word is *harpazō*, and the basic idea is that of stealing. What

the text of verses 28 and 29 means is that Christians should quit
worrying about being stolen by some thief. God is greater than any
robber, and God is stronger than any wolf (see 10:10,12)!

But just in case the believers might still have been worried about
their resources, Jesus reminded them of the unity of the Father and
the Son. Because of this unity, believers ought to be assured that
the Father honors what the Son has said. What a marvelous sense of
dynamic assurance these words offer *to those who "hear," "know,"
and "follow"* Jesus. This is a great assurance text, but one must not
make it into a text of wooden determinism.

John interpreted such a radicalizing of people into two camps as
the die being cast in the world. The alternatives were evident. The
sheep had been assured of the protection of God, and the enemies
were angry and hostile. The Jewish opponents' intention was to stone
Jesus for blasphemy (10:31-33). But the climax to the Book of Signs
needed yet to be furnished.

e. Lazarus and Passover (John 11:1-51). This climax came just prior
to Passover with the sign of Lazarus in chapter 11. The closer one
comes to the crucifixion in this section of John, the more one senses
that Jesus was moving deliberately toward His destiny. Jesus was in
control of His life. He did not start for the south to save Lazarus as
soon as the message of illness was received (11:6). Indeed, Jesus seemingly waited for Lazarus to die. When He knew Lazarus had died,
He began the journey to Bethany. He knew the disciples would learn
an important lesson in believing (11:14-16). Moreover, Jesus knew
that He would raise Lazarus. Before He did, He instructed Martha
about Himself in terms of resurrection theology (11:23-26). John
viewed the high priest's statement as a divinely sent prediction of
truth that flowed from an officeholder in spite of himself (11:48-52).
The divine dimension is definitely in the foreground here.

The human dimension was not removed from the story. The disciples
were afraid to go south because they knew that the Judeans wanted
to stone Jesus (11:8). The conversation of the disciples with Jesus is
a prime example of how Jesus tried to lead His people when their
minds were stuck in a parking gear because of their intense fear of
opposition. Indeed, despite the fact that Jesus their Lord was with

them—the One whom they had earlier refused to abandon because
He had the words of life (6:68)—they were petrified by the hostility.
But Thomas, the realist, stands out because he was *at least* willing
to make the decision to follow Jesus, even though he was convinced
the trip would end in his own death (11:16).[53] In this climactic scene
from the first half of the Gospel, John prepared the reader to meet
Thomas in the last scene of the last half of the Gospel. But the irony
of this story is that Jesus was going to bring life, while the disciples
only thought of death.

The story then takes an interesting twist with Martha and Mary.
They were willing, like the disciples, to believe in Jesus and His
power. But their belief also had its limits, namely, the cold reality
of the tomb. The boundary of their believing stopped with the death
of their brother. They both said to Jesus: "If only you would have
been here!" (11:21,32). I have heard many preachers praise Martha
for her subsequent marvelous confession, "I believe that you are the
Christ, the Son of God, he who is coming into the world" (11:27).
This statement is the climactic confession of the first half of the Gospel.
It is an important model statement of believing. The problem, however, is that in this context Martha's confession is not the end of the
story! Her next statement to Jesus was, "Lord, . . . he stinks!" (11:39).
The person John chose to be the *model for statements of believing*
in this climactic scene of the Festival Cycle is *also a model of not
believing!* Therefore, Martha becomes a warning to all readers who
confess believing but do not exhibit it in living. As a result, the reader
is thrust into the middle of an unresolved Johannine tension between
assurance and warning.

The raising of Lazarus was the sign which the Jewish leadership
could not tolerate, and a plot to kill Jesus was hatched at the highest
level. For John the death of Jesus was imminent, and the anointing
scene was fittingly set in this context as a sign for the end. The sensitive
reader, however, cannot help but notice John's insistence on associating this death process of Jesus with Passover (11:55 twice; 12:1).

f. The conclusion to the Festival Cycle (John 12:1-50). With the
emphasis on Passover, chapter 12 forms a natural conclusion to the
Festival Cycle and a general conclusion to the first half of the Gospel.

Of particular importance in this chapter is the feeling that Jesus' destiny was being fulfilled. Jesus did not permit Judas, the thief, to stop or call into question the anointing. The issue was not determined by Judas—it was *not* money and the poor. Instead, the issue was the sign of Jesus' death (12:4-8). The entry into Jerusalem similarly is portrayed from the perspective of Jesus' destiny. The entry was nothing less than the expected coming of Israel's King-Messiah (12:13-15). The hostile Pharisees were powerless to stop the people's rejoicing (12:19). At this point, even the Greeks of the Diaspora wanted to get into the act and make Jesus a hero. But *the decisive hour had come* (12:20-23)! Therefore, Jesus added another of His important "truly" statements. This one hinted that a wider ministry was to come that Jesus' followers would establish (12:24).

Destiny was set before Jesus. Yet this destiny must not be interpreted in terms of an inevitable fatalism. Jesus still had to struggle with a choice. He did not like the struggle. The question He faced was: Should He abandon His destiny in order to save Himself? His answer was the rejection of self-assertion and the acceptance of submission to the Father (12:27). Unlike the Synoptics, John used the idea of the *voice* from heaven *not* at the baptism of Jesus *but* at the acceptance of the final stage of His ministry! The voice of God thundered that God had glorified His own name in Jesus and that He would do it again (12:28)!

From the vantage point of Jesus' confirmation in His servanthood to God, the reader is introduced to Jesus as Judge. As indicated in connection with chapter 3 of this Gospel, salvation is not a game! The cross is the dividing point of history. In the cross, Jesus judged the world; through the cross, Jesus drew humanity fully to Himself.

What then of the human dimension in chapter 12? Like Jesus, the believers needed to learn the meaning of the death perspective. Therefore, Jesus said, "The one who loves his life shall lose [ruin] it, but the one who hates his life in this world shall guard it unto life eternal" (12:25). Here is the *secret to true assurance,* namely, life that is lived like Jesus lived His life. In following Jesus, we have the security of being with Him (12:26).

But such a pattern is difficult for humans to accept. We tend to choose the way of the others in this chapter. Some believed, but they did not carry their belief very far because "they loved the praise of men rather than the praise of God" (12:43). Because Jesus knew such a pattern was typical, He called humanity to an authentic discipleship of believing and to the abandonment of darkness (12:44-46). Jesus' summary cry about believing was actually a twofold announcement. He *assured* us that His intention in coming into the world was to save the world. But He also *warned* us that whoever rejected Jesus and His sayings would be judged by what He said (12:47-50; see 3:17-19).

The Festival Cycle is, thus, complete. It began with an unstated feast and with the Jews condemning Jesus on the basis of a legalistic misconception of Scripture. It also pointed to Jesus, who preserved the tension of Scripture. Second, it turned to Passover and illustrated the Jews' erroneous evaluation of Jesus on the basis of a misconception of God's gifts of manna and bread. It also focused on the marvelous assurance that comes from receiving this bread, yet at the same time it reminded us of the uneasy question of His departure. Third, it turned to the Feast of Tabernacles, and it highlighted the Jews' rejection of Jesus on the basis of misconceptions of messiahship and inheritance as children of Abraham and of God. It also revealed the tension in discipleship. Fourth, it turned to the Feast of Dedication and the readiness of the Jews to stone Jesus because of their misconception of the nature of the shepherd. But it also underlined the assurance which believers can gain in times of persecution without diminishing the responsibility of the Lord's strict call to follow Him. Finally, the cycle returned to Passover and the Jewish plot which resulted from the human misconception of Jesus, the lifegiver. But here it also pointed to the uneasy tensions both of believing and living and of the Christian's understanding of destiny and the struggle which is a part of human choice.

C. Assurance and Warning in the Book of Glory (John 13:1 to 20:29)

The second major section of the Gospel, the Book of Glory, can be conveniently divided into two parts. The first part is concerned with farewell instructions of Jesus to His disciples and has here been designated as the Farewell Cycle. The second part involves the Johannine portrait of the death and resurrection of Jesus.

1. THE FAREWELL CYCLE (JOHN 13:1 TO 17:26)

The Johannine farewell discourses of Jesus are an intricately interwoven set of instructions to the disciples. The reader might well have anticipated that with the conclusion of chapter 12 John would have moved immediately to the death and resurrection events. But the intention throughout this Gospel has been to direct the reader to an authentic life of discipleship. These final instructions, therefore, form an incredibly important message for Christians. They are a kind of Johannine last will and testament from Jesus, and they are meant to be taken with great seriousness. The discourses together form another cycle which begins and ends with the motif of glory (13:31-32; 17:1-4,24). This theme of glory sets before the reader the fact that these instructions have been given with the death of Jesus clearly in mind. The cycle begins with a command and ends with a prayer. This phenomenon is a reflection of the familiar two-dimensional perspective of John.

a. The Love Command (John 13:1-38). At the beginning of chapter 13, John reminded the reader of the crucial nature of the setting. He referred to the Passover, to the hour, to Jesus' departure, to His love for His own, to the devil, to Judas's betrayal, and to Jesus' date with destiny in terms of the fact that from that point on it all rested in Jesus' hands. In such a setting the first instruction to the disciples came in the vivid form of a living example of Jesus washing their feet. It was a lesson in being a servant; Peter, who here spoke for the disciples, was unfortunately a miserable failure. Peter's failure really involved a lack of submission—in effect a rejection of the implications of being *a follower of the Servant,* Jesus. When Peter was forced to face his error, he tried the quick-fix technique of overcorrection. He asked for a bath! But Peter's error served John's purpose as a means for introducing some special instructional warnings. Percentage of cleanness or purity for the Christian was not determined by the number of body parts that were washed. Feet were important here (13:10). Discipleship was to be viewed as a matter of servanthood.

In one of His incisive "truly" statements, therefore, Jesus announced that Christian servants should not think they would be greater than *their servant Master*. But He added that those who practiced these words would be blessed (13:16-17). Servanthood, indeed, was to be the theme of the disciples' lives and blessing was the expectation.

But the blessing did not include all those in the circle of disciples because Judas was still present (13:18). Judas's betrayal greatly troubled Jesus (13:21). Of course, He knew that one of His intimates would kick him (Note: the foot metaphor is continued.), as the Scripture had indicated (13:18; see Ps. 41:9). Yet the reality of Scripture did not reduce the pain of betrayal. The coming of Jesus' hour meant the coming of Judas's hour also. The sign of the dipped bread which passed from Jesus to Judas permitted the satanic power to work its worst (13:26-27). The self-dimension here is very strong both for Judas and for Jesus. Judas decided, and so did Jesus! But the timing of the crucifixion, John indicated, was given by Jesus. This fact is very important. If it is missed one might become fuzzy on the divine dimension in John and use such timing statements to submerge the human dimension.[54] Neither Judas nor Jesus are pictured as robots in John. They certainly fulfilled Scripture, but they were also responsible for their actions. With respect to Judas, Jesus said, "What *you* are doing." Since Jesus was in charge, He instructed Judas to carry out the plotted deed quickly (13:27). With that command the betrayer departed, and the story increases in intensity as John commented, "It was night" (13:30). Winter had arrived earlier (10:22). Now the night had followed!

It was time for the Son of man to be glorified, but it was also time for the commandment of love to be given to the disciples. Like Jesus' admonition for the disciples to be servants to one another (wash one another's feet, 13:14), the commandment to love one another was a test of discipleship (13:34-35). Active love was what Jesus chose as the sign by which all people would know those who were His disciples. The human dimension was thus brought to center stage in this opening chapter of the Farewell Cycle. The church chose, from all of the events that occurred on the Thursday before Black Friday, to remember that day as Maundy Thursday. *Maundy* is a defective form of the Latin verb for "command" (*mando*), and it points directly to this command of Jesus which is found only in the Gospel of John.[55] As Christians we need to be grateful for a day that calls our attention to the admonition to love one another. We also need to receive this command as a *goal* for every day and as a *warning* against our backbiting, gossiping, and mistreating our brothers and sisters in Christ. To love does not merely mean to *say* that one loves; it means to *act* in love! Christ knows the difference, and so do most of us.

In the transition to the next subject, Peter was once again used as a foil. The reality of Jesus' departure had begun to set in, and Peter's hasty offer to follow Jesus even to the point of death was met by the knowing Jesus with the prediction of Peter's denial (13:36-38). Discipleship, like love, is part of the human dimension which requires more than intention and words. Hasty words without life commitment bring the warnings and judgments of the Lord. Peter was, thus, a picture of the tragic split between human desire and actual life.

b. Assuring Comfort (John 14:1-31). Producing hopelessness, however, was not the purpose for the Farewell Cycle. Providing assurance and comfort was. Jesus, therefore, assured the disciples that they did not need to be worried because God had a place for all of them, and Jesus' going and coming was part of the preparation (14:1-3). Should not such statements have given the disciples assurance? Did they not know where He was going? The practical realist Thomas, however, argued that it was time for a decisive road map (14:4-5). To which Jesus responded with another "I am" announcement that indicated that road maps did not provide assurance for this type of truth and life. Jesus Himself was the assurance; if the disciples knew Jesus, they would recognize the Father (14:6-7).

Unfortunately, Philip's reply revealed that the disciples were stuck on words and that they had difficulty thinking beyond a firsthand assurance or confirmation from the Father. Philip did not realize what he was requesting. Nobody had ever seen God (see 1:18), and the Jews knew that it was extremely dangerous even to meet a representative or messenger from God (see Isa. 6:5). But by sending Jesus, God had taken a giant step for humankind in providing assurance.

The time had arrived for the disciples to realize that the human dimension of believing was tied intimately to the realization that assurance came from the Father through the Son. Jesus said that believing in the identification of the Father with the Son was critical for the disciples. But they had problems understanding His works; therefore, He called them at least to recall His words (14:9-11). Indeed, He assured them that their believing would lead them to do even greater works than His if they would prayerfully ask in His name (14:12-14).

Jesus' concern for the disciples' assurance went beyond their human dimension of prayer to the divine dimension of presence. They would not be orphaned by Jesus (14:18) because they would be given another, the Paraclete (*paraklētos:* Supporter, Advocate, Comforter, and/or Counselor) who would identify intimately with them (14:15-17) and help calm their troubled hearts (14:26-27). In addition, although the world would not comprehend the resurrection, they would see the living Jesus and then know for sure the reality of their Lord's divine sonship (14:19-21). The resurrection of Jesus and the giving of the Spirit were to be viewed as the great symbols of Christian assurance.

The theme of assurance is woven into the very fabric of the Farewell Cycle, but it is never removed from the theme of Christian responsibility. The balancing of these themes seems to come with such regularity that one is forced to reflect on the deliberate nature of this balance and what John was intending to say to Christians about the nature of discipleship through this alternation of themes. Christian responsibility is introduced into the heart of an assurance passage when Jesus said, "The one who has my commandments and keeps them is the one who loves me" (14:21). What follows next was definitely an assurance statement to the effect that such a person would be loved by the Father. But the basic presupposition of obedience is asserted here. This theme of loving obedience is intensified by the instructions in John 15.

c. Instructions about the Vine and the Branches (John 15:1-17). In chapter 15 one meets another *mashal* (parable or allegory). This *mashal* of the vine provides a delicate balance to the *mashal* of the shepherd in chapter 10. Both are necessary to adequately understand John. Jesus is pictured as the vine, the Father as the vineyard keeper, and Christian disciples as the branches. The role of Jesus, the vine, is described as that of supplying the needs of the human branches.

Thus, a branch is to remain attached to the vine; otherwise, it will die (wither). The Father's role is explained as that of the pruner. The pruner's task is to cut off the unwanted twigs, so what is left will be more productive. Lastly, the role of the believer is interpreted as a bearer of fruit. It is pointless in this *mashal* to argue whether the fruit should involve evangelism. Of course, it should. But evangelism is only one aspect of discipleship.[56] The point of the *mashal* is obedient attachment to Jesus which results in the authentic life of discipleship whatever that might entail. Abiding assuredly will bring fruit!

Several significant warnings are sounded in this *mashal*, the missing of which can only lead to the distortion of the Johannine theological picture. The first warning concerns identity. Jesus is the vine, and the disciples are dependent branches (15:5). For disciples to mistake their identity would be to repeat the classic sin of humans evidenced in the stories of the Garden of Eden and the Tower of Babel (Gen. 3:5-7; 11:4). The Christian is not God, and disciples have been acutely warned not to mistake who they are and exalt themselves. Jesus warned Christians not to think that they are beyond the pale of such pride— a particularly terrible temptation for ministers! Jesus also admonished them to recognize that a continual dependence upon (abiding in) Him was an essential mark of Christian discipleship. Without Jesus, the believer is helpless (John 15:4-5).

The second warning concerns judgment. Jesus said that if a person does not remain in Him that person would be thrown out and would die (wither). Such dead branches would then be destroyed by fire (15:6). This verse is very hard for many Christians to accept. They prefer that it not be in the New Testament. But it is just as much a part of this Gospel as the assuring nonstealing text (10:28). Thus, we would be hiding our theological eyes if we fail to see a warning here for Christians. The entire context deals with the true meaning of discipleship. The text must be taken seriously; otherwise, it affects far more than our preconceptions on salvation. It affects our very view of God and the Bible.

John followed these warnings with a parallel statement of assurance which seems to suggest astounding implications. Jesus announced that

God would answer an incredible range of prayers from the disciples (15:7). Lest the disciples felt their heads swelling with the importance of their own prayer power, the assurance statement, like the previous warning, carried a condition, "if you remain [abide] in me." Thus, verse 7 is a statement both of warning and of assurance. The balance of the human and divine dimensions is surely one of the startling realities that continually confronts the reader of the Gospel of John.

This balance might be thought to vanish in the later repetition of Jesus' promise for the Father to answer prayer (15:16). Indeed, in that setting the promise was immediately preceded by the statement that the disciples did not choose Jesus, but that He chose and appointed them to bear fruit which should abide (15:16). There is no question from the Johannine perspective that the action of God always precedes the action of humanity. In the choosing statement, however, an additional aspect was added to the discussion that should remind the reader of the context. The context is the appointment to bear fruit, and the context throws us back to verse 8 where the Father is said to be glorified in fruit bearing. Fruit bearing in turn is linked to being disciples. Discipleship is united with the themes of love and of keeping Jesus' commands (15:9-10). These commands of Jesus are, thus, forcefully summarized here again in the repetition of the new commandment to love one another (15:12; see 13:34-35). When John discovered the idea of love, he hung on to it like a bulldog. Jesus' love is shown to be the model for Christians because He laid down his life for His friends (15:13). The disciples were categorized as friends "*if*," according to Jesus, they "do the things" which He commanded (15:14). The condition is once again important for understanding the text. Only after clearly stating the condition "if" did John return to his assurance theme in which Jesus spoke of choosing and appointing disciples. One must not miss the fact that Jesus tied the argument together when He concluded the *mashal* with a forceful command, "Love one another" (15:17).

Choice or election by Jesus in this *mashal* and in the entire Johannine Gospel must not be understood in a vacuum, as though it were some divine fiat unrelated to life. *Choice was for a purpose*, and *it carried a condition*. The choosing, therefore, implies *both assurance and warning.* To understand the two-sided nature of choosing or election (*eklegomai*) in this Gospel, one needs only to be reminded of Jesus' thunderous words in John 6:70: "Did I not choose twelve, and out of *you* [pl.] one is a devil!" The divine dimension of choice does not eliminate the human dimension of responsible obedience. The life of a follower was not viewed as being easy. It demanded commitment in the face of difficulty. Therefore, the disciples needed assistance.

d. The Paraclete and Persecution (John 15:18 to 16:33). Jesus' desire for the disciples was not viewed by John from the goal of judging the disciples but from the perspective of giving them the crucial support and assurance they needed in the face of an antagonistic world (15:18). The words of Jesus and the gift of the Paraclete (Supporter, 15:26) are clear indications of our Lord's concern for Christians. The hostility of the world was to be understood by Christians as a given factor of life. In this context of animosity, Jesus requoted the saying He used at the beginning of the Farewell Cycle concerning the servant not being greater than his master (13:16), but here He moved the focus from humility to persecution (15:20).

The purpose for this vivid appraisal of hostility, as Jesus stated very clearly, was: "These things I have said to you in order that you might not be *scandalized*" (16:1). The translation in the Revised Standard Version of the Bible, "to keep you from falling away," is quite possible while that in the King James Version of the Bible, "ye should not be offended," is far too mild for an adequate rendering in English of the Greek word *skandalizō*. The temptation with which the early Christians were faced when they were excommunicated from the synagogues and persecuted by those who believed they were doing God's work was nothing less than the *enticement to renounce* their Lord (16:2). To prepare the Christians for the rigors of such hatred and persecution, Jesus called Christians to "remember" that He had expected that true disciples, like their Lord, would also experience *the hour* of such hostile reactions (16:4).

With this note the Farewell Cycle began the turn toward its conclusion. The statements of assurance and warning in fact summoned Christian readers to a realization that *destiny* of life was *not merely* assigned to Jesus but that destiny had *also* been assigned to the servant-disciples who would follow their Lord. Theologians, ministers, and Christian laypeople who are safe from the rigors of real persecution which might lead to their deaths can speculate (as I admit I have often done) on the philosophical meaning of divine choice. We may come to easy theological conclusions. I really began to sense a little more of the tension that is in this Gospel while serving, during a sabbatical, as an educational missionary in Cameroon, West Africa. There I began to perceive more clearly the twofold meaning of assurance and warning in dominical instructions like John 15:18 to 16:4*a*.

The assurance of Jesus in the midst of tribulation and persecution was meant to bring comfort and solace to the disciples. Earlier they would *not* have been able to accept such a way of persecution (16:4*b*). But reality had begun to dawn on them, and the issue was no longer the *intellectual question* of the *road map* (16:5; see 14:5). It had become the *existential question* of *survival*. Jesus told them that their sorrow would be offset by the presence of the Paraclete (Supporter, Advocate) who would act as their public defender as well as the prosecutor of the world (16:6-11). They would know the meaning of being hauled into court, but there was a higher court, and the prosecutor of the divine court would be their guide to truth on earth. They could, therefore, have assurance because their advocate would lead them to understand what they were not able to bear (16:12-15).

But timing was a difficult matter to handle for the disciples. They did not know how to deal with the various statements of "a little while," and they were not certain how to integrate Jesus' words concerning weeping and rejoicing (16:16-22). Yet writing from the post-resurrection perspective, John already knew the answer; he expected his readers to understand. The "hour" was, nevertheless, a riddle to the earlier disciples. Even though they thought they understood Jesus plainly and even though they thought that they had finally resolved their belief questions (16:29-30), Jesus pointed them beyond the reality of their intellects to the reality of persecution. The reality of "tribulation" was to prove their believing, and Jesus wanted them to understand beforehand that He had modeled for them how to deal with that "hour." True assurance for the disciples was found not in words but in Jesus who saw the other side of tribulation and beckoned His disciples to follow. Thus He said, "Be courageous, I have conquered the world!" (16:33).

e. The Great Prayer (John 17:1-26). The Farewell Cycle turned fully to its conclusion with John 17. This chapter is not another instructional lesson. The instructions had been completed with the assurance for the disciples that there was to be victory in Jesus. The form and function of chapter 17 are, therefore, a little different than in the other chapters. The form is not a didactic (instructional) statement. The form is a prayer. The function of the prayer was not to provide information, except perhaps as a summary of the previous instructions. But its purpose was to give the reader an open window on the heart of Jesus. The Gospel writer seemed to sense that assurance was not ultimately captured in logical statements, though statements are important. Assurance, whether it is given by a parent, a spouse, a professor, a minister, a co-worker, a friend, or by Jesus Himself, is received best when the receiver senses the caring, loving heart of the person seeking to communicate assurance. John included this prayer to reveal to the reader the heart of Jesus.

The prayer opens with a reference to the themes of both hour and glory. The hour, which was introduced in chapter 2, has been reached; therefore, Jesus prayed that, because He had obediently honored the Father, the Father would bring to completion the reality of glory (17:1-4). This servant pattern of Jesus, however, in no way diminishes the exceedingly high Christology of John in which the preexistence of the Son before creation is affirmed (17:5; see 1:1-4). This high Christology in the prayer forms the foundation for the sense of assurance which one could receive in the petitions. The preexistent Son's concern about the weak ones of the world is the premise of the prayer.

The assurance theme was brought to focus by John when Jesus prayed for Christians as God's own people who were given by God to Jesus for His instruction of God's words (17:6-7). The "reception" of Jesus' words and the "believing" that He came from God, however, introduced the human element in assurance (17:8). The combination of both the divine and the human dimensions formed the reason the prayer has been so important. Because humans are not robots of God in the salvation process, God's Son is concerned about human life, especially about the believers. This prayer of Jesus, therefore, was clearly focused on behalf of believers rather than the world, and this prayer has several very significant facets.

First, it is a prayer for protection. Jesus prayed, "Holy Father, keep them by your name" (17:11). Living in the world was dangerous, and Christians needed to be guarded. This prayer implies a serious danger of loss. Many theologians have great difficulty with John's idea of loss. We all have presuppositions, but the biblical texts ought not to be forced into the molds of our presuppositions. The prayer is definitely a prayer for protection. Jesus said that while He was on earth He was the keeper who guarded (protected) the disciples and none was destroyed (lost, *apōleto*) except the son of destruction (*apōleias*). Thus, Jesus had fulfilled both His destiny and the Scripture (17:12). But the departure of Jesus from the world meant a change. The resurrection would certainly bring the disciples joy, but there was more than joy. There was also danger. Therefore, the disciples needed to be ready to face a hostile world (17:13-14).

One option that Jesus obviously considered was to put the disciples in a germ-free environment where sin was not present. But that option would have meant taking them out of the world and teleporting them to heaven. Jesus knew that that option was impossible because it would also have meant the abandonment of the world to the evil one. Therefore, he prayed that, although they would be left in a hostile world, they should be kept out of the grip of the evil one (17:15).

The disciples' need to live in this hostile world led to the second facet of Jesus' prayer. Jesus next prayed for their holiness or sanctification in the truth (17:17). This prayer was a direct result of the fact that Jesus would not abandon the world. He had truly been sent by God to the world. In turn He sent His disciples to the world (17:18). They had a mission. But in order to do it, they needed the strength and assurance that came from a holy life, a holiness which was backed by the holiness of Jesus. Jesus responded to their need by a reconsecration or recommitment of Himself to holiness (17:19). Think of the implications of the Son of God following the incarnational pattern to such a point in His concern for His disciples that *He* committed Himself to holiness for us! Whatever John meant by this statement, its full significance is staggering. The holy Son of God chose to be holy for our sakes.

The third facet of the prayer has received considerable attention in the twentieth century. It was the prayer for oneness (17:21). Like protection and holiness, oneness is another aspect of assurance. Anyone who has participated in dialogues with Christians of other traditions knows both the frustration of dealing with people who think a little differently than he does and the sense of joy that comes from the discovery that there are some wonderful brothers and sisters in Christ in other traditions. Friends, when one has had the experience, as I have, of being in dialogue with other Christians from traditions whose forebearers persecuted his recent ancestors, he begins to learn something of the meaning of Jesus' prayer. The prayer for oneness was no mere prayer for organizational unity. At its core, the prayer involved mission ("that the world may believe," 17:21)! Organization is one thing, but unity which flows from a love for other Christians and a commitment to win the world for Christ is quite another.

To be at peace with brothers and sisters in Christ can bring to the Christian a marvelous sense of assurance. That one disagrees with others does not mean that we cannot be brothers and sisters. We may not agree with each other, yet we can really love one another, and that is precisely why Jesus reintroduced the idea of love (vv. 23,26). Emile Cailliet warned that we as humans tend to colonize the reality with the intelligible.[57] To put these words in other down-to-earth terms, *none* of us *can*, thankfully, ever *succeed in pouring the ocean of God's truth into the teacups of our minds. But we can love!* Yes, we can love one another.

My sense of the text tells me that John saw in the prayer of Jesus a two-sided heartbeat. Clearly the most obvious side was a genuine heartfelt longing for Christians to live above the ways of the world. Thus, Jesus prayed for our protection. Moreover, He prayed for us to be holy and to be one. But He also prayed that we might reach our ultimate destinies and be with Him where He would be in order that we might behold His glory (17:24). What a magnificent sense of assurance can flow from this prayer. When we Christians look honestly at the elements of this prayer, we may recognize why it was a *prayer*. We are not overwhelmingly effective with either oneness or holiness. And if we desperately need prayer in these matters, may it not be possible that we desperately need prayer for our protection and destinies as well? It would be to our benefit to humbly join our Lord in these four petitions, not only for ourselves but also for others.

Thus ends the Farewell Cycle. It was introduced by a proclamation that the hour had come and by a command for us to love. Once again we are faced with the intersection of the divine and the human. The cycle turned next to the question of human hopelessness and God's assuring provision. But it also warned us to remember the condition of love which became the focal point of the vine *mashal* with its assurances and warnings. The cycle turned to the existential question of persecution, but it also brought us to the assuring promise of the Spirit who dwells in the lives of Christians. As the dangers associated with persecution and tribulation came into full focus, the cycle turned for its final time to the prayer of the Son of God who, in stooping to concern Himself with His very human disciples, had prayed for their protection, holiness, oneness, and destiny in the midst of a threatening evil world. Christ cares, and His care means assurance; Christ also holds us responsible, and therefore, His concern means warning as well.

2. THE FINAL EVENTS OF THE BOOK OF GLORY (JOHN 18:1 TO 20:29)

The conclusion to the Farewell Cycle ushers in the final events in the coming of Jesus to the world. For the purpose of study, these events can be helpfully divided into the death and resurrection stories.

a. The Death Story (John 18:1 to 19:42). The Johannine death story is exceedingly significant because of the striking contrast between the divine dimension, as represented in Jesus, and the human dimension, as represented in figures like Judas, the soldiers, Peter, the Jewish authorities, and Pilate. The struggle of Jesus' troubled heart concluded when the voice from heaven announced His victory (12:28).

His instructions in the Farewell Cycle were given from the vantage point of the victor; in the death story, the God-man was definitely in control.

From my perspective, the word *passion* (which in its Latin derivation suggests a suffering as the result of some external force) is an inadequate description of the Johannine story. If anyone was being acted upon in this Gospel, it was not Jesus. Unlike Mark (15:34) and Matthew (27:46) John recorded no cry of dereliction ("My God, my God, why have you abandoned me?"). The portrait is every bit as serene and confident as the Lucan death story. To the Christian reader who seeks a testimony of assurance, the Johannine record of the final events in the earthly life of Jesus is filled with confidence. Jesus was in control at every turn.

But when one looks at the human figures in this record, the reader finally senses where assurance is located. Judas had left the supper during the first stage of the Farewell Cycle, and John said that it was night (13:30). Judas went to the garden with fully armed soldiers who needed the help of lanterns and torches. Jesus was fully in control and stepped forward with a self-identification. At that point, the careful reader of John should be able to guess what those identifying words were. They were none other than *egō eimi* ("I am," 18:5). Whenever mere mortals have confronted the revelation of God, there has been only one result. So it was in this story. The armed soldiers were sent straight to the ground (18:6). Jesus gave them permission to advance and take Him, but He also ordered the soldiers to let the disciples go (18:8).

At that point Peter (His name was not mentioned here in the other Gospels), tried to get into the act with a fruitless attempt at courage. This attempt was promptly stopped by Jesus who warned Him not to try to take the Lord's destiny into His own hands (18:11). Well-intentioned brashness was certainly a quality of Peter. Like many of us, He acted on incomplete knowledge and felt quite capable of deciding what was best for God.

But Peter soon had his chance for courage, and he soon had an opportunity for self-identification. When he was asked the question by the maid, John focused on the stark contrast of his answer when he said, *ouk eimi* ("I am not," 18:17; see 18:25). Even with two more chances, the last one being a positive identification by a relative of the man who suffered from Peter's foolhardy attempt at courage, Peter could not admit his discipleship (18:26-27). What an illustration of the reason we as humans need the prayer of Jesus in John 17.

At the same time as Peter yielded to denial, Jesus stood firm. He would not knuckle under to Annas. He had done nothing for which he was ashamed and said nothing in secret which he desired to be hidden (18:19-24). It was almost as though John wanted to make sure that Christian readers received a clear message that their assurance was not in Peter but in Jesus.

The scenes which followed next moved with the regular beat of a funeral dirge and reveal the manipulative inconsistencies of sinful humanity. The priests were absolutely unwilling to defile their external selves by entering a Gentile praetorium (the judgment hall) before Passover. But they were fully willing to condemn the Messenger from God and to turn Him over to a Gentile judge at Passover time (18:28-32). Inconsistent means have frequently been used to serve what was thought to be just ends even in the religious world; such a process hardly guaranteed security then, and it certainly does not now.

The Gentile governor who represented the mighty Roman imperial power was also, for John, just a shadow of a man in the presence of King Jesus. The governor's questions—"Are you the King of the Jews?" "Am I a Jew?" "What is truth?"—sounded like hollow words in comparison to Jesus' responses. As though putting Pilate on trial, Jesus asked, "Are you saying this from yourself or did others speak to you about me?" Then Jesus proclaimed the truth of His kingship which laid beyond the restricted borders of the governor's world (18:33-38a). What a sense of hope and assurance Jesus' words must have engendered among Christians who faced the threatening judgment seats of Rome!

The governor was on trial, not Jesus. Pilate tried the easy answer of custom to secure Jesus' release; it backfired, and he had to release a robber (18:38b-40). He tried the harder answer of pity, but the people saw blood and wanted more (19:1-7). He tried out of fear to reason with Jesus, but Jesus was silent (19:8-9). He then tried to

threaten Jesus with his power, but Jesus told him that even the governor was powerless to deal with sin (19:10-11). As a last resort, Pilate
tried to reason with the bloodthirsty crowd; at that point the chief
priests committed the ultimate apostasy for Israel when they responded for the people, "We have no king, except Caesar!" (19:15).
Pilate lost his case! He, too, was guilty of expediency and gross injus-
tice. The time for the crucifixion had come. Jesus permitted it. It
was his hour!

But in John the crucifixion is not represented as a sorrowful failure.
There was no via dolorosa (the way of sorrows). John did not include
Jesus' being too weak to carry His own cross (see Mark 15:21; Luke
23:26). The charge on the cross was simply "The King of the Jews";
John said that the charge was written in the world languages of Hebrew, Latin, and Greek (19:20-21).[58] In John the chief priests attempted to have the charge changed from a general title to a mocking
self-affirmation, but Pilate finally would have nothing of their manipu-
lation. Undoubtedly in this charge, John saw a universal affirmation
of Jesus' kingship. Here again was assurance for the weak heart.

The other events of the last day portrayed no less a forceful picture
of Jesus. The parting of the clothes by the quaternion (the squad of
four, only in John) and the lot casting for Jesus' seamless tunic was
for John a fulfillment of Scripture (19:23-24). The Johannine transfer
of Jesus' mother to the beloved disciple, whether given according to
an adoption formula or not, indicated Jesus' superintending concern
even from the cross (19:25-27).[59] That Peter was not even present at
the cross seems evident, but it is not profitable here to press this
point. Then came the thirst which was also a fulfillment of Scripture
and, finally, the last words from the cross: "It is finished"!

"It is finished," which is not recorded in any other Gospel, formed
for John the incisive summation of the completion of God's will by
His incarnate Regent on earth (19:30). The death of Jesus was according
to divine timing! He gave up His spirit; they did not kill Him! They
came to break His bones, but He was already dead. The act of piercing
His side only confirmed again that His death was for the sin of the
world, and the *witness* confirmed this fact (19:35). The way of Jesus'
submission to God was the way of assurance because John saw here
again the fulfillment of Scripture (19:36-37).

Finally, the burial was not some hasty event. It was a deliberate act of Joseph and Nicodemus, the night seeker (3:2). In this act, Nicodemus fully came out of the closet (see 7:50-51) and John saw a signal that something was to occur beyond the crucifixion. The hundred (Roman) pounds of spices were enough to bury a king.[60] And with these preparations completed, John noted that they observed the day of *Preparation*.

The sense of assurance given through this death story pointed the believing reader to the exciting expectation of the resurrection story. But the death story's dark side concerning Judas, the soldiers, Peter, Pilate, and the high priests added a warning for everyone concerning the fallible nature of humanity.

b. The Resurrection Story (John 20:1-29). The resurrection story begins with the discovery of the empty tomb. Here again the Johannine tomb narrative has its unique elements. The account starts like the Synoptics with a focus on a female visit to the tomb,[61] then quickly shifts to a tomb visit by two of the disciples. Mary's reaction to the empty tomb was one of frustration over what she thought was the theft of the body of the Lord (20:2). One might project her probable insecure reaction as: "Can they not leave Him alone yet?"

But the disciples were not concerned with her insecurity at her sense of loss. Notice how John divided the account of Mary into two parts with the disciples and their agendas in the middle. The other disciple is said to have reached the tomb "first." (John seemed to consider it necessary to repeat this fact.) The other disciple paused, looked in, and when Peter arrived, he followed Peter into the tomb. Peter saw the burial clothes and the head wrapping, but the Gospel writer asserted that the other disciple saw and believed (20:3-8).

Setting aside the Peter question which has already been raised earlier, the reader should remember that one of the major themes of John has been seeing and believing. Here the other disciple was highlighted for attention as the first in a series of postdeath believing accounts. The empty tomb and the grave clothes were apparently enough assurance for this disciple to believe. His believing, John added, was prior to the rest of the community's reflection and understanding of the Scripture (20:9). Indeed, it was seemingly prior to any resurrection appearance of Jesus! This phenomenon was definitely unique in Gospel literature because post-crucifixion believing seemed to follow not precede appearance experiences. Whatever position some may take on the resurrection issue, it seems quite evident that John's view of resurrection assurance started with the empty tomb.[62] This believing seems to have begun when it was early but was *still dark* (20:1). The day, however, was coming again!

In the second account, which is a continuation of the Mary story, another stage of assurance is brought into focus. Not only were two angels in the tomb as symbols of divine action, but the caring Jesus is introduced and was finally recognized by His personal naming of Mary (20:16). Her immediate reaction upon recognition was to try and grab onto Jesus. While many pages have been written on the issues of the touching and the ascension in connection with this account, the intention of John with respect to assurance here seems to be fairly clear. The bodily presence of Jesus was not to be the way of sensing Christian assurance.[63] Holding on to some kind of a physical Jesus was impossible. Jesus' ascension meant that He was to be with the Father (20:17). But Mary did have a kind of assurance she carried with her and reported to the disciples, "I have *seen* the Lord" (20:18).

The two-part concluding story of the book involving the disciples and Thomas has already been discussed in some detail. At this point, it is sufficient to recall that the double appearance story of Jesus which included the receiving of the Holy Spirit, the commissioning of the disciples, and the confession of Thomas seems to suggest a movement out of darkness (20:19) into a time of transformation. And it was not meant merely for the benefit of the first disciples. The two-fold story was meant to assure the *readers who would follow* that the appearances of Jesus to the disciples were the kind of appearances that were unrepeatable. Nevertheless, they were worthy of accepting as the basis for believing. This combined story served as a warning that if one required firsthand confirmation before believing one would miss the blessing of Christian believing (20:29).

Christianity is more than proven facts. Proof will never be enough for the unbeliever who, like the Jews, will not believe. For John Christianity was a way of living in dependent believing on Jesus as the Son of God. Enough signs were provided to open the door of the human will so that God can provide the living assurance that the Jesus of the Gospel signs is indeed, "My Lord and my God!" (20:28). *John did not speak of proof but of witness.* God has not provided a sign greater than that of the risen Jesus. Humanity is called out of darkness to see these signs and "believe that Jesus is the Christ, the Son of God" (20:31). With this purpose statement, the Gospel originally ended.

D. Assurance and Warning in the Epilogue (John 21:1-25)

While the book was at first completed with chapter 20, there is no textual record that it ever circulated without the Epilogue.[64] The matters of authorship and style for the Epilogue are far too involved to handle here. It is sufficient, however, to say that there are many similarities with the first twenty chapters. As I have briefly indicated at the beginning of this discussion on the Gospel of John, the picture of Peter in this Epilogue was not vastly different from the one in the earlier chapters.

But there is one major concern which had to be addressed. Peter needed to be restored to the community. Such a restoration, indeed, was done through the beloved disciple who, as the *day was dawning* (21:4), identified the Lord for Peter (21:7). We need to focus on the restoration itself because this story of Peter's restoration has become one of the most moving stories in the New Testament. Three times Peter denied his Lord (18:15-18,25-27). Three times he was asked concerning his love for Jesus (21:15-17). When Jesus asked the question of love the third time, John pictured the personal agony as very intense. The dialogue did not focus on a mere play of words for *love*, as it has sometimes been proposed. The emphasis was on the threefold question of Jesus.[65] Peter's denial had been serious, and Peter's restoration was painful. Denial for a disciple was not treated lightly by Jesus. It was a very serious matter, and the Gospel of John treats denial seriously.

Peter's grief, however, was part of the healing process, and his restoration was announced in the last of Jesus' "truly" statements. *He received a sign*, a sign he would rather not have had. It was a sign of his martyrdom (21:18-19). Who wants to die? Who wants to die alone? Therefore, Peter asked about the other disciple. To this question Jesus sternly replied that such a matter was none of his business (21:22). Peter's business was *his* sign. If Christian readers perceive correctly the sign, they will see that it was both a clear and assuring sign of Peter's restoration, even though it was a sign of his death.

To the early reader who struggled with faith in the time of persecution, this story of the restoration of Peter was a magnificent promise of hope and assurance. If a martyr such as Peter could also have been a denier, then what about a later renouncer of the Christian faith in the fiery times of persecution? Again and again the early church had to wrestle with cases of renouncers. What was to be their lot when the fear of persecution had passed? The answer was not an easy one because many Christians had stood firm and had died for their faith. The model of Peter, however, was a model that the early church could not easily forget. Restoration was possible.

The way Jesus handled Peter's wrenching question, "What about him, Lord?" is also very telling. It was none of Peter's business what the risen Christ would demand of the beloved disciple. Peter's business was his personal responsibility to God. His call was to "follow" Jesus. That call was a final warning not to deviate from the way of the Lord.

The Epilogue, therefore, is a word of assurance; but it is not an easy word. It is a word that takes very seriously human sin and human responsibility, and in so doing it also warns the reader that Christian discipleship may demand the ultimate price. Peter may have ignobly escaped death through denial the first time, but restoration and following Jesus still meant his death. He still had to face his destiny. His response the second time was very different. By the time this Gospel was written, Peter had paid the ultimate price for following Jesus. Peter had been restored. Thank God for restoration! Chapter 21 was, indeed, added as an Epilogue. But what an Epilogue!

Conclusion

In conclusion, it is evident that John consistently maintained the balance between assurance and warning throughout this Gospel, even in the Epilogue. The divine dimension is punctuated with warnings related to the human dimension. The human dimension is given assurance by the constant interjection of the divine dimension. For Christian interpreters to emphasize either of the dimensions and reduce the other is to misunderstand the marvelously balanced message of this Gospel. While the Gospel of John was undoubtedly scheduled to be completed with the end of chapter 20, chapter 21 was a necessary Epilogue. The Epilogue is not an irrelevant postscript to the Gospel. It has become, instead, an incredibly important second ending which repeatedly forces the reader to confront in exemplary fashion the twofold question of assurance and warning. This Gospel constantly reminds Christians who struggle with life's turmoils and traumas that they are not alone in their difficulties, that others have traveled that way of life before them. They can be assured, therefore, that the caring Jesus has prayed for them, has provided them with the resource of the Paraclete, and has given to them a model of restoration. To those who sin, deny their Lord, or take lightly the meaning of believing in Jesus, these words of warning stand as an unbending sign of the absolute necessity for return, restoration, and the resumption of God's demands on their lives. This Gospel is, indeed, an inspired word of assurance and warning for those who believe in Jesus Christ, the Son of God, the Lord of the church!

Notes

1. G. L. Borchert, "The Fourth Gospel and Its Theological Impact," *Review Expositor* 78 (1981): 249.

2. In the ninth grade, while confined to an isolation hospital, I memorized most of this Gospel, but it was not until my doctoral studies after having taken five courses in this Gospel that I genuinely felt a sense of understanding the multidimensional nature of this masterpiece called the Gospel of John. In the quarter of a century of teaching the Gospel since that time, I have been thrilled time and again by the experience of leading students and lay people to discover the marvelous meaning of the complex simplicity of this written gift from God.

3. Borchert, p. 249.

4. A. H. Strong, *Systematic Theology*, 3rd ed. (New York: A. C. Armstrong and Son, 1890), p. 491.

5. Dale Moody, *The Word of Truth* (Grand Rapids: Wm. B. Eerdmans, 1981), p. 357.

6. D. A. Carson, *Divine Sovereignty and Human Responsibility*, New Foundations Theological Library (Atlanta: John Knox Press, 1981) and I. H. Marshall, *Kept By the Power* (Minneapolis: Bethany Fellowship, 1969).

7. R. E. Brown, *The Gospel According to John I-XII*, The Anchor Bible (Garden City: Doubleday & Company, 1966) 29:xxi-cxliv; W. E. Hull, "John," *The Broadman Bible Commentary*, ed. C. J. Allen (Nashville: Broadman Press, 1970) 9:189-208; Leon Morris, *The Gospel According to John*, The New International Commentary on the New Testament (Grand Rapids: Wm. B. Eerdmans, 1971); Rudolf Schnackenburg, *The Gospel According to St. John*, 3 vols., trans. K. Smith (New York: Crossroad, 1982); Stephan Smalley, *John: Evangelist and Interpreter* (Greenwood, S. C.: Attic Press, 1978); G. A. Turner and J. R. Mantey, *The Gospel According to John* (Grand Rapids: Wm. B. Eerdmans, n.d.), pp. 1-50. B. F. Westcott, *The Gospel According to St. John* (Grand Rapids: Wm. B. Eerdmans, 1954). C. H. Dodd, *The Interpretation of the Fourth Gospel* (Cambridge: University Press, 1958) and *Historical Tradition in the Fourth Gospel* (Cambridge: University Press, 1963). Robert Kysar, *The Fourth Evangelist and His Gospel: An Examination of Contemporary Scholarship* (Minneapolis: Augsburg Publishing House, 1975) is a helpful review of scholarly works on the Gospel.

8. Donald Guthrie, *New Testament Introduction*, 3rd ed. (Downers Grove: Inter-Varsity Press, 1970), pp. 237-335 and W. G. Kümmel, *Introduction to the New Testament*, trans. H. Kee (Nashville: Abingdon Press, 1975), pp. 188-247.

9. Following the discoveries of the Gnostic texts at Nag Hamadi (Chenoboskion) and the Dead Sea Scrolls at Qumran, Wm. F. Albright posited a date prior to the seventies for a basic document behind John. See his article "Recent Discoveries in Palestine and the Gospel of John" in *The Background of the New Testament* (C. H. Dodd Festschrift), eds. W. D. Davies and D. Daube (Cambridge: University Press, 1956), pp. 153-173. In 1958 while addressing pastors in Philadelphia, Albright suggested that the basic document could be as early as the forties or fifties of the first Christian century. J. A. T. Robinson in *Redating the New Testament* (Philadelphia: Westminster Press, 1976), pp. 259-285 has likewise argued for an early dating of John. These views have not generally received a favorable response from most scholars.

For a discussion of late dating for the Gospel in the second century, see the discussion of W. Kümmel, *Introduction to the New Testament*, pp. 217-228 and the view of Rudolf Bultmann, *Theology of the New Testament*, trans. K. Groliel (New York: Charles Scribner's, 1955), pp. 6-10. These views likewise, for my part, are quite unsatisfactory.

10. R. A. Culpepper, *The Johannine School*, SBL Dissertation Series 26 (Missoula, Mont.: Scholars Press, 1975). For a discussion of the Johannine community see Raymond E. Brown, *The Community of the Beloved Disciple* (New York: Paulist Press, 1979).

11. F. V. Filson, *The Gospel According to John*, The Layman's Bible Commentary (Richmond: John Knox Press, 1963), pp. 19-26.

12. C. H. Dodd, "The First Epistle of John and the Fourth Gospel," *Bulletin of the John Rylands Library* 21 (1937): 129-156.

13. See G. H. C. MacGregor and H. W. Morton, *The Structure of the Fourth Gospel* (Edinburgh: Oliver & Boyd, 1961).

14. Borchert, p. 252.

15. For a discussion of the relationship between Christians and Jews at this time see Leonard Goppelt, *Apostolic and Post-Apostolic Times*, trans. R. Guelich (Grand Rapids: Baker Book House, 1970), pp. 117-123. See also G. Borchert, "The Lord of Form and Freedom: A New Testament Perspective on Worship," *Review and Expositor* 80 (1983), 8-9.

16. The idea of Jamnia has been recently debated. Whether Jamnia is said to represent a specific formal council or a collective idea within Judaism does not seem to make much of a serious difference to my thesis here.

17. While I might not state the issue as stridently as Carson, I find myself in basic agreement with him at this point. See *Divine Sovereignty*, p. 152.

18. For a comparison of a Gospel with other ancient literature see Ralph P. Martin, *New Testament Foundations: A Guide for Christian Students*, *The Four Gospels* (Grand Rapids: Wm. B. Eerdmans, 1975) 1:13-29. See Charles H. Talbert, "The Gospel and the Gospels," *Interpreting the Gospels*, ed. J. L. Mays (Philadelphia: Fortress Press, 1981), pp. 14-26. This book is a series of reprints from earlier essays published in *Interpretation*. See also Talbert's earlier work, *What Is a Gospel?* (Philadelphia: Fortress Press, 1977) and his article "Ancient Biography," *Anchor Bible Dictionary*.

19. Hans Conzelmann, *An Outline of the Theology of the New Testament*, trans. J. Bowden (New York: Harper & Row, 1969), pp. 60-61, does not consider the Greek background very helpful in discussing the idea of gospel. While I think he is correct with respect to content, I think there are some interesting side ideas which are important for understanding the development of the document idea.

20. Approximately 80 percent of the uses of the term occur in the Pauline letters. See U. Becker, "Gospel, Evangelize, Evangelist," *The New International Dictionary of New Testament Theology*, ed. Colin Brown, trans. and rev. (Grand Rapids: Zondervan Regency Reference Library, 1976) 2:107-115.

21. J. A. Fitzmyer, *To Advance the Gospel: New Testament Essays* (New York: Crossroad Publishing, 1981), pp. 158-160.

22. F. F. Bruce, *The Defense of the Gospel in the New Testament*, rev. ed. (Grand Rapids: Wm. B. Eerdmans, 1977), p. 3.

23. For a discussion of the issues involved in the Synoptic problem see D. Guthrie, *New Testament Introduction*, 3rd ed. (Downers Grove: Inter-Varsity Press, 1970), pp. 121-187. For the theory of the priority of Matthew see W. R. Farmer, *The Synoptic Problem: A Critical Analysis* (Macon, Ga.: Mercer University Press, 1969/1976). I personally am not inclined to accept Farmer's updated Griesbach hypothesis.

24. For a copy of the *Diatessaron* see J. Hamlyn Hill, *The Earliest Life of Christ Ever Compiled from the Four Gospels, Being the Diatessaron of Tatian* (Edinburgh: T. & T. Clark, 1894); Edwin Preuschen, *Tatian's Diatessaron* (Heidelberg: Carl Winters Universitätsbuchhandlung, 1926); or A. S. Marmardji, *Diatessaron De Tatian* (Beyrouth: Imprimerie Catholique, 1935).

25. For a helpful introduction to the idea of the Gospels as portraits see the helpful discussion of my former colleague Robert Guelich, *The Sermon on the Mount* (Waco: Word Books, 1982), pp. 24-25.

26. R. E. Brown, *The Churches the Apostles Left Behind* (New York: Paulist Press, 1984), p. 84. The italics are his.

27. Alfred Loisy, *Le Quatrieme Evangile*, 2nd ed. (Paris: Emile Nourry, 1921), p. 514.

28. Borchert, "The Fourth Gospel," p. 252.

29. Brown, *The Churches the Apostles Left Behind*, p. 93.

30. Brown, *The Gospel According to John I-XII*, pp. 3-4, considers the prologue to be a four strophe hymn with insertions. J. T. Sanders, *The New Testament Christological Hymns: Their Historical Religious Background* (Cambridge: University Press, 1971), pp. 20-24, is not convinced that the poetic style was a hymn, C. K. Barrett, "The Prologue of St. John's Gospel," *New Testament Essays* (London: SPCK, 1972), pp. 27-48.

31. R. A. Culpepper, "The Pivot of John's Prologue," *New Testament Studies* 27 (1980): 1-31. For those not familiar with chiasm, it is a form of logic where the first and last statements are parallel and the format becomes something like a, b, a, d, ć, b́, á.

32. G. Borchert, *Great Themes from John* (Buffalo: Baptist Life Association, 1965), p. 6.

33. Both names are related to the idea of "rock," and both names may reflect a time after the confrontation between Peter and Jesus in which Peter is linked with the idea of rock. See Matthew 16:18.

34. Note the problem which the Tatian synthesizers have with the plural here when the second sign does not come until chapter 4.

35. The rich/young/ruler is a composite title for a man in the Synoptic stories of Mark 10, Matthew 19, and Luke 18. The one additional command of Jesus completely upset the tenuous balance of life that the man had constructed for himself. In other words, while he argued that he was directed by God, his theological construct was, in fact, oriented to the earth, and

Jesus added a command that challenged him to reevaluate his construct in terms of real trust in God. That prospect was too threatening for him. Unfortunately, like this man, many Christians have not brought their thinking truly under the scrutiny of God.

36. The translation "eternal" in English is probably to be preferred to "everlasting" since it includes a qualitative sense as well as quantitative temporal sense.

37. For those interested in his thinking, see Emile Cailliet, *The Christian Approach to Culture* (New York: Abingdon-Cokesbury, 1953) and Emile Cailliet, *The Dawn of Personality* (Indianapolis: Bobs-Merrill, 1955).

38. The original title of Rudolf Bultmann's Gifford Lectures on history and eschatology from the existentialist position was *The Presence of Eternity* (New York: Harper & Brothers, 1957). See the discussions at 3:18 in Rudolf Bultmann, *The Gospel of John: A Commentary*, trans. G. R. Beasley-Murray (Philadelphia: Westminster Press, 1971).

39. G. L. Borchert, *The Dynamics of Evangelism* (Waco: Word Books, 1976), pp. 61-62.

40. The Samaritans were the half-breed descendents of the mixed marriages both from the inhabitants of the Northern Kingdom (Israel) left after the destruction of Samaria in 720 BC by Assyria and from the non-Jewish inhabitants which the Assyrians forcibly transported to Samaria and forced to settle there. The intermarriage of the races created for their foreign rulers a new less-hostile group of settlers. These half-breeds were despised by the returning Exiles in the time of Nehemiah, and antagonism quickly erupted between the Jews and the Samaritans. During the Maccabean period, John Hycannus forcefully subjugated the Samaritans.

41. For discussions on church growth see for example D. A. McGavran, *Understanding Church Growth* (Grand Rapids: Wm. B. Eerdmans, 1980); D. A. McGavran with W. C. Arn, *Ten Steps for Church Growth* (San Francisco: Harper & Row, 1977) and *How to Grow a Church* (Glendale: Gospel Literature International, 1973); C. P. Wagner, *Your Church Can Grow* (Glendale: Gospel Literature International, 1976) and *The Pastor's Church Growth Handbook*, 2 vols. (Pasadena: Church Growth Press, 1979 and 1982). See also D. Miles, *Master Principles of Evangelism* (Nashville: Broadman Press, 1982) and *Church Growth—A Mighty River* (Nashville: Broadman Press, 1981).

42. While there are no direct parallels to this story in the Synoptics, some elements in the stories of the centurion's sick servant and Jairus's dead daughter (Luke 7:1-10; 8:40-42, 49-56; and parallels) are similar, particularly the importance of faith.

43. See Aïleen Guilding, *The Fourth Gospel and Jewish Worship: A Study of the Relation of St. John's Gospel to the Ancient Jewish Lectionary System*

(Oxford: Clarendon Press, 1960). While I would not accept all of her thesis, I do think she has shown conclusively that at least part of the Gospel focuses on the Jewish festivals.

44. Most modern versions correctly omit the last part of verse 3 and all of verse 4 as a scribal addition to the text. A brief glance at any critical edition of the Greek New Testament will indicate how great the manuscript probability is for the omission of these words. See for example Nestle-Aland, *Greek-English New Testament* (Stuttgart: Deutsche Bibelgesellschaft, 1979), pp. 259-260.

45. See Borchert, "The Lord of Form and Freedom," pp. 7-8.

46. For an example of this process see Joseph Klausnean, *Jesus of Nazareth*, trans. H. Danby (London: George Allen Unwin, 1925). The quest for the historical Jesus was a continual pattern of rewriting. See Albert Schweitzer, *The Quest of the Historical Jesus*, trans. W. Montgomery (New York: Macmillan, 1954). For an interesting example of a battle among Talmudic scholars see Jacob Neuser's conflict. See Saul Liberman, "A Tragedy or a Comedy?" *Journal of Oriental Studies* 104.2 (1984): 315-319 and the *Biblical Archaeology Review* 11 (Mar.-Apr. 1985): 12-16.

47. This chapter has been a battleground between sacramentalists and non-sacramentalists. A few years ago J. Ramsey Michaels sought to argue at one of the Society of Biblical Literature meetings that this text has little or no relationship to the Lord's Supper. In spite of my friendship with Michaels and others who take this tack, I disagree. Although John does not include Jesus' baptism and the Last Supper per se and although flesh here is used rather than body, this does not mean John's theology is unrelated either to baptism or the Lord's Supper. But I do consider that the ordinance is associated with love and service in the spirit of John 13.

48. See for example the discussion of Kenneth S. Latourette, *A History of Christianity* (New York: Harper & Brothers, 1953), p. 82.

49. For discussions of this difficult problem see for example Carson, *Divine Sovereignty*, pp. 167-168,184-186, etc.; Marshall, *Kept by the Power*, pp. 181-182 and Moody, *The Word of Truth*, p. 356.

50. For a discussion of *mashal* as it pertains to this story see Brown, pp. 390-391.

51. The Antiochans were famous for giving nicknames to people as they did to the followers of Jesus when they called them Christians (See Acts 11:26). In case of Antiochus IV who called himself Epiphanes which meant that he was a "manifestation of God," the Antiochans suggested instead that he be called Epimanes which means "madman." The story of this period which saw the rise of the Maccabeans (later called the Hasmonean dynasty) should be known to Bible students. A helpful little introduction to the times

known as the intertestamental period is Norman Snaith, *The Jews from Cyrus to Herod* (Nashville: Abingdon Press, n.d.).

52. For the problems inherent in a doctrine of reprobation see Harry R. Boer, *The Doctrine of Reprobation in the Christian Reformed Church* (Grand Rapids: Wm. B. Eerdmans, 1983).

53. Tradition suggests that Thomas died as a martyr in India where he became the founder of a church there. One of the national Indian churches is called The Mar Thoma Syrian Church.

54. While it may be only my personal perception, I genuinely consider that the human dimension has been reduced to a function of the divine in Carson's work. See *Divine Sovereignty.* The balance is so difficult to maintain, and Carson has genuinely sought to consider the nature of the tension. My criticism is that his commitment to Calvinism makes it difficult for him in the end to live with the tension.

55. Borchert, *Great Themes from John*, p. 12.

56. I am committed to evangelism, as is evident in my book on evangelism, but evangelism must not be isolated from other aspects of discipleship such as social concern. See Borchert, *The Dynamics of Evangelism*, p. 20 where I reject some common bifurcations of Christian proclaimers.

57. See the discussion related to note 37 in this chapter.

58. John likely saw in this language notation an indication of the universality of Jesus' messiahship.

59. See the discussion of Raymond Brown, *The Gospel According to John, XIII-XXI* (Garden City: Doubleday & Company, 1970) p. 907.

60. For a discussion of the amount and procedure of burial see ibid, p. 941 and Morris, pp. 825-826.

61. For a detailed discussion of the women at the tomb see E. L. Bode, *The First Easter Morning: The Gospel Accounts of the Women's Visit to the Tomb of Jesus* (Rome: Biblical Institute Press, 1970).

62. For a contrasting opinion see for example R. H. Fuller, *The Formation of the Resurrection Narratives* (Philadelphia: Fortress Press, 1971, 1980), pp. 135-136. See G. E. Ladd, *I Believe in the Resurrection of Jesus* (Grand Rapids: Wm. B. Eerdmans, 1975), p. 89.

63. See Brown, *John, XIII-XXI* pp. 992-993.

64. For a discussion of this issue see Westcott, p. 359.

65. While many sermons have been preached on the basis of a distinction between the two Greek words here for love (*agapaō* and *phileō*), it seems unlikely that a philological nicety was intended. Besides in Hebrew and Aramaic, the word would be the same for both Greek words. Moreover, there was no distinction of meaning made in the Greek words when used elsewhere in this Gospel. The emphasis fell here not on the change of words but on

the fact that Peter was grieved that Jesus asked him the third time (John 21:17). Preachers must take care not to be led astray by such linguistic niceties but watch for what the text itself indicates are the clues to understanding.

By the way, the "neat" distinction that Anders Nygren suggested between *agapē* and *eros* is an interesting study in motifs, but it is not very helpful when applied to the New Testament because *eros* does not appear anywhere in the New Testament, and *agapē* in the New Testament means far more than just self-giving love. See *Agape and Eros*, trans. P. Watson (Philadelphia: Westminster Press, 1953).

4

Assurance and Warning
in Hebrews: A Sermonic Style

"The book of Hebrews is one of the great theological treasures of the Christian faith."[1] It is unique in the New Testament canon. Although Hebrews has an epistolary ending, it is not a true letter. It is much closer to a sermon than to an epistle. It is, moreover, a magnificent model of sermon style. It has a superb way of alternating between theological exposition (the way of stating the meaning and purpose of God's saving work in Scripture) and exhortation (the applying of scriptural insights to life.)[2] As education specialists inform us, a story that has to have a moral tacked on at the end is far weaker than if the moral or lesson is integrated into the narrative itself. The writer to the Hebrews was a great biblical artist. He did not need to say: "The moral of my work is. . . ." He wrote with a marvelous understanding of his readers and his applications were constantly present throughout the book.

But the artistry of this writer and his alternating between exposition (theology) and exhortation (life practice) may cause great problems for those interpreters who seek simple and easily constructed definitions of doctrine. It is easy to miss this preacher's intentions for his great work, if we look for simple formulas. The writer was a brilliant communicator of the first century, but he does not necessarily fit the mold in twentieth-century patterns of thinking. It is absolutely crucial to realize this fact if one is to understand Hebrews and if one is to evaluate the various interpretations which are given to this book. It is precisely in the subject area of assurance and warning that the theological frustrations of interpreters are most evident.

For many Christians, Hebrews is a book to be avoided like the plague, except perhaps for some well-selected texts in chapters 1, 11, 12, and 13. Because of the warning texts in this book, many Christians have, in fact, followed the lead of Martin Luther in assigning the Book of Hebrews to the nonworking section of their Bibles. Luther absolutely detested the theology of Hebrews 6:4-6 concerning the impossibility of a second repentance.[3] Moreover, the Calvinistic representatives of Protestantism, who have descended from Augustine through John Calvin and John Owen to the present day,[4] have found the warning passages of Hebrews to spawn migraine headaches for their theological or intellectual systems.

The Difficult Problems of Authorship, Dating, and Form

Before turning to the argument of Hebrews a few matters of introduction need to be mentioned briefly. For a longer discussion concerning these very difficult issues, the reader is referred to my study in the *Review and Expositor*[5] or to introductions by Donald Guthrie and W. G. Kümmel[6] or to commentaries, such as those by F. F. Bruce and G. W. Buchanan.[7]

Authorship

For the purposes of this study, it is important to remind ourselves that differences of opinion over the authorship of Hebrews have a long history. The early church fathers, like Irenaeus and Hippolytus from the Western church (who were in the forefront of the fight against heresies), did not consider Paul to be the author. But the Eastern tradition, from Pantaenus through Clement of Alexandria (not generally regarded as the pillars of orthodoxy), supported Pauline authorship. Origen in the East, however, was probably correct in concluding: "who wrote the epistle, God knows for sure!"[8] Many suggestions have been made concerning the author which include possibilities such as: Apollos, Barnabas, and Luke; as well as unlikely candidates such as: Clement of Rome, Philip the Caesarean deacon, and Priscilla. The heading in our King James Bibles concerning Paul is a very late addition to the text.

About all we can say at this stage is that the writer was probably a second generation Greek-speaking Jewish Christian. He told us himself that he did not know Jesus personally (Heb. 2:3)—a statement Paul would have forcefully denied (for example, 1 Cor. 9:1; 15:8)—but he seemed to be familiar with Paul's associates (Heb. 13:23).[9]

Dating

The dating is also difficult. The latest possible date for writing Hebrews is the mid-nineties because some passages from Hebrews seemed to be in the mind of Clement of Rome when he wrote his epistle to the Corinthians (1 Clement 9:4; 12:1; and 36:1-2). At the early end of the spectrum, however, it is much more difficult to decide. As I have argued elsewhere the theory that the Temple is still standing, most strongly proposed by J. A. T. Robinson, is filled with suppositions.[10] In spite of B. F. Westcott, Buchanan, Robinson, and others, it is imperative to remember that Hebrews nowhere suggests a temple motif. "Sanctuary, yes; tabernacle, yes; priest, yes; sacrifice, yes; and levite, yes. But why must we draw the conclusion that the reconstructed second temple of Herod is in mind?"[11] Moreover, as I have also indicated, the motifs throughout the book are pre-Solomonic and nontemple and the specific history of Israel which was the concern of the writer even in chapter 11 comes only up to David. Everything else is by vague allusion.[12] The date is, therefore, very difficult.

Title

The title designating the recipients "to the Hebrews" was first mentioned by Tertullian.[13] How reliable was his tradition is a matter of discussion. The conclusions which are drawn by scholars are primarily the result of theological inferences and not historical witnesses. From the point of our study, it matters very little whether the recipients were Palestinian Jewish Christians, Diaspora Jewish Christians, Gentile Christians, or a group of Christians in general. As I have previously discussed at length, there is certainly some attachment to Rome (Heb. 13:24) though these arguments do not need to be repeated here.[14]

Language and Style

With respect to language and style, even the novice Greek student realizes that a superb writer was at work. The language is complex, variegated, and in style very different from anything else in the New Testament. The writer was a genuine artist who "was able to communicate the dynamics of oratory in written form."[15]

Unity

With respect to form, some scholars have argued that chapter 13 is a later appendix which was added to give it an epistolary appearance so that it would be joined to the Pauline Epistles. Floyd Filson, however, is undoubtedly correct in his analysis to the effect that the book is a unified product.[16] But such a statement does not mean that the work did not pass through several stages in the mind of the author before reaching its present form. It could well have begun as Midrashic notes (a Jewish type of commentary on Old Testament texts) and then developed into a sermon which was (later perhaps) set down in writing.[17]

The Nature and Purpose of Hebrews

In its present form, Hebrews is a *sermon* to Christians, *and more*. Indeed, it is a forceful call to Christians to live up to their destinies. The interweaving of expositions and exhortations has been brought to a thematic focus in Hebrews in terms of the superiority of the salvation which is available through Jesus. This salvation is set over against the salvation which was available in the Jewish faith. In every aspect of the faith, Hebrews shows Christ to be far superior. Accordingly from the point of view of Hebrews, there is no legitimate reason for any Christian to capitulate or give up in the face of persecution and the plundering of his or her personal possessions (Heb. 10:32-34).

The purpose of Hebrews is thus a homiletical (sermonic) summons to endurance in the face of hostility. The foundation of this summons is the conviction that victory is in the exalted Jesus (10:12) who has set the standard and provided the model for Christians to follow. Donald Hagner recently suggested that "probably *the* major purpose of the book" is "to warn readers of . . . danger and to exhort them to faithfulness."[18] There is little doubt that Hagner is on the right track. More particularly, I would say that the purpose involves: (1) *clarifying* the ultimate nature of Christian salvation so that those who misunderstand the uniqueness of Christianity might do so no longer; and (2) *helping strengthen* those who are tempted, in the face of intense pressure, to return to Judaism (or any other religion) so that they might endure to the end. This book was thus conceived to be both a strong statement of assurance concerning the greatness of the Christian faith and a stern warning not to abandon hope in Jesus.

The writer of Hebrews had very little interest in doctrinal or academic disputes about the possibility or impossibility of apostasy. Our arguments and our syllogisms would be for him an example of the fact that we were playing a game with Christianity, even though we might be intensely serious in our little game. The writer of Hebrews was not playing a theological game. He was in the midst of a crisis, and he was absolutely serious about assisting weary pilgrim readers to reach the promised land! He was not debating the apostasy/security issue. He was seeking to ensure that believers might understand God's ultimate answer to the problems of humanity.

Only after I left the haven of North America and lived for a time in the Third World did I begin to understand the life and death issues of Christianity and to sense the wearying effect of persecution. Being in crisis situations, where witnessing for Jesus is illegal, helps one understand Hebrews. It was addressed to potentially exhausted Christians. Remember as you read this great work that Hebrews is a sermon. As a sermon, Hebrews is a masterpiece. Let us read it as the Word of God.

The Book of Hebrews needs to be studied as a whole or as a unit. Indeed, it needs to be *experienced holistically* as a sermon or as an oratorical address. The book's purpose is motivational. It is an apology concerning the way of living for Jesus. It contains exhortations to live up to one's Christian potential, and it includes warnings for weary pilgrims who needed to be reminded that in this life Christians are called to perseverance (12:1). The way of Jesus, the Christian's model, is the way of endurance (12:2). In the midst of persecution and trouble, therefore, those Christians were exhorted not to grow weary (12:3) but to sense the significance of painful discipline in gaining the eschatological assurance of their hope (12:4-11,26-29). The Christians in Hebrews were people *en route*. They were pilgrims.[19] They needed to be called to be strong in their times of weakness (12:12-14). They needed to be warned of pitfalls (12:15-16). Assurance and warning were given to help them attain their desired end—the kingdom of God (12:18-29).

For the reader who is fresh from studying the Gospel of John or the Epistles of Paul, the mind-set of Hebrews will seem a little different. There are verbal similarities, but there are quite different shades of meaning given in this book to ideas such as faith, law, soteriology (salvation), flesh and spirit, covenant, and priesthood. If one imports a full-blown theology of John or Paul into Hebrews, one will most certainly misunderstand the power of this marvelous book. It is not a question of the inspiration or the authority of Scripture. It is a case that words mean different things in different settings. That is the problem of proof texting from the Bible. The force of a biblical idea is to be found in the context where the idea appears. Recognizing the uniqueness of a great book like Hebrews is basic to an adequate hermeneutic or method of interpreting Scripture. Failing to see the uniqueness in a superb work like Hebrews is frequently a problem for interpreters.

One who is open to the text of Hebrews may discover a marvelous sense of *balance* between the divine and the human dimensions. The reader's task involves a struggle to discover the focus for both the divine and human dimensions which were drawn together by the writer. The pursuit of this task is our way of being faithful to the authoritative message contained in this great book.

To be faithful to the Bible is to recognize the uniqueness of its parts. It is also to discover a greater depth concerning our God who can use various writers with different gifts to communicate the marvelous message of the unique way of salvation in Jesus Christ our Lord. If God could have given us the total message in one letter or one Gospel, there would have been no need for the rest of the books. Our task, therefore, is to discover in all of the works the greatness of our God and of our salvation. Hebrews is a part of God's wonderful message of assurance and warning.

The Organization of Hebrews

The Book of Hebrews has been outlined by scholars in several ways, but it is important to recognize a number of natural divisional points. I prefer the following outline.[20] Following the Introduction (1:1-4), I am inclined to combine several subdivisions and designate the first section as "A Superior Person or Model" (1:5 to 4:13). I divide the large central segment of the book so that the second section becomes "A Superior Priesthood" (4:14 to 7:28) and the third section is designated as "A Superior Covenant" (8:1 to 10:18). The fourth section I entitle "A Superior Faith" (10:19 to 12:29), and the final section I call "A Superior Life" (13:1-25).

The Sermon Called Hebrews

A. Assurance and Warning: The Beginning and the End of Hebrews

THE PROLOGUE

Like the Gospel of John, the Book of Hebrews begins with a very exalted picture of Jesus, the Son of God (Heb. 1:1-4). Jesus' activity in creation is forcefully affirmed at the very start (Heb. 1:2) just as it is in John 1:3. Moreover, the divine nature and intimate relationship of the Son with God, as asserted in John 1:1-2,18, is indelibly stamped upon the Son in the Prologue (Introduction) to this sermon (Heb. 1:3). And the glory of God, which is one of the focal motifs in John 1:14, was also employed by the preacher for the purpose of identifying Jesus as the true mirror of God to the world (Heb. 1:3).[21] As in the Gospel of John, the divine dimension is set clearly in the forefront of thought at the beginning of this profound sermon.

It is important, I believe, at this stage to emphasize the fact that Christian faith is absolutely dependent upon God being understood as the first actor in the salvation process. Only because God has acted first (and continues to do so) is there any possibility of the assurance of faith for us as weak humans.

Moreover, the fact that the Son is placed so high in the Prologue of Hebrews is to be viewed as a signal to the reader that all other bases for faith have paled into insignificance before the Son, whether those other foundations be patriarchs, prophets (1:1), angels (1:5 ff.) or anything else.[22] The Son is accordingly presented as the only secure basis of assurance among weak and sinful humans. The preacher made it indelibly clear that we do not cleanse ourselves from sin, the Son does (1:3). In the Son, therefore, is our hope of relating to the majestic God of heaven and earth.

THE ENDING

When turning to the concluding portions of Hebrews, one can hardly fail to notice that chapters 12 and 13 are filled with a series of exhortations for Christians to follow the model of Jesus and to avoid the pitfalls of human life. The sermon thus moves deliberately from the divine exalted Lord to the human dimension of failure and weakness. The preacher's theology is beautifully balanced because where humanity is brought into the picture one finds warning and exhortation.

But the orator's attention did not bog down in the swamp of human weakness. As the sermon nears its conclusion, it moves back briefly to remind the reader of assurance from the divine dimension both in chapters 12 and 13. In chapter 12 the writer assured the reader that God has yet a final shaking of the world to perform in order to establish the unshakable kingdom (12:26-28). Moreover, in chapter 13 the writer added a prayer before his final exhortations and benediction. In this prayer he called to mind the only mention of the resurrection power and the shepherding role of the Lord in the Book of Hebrews (13:20).[23] Undoubtedly the purpose of these statements was to assure the readers that they were not on their own because God was working in them through Jesus Christ, to whom belongs the glory for eternity (13:21).

The movement from the beginning to the end of Hebrews provides the reader with a strategic insight into the threatening nature which persecution and hostility presented to the early Christians. The head-on confrontation of the situation in the face of danger exemplified by Hebrews is an important model for Christian leaders of all ages. It is a good example for leaders who seek both to support believers in the midst of persecution and to help those who are tempted not to retreat from the Christian faith. Christian leaders must be ready to confront all forms of persecution with integrity. The *warnings* must be *sounded with clarity,* and they must be *coupled with an overwhelming sense of assurance based* on the *God* who in *Jesus Christ* has acted uniquely, is acting continuously, and will act decisively to secure the salvation of His faithful followers. We will now direct our attention to a specific discussion of this sensitive balance in Hebrews.

B. Assurance and Warning:
A Superior Person or Model (Heb. 1:5 to 4:13)

In this section of Hebrews, Jesus, the Son of God, is compared first to angels and then to Moses and Joshua—Israel's deliverance figures.

1. THE SON AND A COMPARISON TO THE ANGELS (HEB. 1:5 TO 2:18)

The writer of Hebrews began with a comparison to angelic figures, confronting immediately the issue of the supernatural power in the world. The spiritual environment of the first century was marked by a sense that spiritual powers were loose in the world, and they greatly affected the well-being and destinies of mortals. In the Hellenistic world, the role of the Fates (the supernatural determiners of human destiny) was oppressive. But even in the Judaism of Jesus' day, the spirit world was not viewed only with positiveness. One cannot read many chapters in the Synoptic Gospels (Matthew, Mark, and Luke) without sensing the role that demons played in the thoughts and actions of people. The idea of demons affecting human actions is hardly in the forefront of many people's thought in the sophisticated West. Most today, however, understand power and many at times may be willing to categorize some uses of power as demonic. Yet the idea of loose spirits is hard for many to imagine.

The world of the Bible is not the world of twentieth century Western culture. Ideas like the "spirits in prison" of 1 Peter 3:19 are not seen by many Westerners as spirits but as dead human beings. The principalities and powers in Paul are frequently demythologized into nonspiritual forces. As a result, the opening of Hebrews becomes for many in the Western world only a nice little exercise in theological argument.

But in the first century, the opening chapter of Hebrews, with its comparison of the Son to the angels, must have struck the Christian reader with a tremendous sense of spiritual power. After all, the angels were God's special messengers of hope, of support, of protection, and of judgment. But above all, they were ministering spirits (*leitourgika pneumata*) who were dispatched by God to care for His people (1:14). The angelic task was to protect God's people from the attacks of the demonic realm. Yet, according to Hebrews, these marvelous messengers of God were hardly worthy of mention in the same breath with God's Son.

Employing a collection of texts from the Old Testament and Jewish styles of argument, the preacher of Hebrews asserted forcefully that humanity's great symbols of security and protection in the world—the angels—were placed in a subjective role as they fell in worship before the Son (1:6; see Deut. 32:43, LXX, and Ps. 97:7; also see Odes of Solomon 2:43).[24] They knew their proper places because, as the psalmist acknowledged (Ps. 45:6), they realized that the Son's throne was eternal (Heb. 1:8). The Son was active in creation, even the creation of heaven (1:10), and He would be around at the end of time when all was rolled up. Indeed, His years would never come to an end (1:12). And even now He is seated at the right hand of God (1:13). What a comparison with angels!

But an important part of the message is that the angels are not merely servants of Christ. Their purpose is to serve Christians (1:14). Christians are the concern of Christ, and the angels who have been viewed as the great forces of God in the world are not to be regarded as unfriendly powers, like the Greek Fates. They are God's servants who are concerned for the welfare of Christians. This opening of the sermon was for weak, persecuted Christians of the first century an impressive basis for Christian assurance.

But the preacher hardly lingered on that subject because he had another agenda. A major concern of his was to deal with the danger of drifting. By employing very forceful sermonic or oratorical methods, he called his readers to pay particular attention to what he had to say (2:1). But he also used a kind of shock treatment by joining himself to them as being in the danger of drifting and by asking them, "How shall *we* flee [escape], if [when] *we* neglect [are unconcerned about] such a magnificent salvation?" (2:3, author's italics). His answer was obvious. He had already reminded them that if the recipients of angelic messages (many interpreters link these messages with the law) disobeyed, they were judged (2:2). There was little hope then of missing severe judgment, the preacher argued, for anyone who disobeyed the Christian message which was (1) delivered by the Lord, (2) received by His disciples, (3) accompanied by signs, and (4) supported by evidences of the Holy Spirit (2:3-4).[25] When the early reader had finished with these verses, the preacher had definitely gained his or her attention. The warning question that was framed to shock the reader required an answer—some kind of an answer! But what could be the answer to such an intense question of warning?

The answer, I submit, burst forth from the writer in the remaining verses of chapter 2. The writer returned briefly to the subject of the angels for the purpose of bringing humanity into the picture. There had been no question of the Son's superiority to the angels. In Hebrews 2:9 the reader meets the first mention of the name *Jesus* in this sermon. This use is made in connection with an incarnation statement, Jesus was the one "who for a short time was made lower than the angels" (2:9; see 2:7; Ps. 8:5, LXX). Such a statement is parallel to the Pauline idea that he "emptied himself" (see Phil. 2:7). For the preacher, the incarnation was the means by which the *Son* identified with humanity and provided God's many *"sons"* (and daughters) with the opportunity of experiencing the divine glory (Heb. 2:10). The incarnate One, who was the lead runner or pioneer of our perfected way to salvation (see 12:2), was identified in this world by nothing less than suffering (2:10)—an experience which was personally understood by most Christians of the first century.

The preacher then carried his incarnation theme further by asserting the phenomenal idea that the incarnate One who makes people holy (sanctifies them) has a common source (*ex henos*) with all of those (us) who are made holy. Accordingly (*aitian*), Jesus was not ashamed to call them His brothers (2:11). Whether this source for the preacher was the commonness of Christian suffering or the commonness of relying on God is not absolutely clear. But the point is that a wonderful relationship between Jesus and Christians is firmly asserted. As a result, the question of the psalmist, "What is man that you are mindful of him?" (Ps. 8:4) in Hebrews 2:6 has in fact been given an incredible answer. Human beings are very important to God, and this concern of God for humanity is the basis for a Christian's assurance in God.

But such assurance did not remove the dimension of human responsibility. Indeed, it seems to have made human responsibility all the more intense. Jesus did not merely come to identify Himself with humanity. He also came to establish a greater ministry to humanity than any of the angels could ever offer. Jesus' identification with humanity led to His death. But through His death, He destroyed the power of the broker of death (the devil) and provided deliverance to those who throughout life were slaves to the fear of death (2:14-15).

The concern of the preacher was obviously not to discuss angels (2:16). He made no attempt to evaluate the first-century readers' view of angels. His concern was with humanity and the descendants of Abraham. The preacher announced that the Son did not choose to become a type of visiting angel. Instead, He became an authentic human being (*kata panta*, "in all respects") so that He personally might bring about reconciliation as the merciful and faithful High Priest for humanity (2:17).

This initial reference in the sermon to Jesus as the High Priest points to the basis for a Christian's assurance. The Son did not merely come to establish a standard for Christian life. The profound message of Hebrews is that, because Jesus experienced suffering and temptation, He is able to help weak humans who are beset by temptation (2:18). *The answer* to the disturbing warning question of Hebrews 2:3, then, is not an academic or philosophical statement of security, but a very practical promise of assistance to those who are undergoing temptation. Such an answer may not seem sufficient for some logicians, but the answer is more than adequate for all those who fear failure and death in the midst of persecution. The assuring answer of Hebrews is not to be found in argument but in the divine presence and personal support of Jesus.

2. Jesus and a Comparison to Moses and Joshua (Heb. 3:1 to 4:13)

In opening chapter 3, the writer addressed his readers as "holy brothers" and "sharers [partakers; *metochoi*] of a heavenly call" (3:1). This language is typical of the preacher and seems clearly intended to identify his readers as Christians,[26] those whom Paul called saints. To these holy ones the preacher of Hebrews directed a summons: "Reflect on Jesus, the apostle [sent one] and high priest of our confession" (*homologia*, from which we get our English word *homily* or sermon). The idea of calling Jesus an apostle may trouble some readers who think that the term only applies to humans who are on mission. But for the preacher, the incarnate Jesus provided God's example of what it meant to be a "sent one."

This Jesus, according to Hebrews, is the ideal model of one who—like Moses, an earlier model—was faithful to God. But in contrast to Moses, Jesus is worthy of a glory which is far superior to Moses. Moses was only a servant *in God's house*, whereas Christ was none other than the Son who was set *over God's house* (3:2-6). On the basis of the Son's faithfulness and worthiness, Christian followers ought to have a great sense of assurance and confidence because they *are God's house* (3:6).

This confidence is carefully conditioned in Hebrews 3:6 by the two little Greek words *ean kataschōmen* ("if we hold firm" or remain faithful). This condition is repeated in verse 14, and it is accompanied by an extended Midrashic interpretation (a rabbic style of interpretation) of Psalm 95:7-11.[27] This method: uses key words such as "today," "harden," "rebellion," "go astray," and "rest" to emphasize the contemporary significance of the text; asks interpretative questions of the text; and interweaves other Old Testament texts primarily from the Torah or Penteteuch to provide support for the thesis of the interpreter.[28] The purpose of this Midrashic argument is clearly to warn the reader to avoid the pitfalls that had been experienced by God's earlier people in the Exodus.

After quoting the text from the Psalms, the preacher immediately sounded the warning, "Beware, brothers, lest there be among any of you an evil heart of unbelief by which you might fall away (apostatize, the Greek is *apostēnai*) from the living God" (Heb. 3:12). Instead of succumbing, however, he called for them to exhort each other daily so that none of them might be hardened as happened to the Israelites in the wilderness (3:13). Then, he provided his readers with a perspective on his view of salvation. Unlike the Pauline and Johannine perspectives of salvation, the perspective of salvation in Hebrews is viewed from the end of life's journey. This difference in perspective has caused many Christians—who have been brought up with a definition of salvation in terms of the start of their relationship with God—to become very frustrated.

Permit me, therefore, to illustrate what I mean by the difference in perspective with what may be an apocryphal story that has been often attached to one of the Baillies of Great Britain, but could easily be applied to almost any theologian. When approached on the street and asked, "Brother, are you saved?" Dr. Baillie is reputed to have answered, "Yes! No! and Partly Yes and No!" The meaning, of course, involves the three dimensions of salvation. Thus, one can say, "Yes, I am justified" (I have begun the Christian life). One can also say, "No, I am not glorified" (in heaven). But one can also add, "Partly, I am sanctified" (I am in the process of becoming totally holy).

For many Christians, the idea of salvation is normally viewed from the perspective of justification, the start of the Christian life. But when one comes to the Book of Hebrews, such a definition does not fit very well. The preacher of Hebrews views salvation more holistically from the perspective of a journey which, when it is finished properly in God, leads to the promised land or to the expected rest (4:1-2).[29] To be saved, according to Hebrews, means to endure to the end, not to fall by the way in the process, and to enter the rest of God (4:11). When one enters the rest of God, one also ceases labor in this world, as God did in the Genesis story (Heb. 4:10; see Gen. 2:1-3). God, of course, did not die in the Genesis account, but rest in Hebrews becomes a picture of the eschatological (future) bliss which follows life in the world. When one understands this perspective of salvation in Hebrews, the reason for so many warnings becomes more intelligible.

When one perceives this perspective of rest in Hebrews, it ought to become clearer why people who define salvation in terms of an initial encounter with God are frustrated by this book. This frustration is emphatically even more true of Christians who try to treat sanctification from a starting perspective like justification. They often say, "I was saved on such a day, and I was sanctified on another day." But such a way of speaking is very unbiblical. And Hebrews, for certain, cannot be shoved into such thought patterns.

Instead, Hebrews is a document which resists most of our well-calculated pinpoint definitions. There was a reason Luther set it outside of his working canon, and there is a reason it is not the most popular book among many Protestants. But as long as Hebrews is in the canon, we are duty bound to learn from it and not to twist it to say what it does not mean. Its warnings are to be taken seriously. One must remember the sermonic style of this inspired document and its basic view of salvation, if one is to make sense of the book.

On the basis of this perspective, the nature of assurance and warning in this section becomes much clearer. The readers can be considered to be partakers (sharers, *metochoi*) in Christ and experience assurance, *if* they remain faithful (3:14). The theme of Hebrews 2:1-3 and 3:1,6 is repeated. Here, however, the theme is more fully developed. With the story of Moses as the setting, the exhortations are sounded for the followers not to harden their hearts lest they become rebellious like Israel in the wilderness and, failing to persevere, never enter their intended rest (3:15-18) because of faithlessness (many versions poorly render *apistian* here as unbelief: 3:19).

Faith (*pistis*) in Hebrews has a different emphasis than it has in Paul, and the word is not used in the Gospel of John. Faith here is better translated as *faithfulness* (see Heb. 11:1 *ff.*)—a meaning not unlike the Johannine verb *pisteuō*, "believe" or "commit oneself to." In Hebrews faithfulness is seen as the key to entering the rest of God, the intended eschatological, or future, hope (4:1-5).

To make certain the readers understood what he was saying, the preacher of Hebrews reminded his people that the *faithlessness* of Israel was in fact disobedience (4:6). Israel's failure to enter its promised rest was directly related to its hardness of heart (4:7). In discussing Psalm 95, the preacher proclaimed the relevance of that text for his own time by warning, "Today . . . harden not your hearts." That warning applied not merely to the time of the Exodus but also to the first century of the Christian era (4:7). One should add that it applies equally to us because *every new day is today!*

Next the preacher introduced Joshua, the other savior figure, who as the servant of God led the people to their rest in the Promised Land after their years of wilderness wanderings. Joshua has been mentioned here briefly to remind the readers that the "rest" that came through him was not the ultimate hope for the people of God (4:8-9). Ultimate rest continued to remain an expectation for first-century Christians, even as it does for us. All are, therefore, exhorted to "make every effort to enter into that rest so that no one might fall" according to Israel's "example of disobedience" (4:11). To this exhortation the preacher added the warning that the word of God is a decisive means of judgment that reaches to the inner thoughts of humanity. The preacher's point was that the readers had to realize that nothing remains hidden from the sight of God (4:12-13). The warning that concludes this section is extremely forceful. It was hardly meant to be a clever word game. It was to be taken seriously by Christians who were threatened by the pressures of persecution.

In summary, it can be said that this section began with an emphasis upon assurance and confidence in Jesus, the one who far surpasses both the angels and Moses. In the course of argument, a conditioned confidence, which is dependent upon the faithfulness of God's servants, emerged. Because faithfulness is so crucial for attaining the hope of the Christian, the preacher of Hebrews was almost overpowering in the warnings which he issued to his readers. The purpose of this section, however, was neither the academic discussion of apostasy nor the practical condemnation of Christians. The purpose was to motivate all Christian readers toward reaching the assurance of the promised land. In pursuing this purpose, the writer was fully aware that Christianity is not merely a matter of words or beliefs, but a very serious matter of obedience and faithful living. The preacher was confident his people would hear his warnings and respond to his exhortations.

C. Assurance and Warning: A Superior Priest (Heb. 4:14 to 7:28)

This section of Hebrews contains exhortations to live in confident assurance and reliance upon Jesus, the Son of God. These exhortations are finely balanced by forceful warnings concerning sluggishness and falling away. Both are set within the context of a realization that the Son is a far superior priest than Aaron and his successors.

1. JESUS, THE GREAT HIGH PRIEST: PART ONE (HEB. 4:14 TO 5:10)

The preacher opened this section with an impressive picture of Jesus as the great High Priest who passed through the heavens. The picture is noteworthy for at least two reasons. First, the Aaronic high priest's most significant task was his annual passing through the veil into the most holy place on Yom Kippur (the Day of Atonement), but Jesus, the High Priest, is portrayed as having a firsthand meeting with God since He has passed through the heavens (4:14). Second, Jesus is "a great high priest," a designation which seems to be quite unusual and was probably intended to give the reader a sense of the overwhelming superiority of Jesus in that role.[30] This exalted perception of Jesus as the surpassing High Priest elicited from the writer another intense exhortation: "Let us hold fast to our confession" (*homologia*, 4:14; see 3:1).

But this exalted role of our High Priest does not mean that He is so transcendent that He is removed from the experiences of humanity. Indeed, our incarnate High Priest is truly able to empathize (or sympathize, *sumpathēsai*) with human weakness because He has fully experienced the trials (*pepeirasmenon;* better rendered by the idea of trial than temptation) of humanity without succumbing to sin (4:15). As a result, Christians ought to have a sense of boldness or assurance because they have been given access to the divine throne or seat of graciousness where mercy and grace are freely dispensed (4:16).

With Jesus, access to the mercy seat is not pictured as an earthly, once-a-year event on the Day of Atonement. Instead, our great High Priest has entered the very presence of God and in so doing has provided assurance of our timely access to the throne of God in periods of need. We, therefore, are able to draw near, not merely to an earthly priest as he returns from the tent of meeting (tabernacle) experience. But we have through Christ continuing full access to the holy God Himself, who dispenses mercy and grace whenever we have need (4:16).

Having thus exhorted his readers to confidence in the person and work of their High Priest, the preacher began to interpret the priestly office and how the Son fits this office. This exposition has two focuses and involves a split discussion in 5:1-10 and 7:1-28. One focus is related primarily to the Aaronic priesthood and the other to the order of Melchizedek. These two focuses are interwoven in such a way that, even though Jesus was not descended from the priestly tribe of Levi, a Levitical family line was regarded as unnecessary because the order of Melchizedek is shown to be superior to that of Levi (7:4-10). This idea of Jesus as the High Priest and the comparison of Jesus to Melchizedek is unique in the New Testament and probably was suggested to the preacher by his reference to Psalm 110, which in that context contains one of the familiar "Son" texts of the Old Testament.

The writer of Hebrews appears not to have argued from the basis of Aaron or Melchizedek to Jesus, but the reverse. Aaron was ordained or appointed on behalf of the people to represent humanity before God with respect to both gifts and sin offerings (5:1). But Jesus is far greater. He is, of course, also appointed by God, but He is sinless; the Aaronic priesthood was subject to all forms of human weakness (5:2,5). As a result, Aaron could hardly have been proud because the sacrifices for sin applied to him as well as to the people (5:3-4). But, by way of contrast, the preacher found it worth noting that, in spite of who Christ is, He was not ambitious and did not glorify Himself (5:5).[31] The preacher may have had in mind a contrast of Jesus with the scheming, proud high priests of the Gospel stories. Indeed, in the days of His flesh Christ is said to have appropriated (learned) obedience from what He suffered. The preacher added that Jesus fulfilled His purpose (was perfected) of becoming the source of eternal salvation for all those who are obedient to Him (5:8-9).[32] Jesus was, thus, the ultimate model of obedience to God, and Christians are to follow that model.

2. A MAJOR EXHORTATIONAL MESSAGE ON ASSURANCE AND WARNING (HEB. 5:11 TO 6:20)

At this point the writer may seem to have sharply broken off or digressed from his discussion of the superior priesthood. But we must remember that his reason for writing this homiletical (confessional) essay was not to discuss the complexity of the priesthood. That subject was apparently significant for him, and he did return to it. Yet the main purpose for his shift in attention was to remind his readers that he was calling them to an accounting. Helping Christians understand the real nature of God's leading in the midst of a crazy, hostile world was the preacher's purpose. He would not be sidetracked from this main purpose, even if the development of his argument might suffer a little. It was almost as though the preacher had previously

delivered this sermon orally and anticipated the reactions of his readers. Whether his audience were composed of Jewish or Gentile Christians did not matter, the argument was important for them to hear.

But they seemed to be so very immature and sluggish in their
learning. They were like sleepy heads and babies (5:11-12). They
should have moved on to the point where they were already becoming
mature teachers themselves. Instead of being ready for an adult diet,
however, they still required a baby-food-type of preaching and Bible
study (5:13). They were still at the stage of learning the basic *ABCs*
of their Christian faith, and they were unable to distinguish (*diakrisin*)
between good and evil (5:14). They were confused, like a number of
Christians today. They were mixed up on what was important and
were fuzzy on what was truly right and wrong. What should have
been giving them a great sense of assurance and confidence in their
great High Priest seemed, instead, to have been touching imperceptive
ears. What was the preacher to do?

His decision, as Bruce suggested, was to try and feed them something that would "take them out of their immaturity."[33] From the
preacher's perspective, it was time for these folk to receive more
than a repetition of the introductory matters with respect to Christ
(6:1). His goal was to carry them beyond their *ABCs*, which he enumer-
ated in three pairs of introductory teachings: (1) repentance (from
dead works) and faith (in God), (2) baptisms (washings) and laying on
of hands, and (3) the resurrection from the dead and eternal judgment
(6:1-2).[34] Have you ever stopped to consider how much preaching
today seldom gets beyond introductory teachings, such as coming to
Christ, baptism, church membership, and rewards and punishments?
Perhaps we can learn something from this inspired preacher.

What follows this review, however, was in all likelihood totally
unexpected by the reader, even though the stage had been set for a
major warning by previous statements (see 2:1-3; 3:12-19; 4:11-14).
The warning in Hebrews 6:4-6 is one of the most debated texts in
the New Testament. The word "impossible" in verse 4, when linked
with renewal to repentance in verse 6, not only has challenged inconsistent Christian living but also has frustrated many doctrinal formulations on the security of the believer.

In analyzing the purpose of this warning and in order not to turn off contemporary insecure readers, I think it is imperative to note at the outset of our discussion that this is not the only occurrence of the term *impossible* (*adunaton*). It also appears in the subsequent assurance statement in verse 18. The writer affirmed the fact that there are *two* unchangeable (*ametathetōn*) realities, not just one (6:18)! One reality has to do with the dimension of humanity; the other, with the dimension of God. The preacher of Hebrews was concerned with the intersection of these two realities. This intersection has plagued human logic throughout the centuries. An adequate understanding of the meaning of the warning statement in Hebrews 6:4-6 includes the assurance statements in the concluding verses of Hebrews 6. This chapter is a finely tuned statement which balances both warning and assurance. While warning is the first focus of attention, assurance is not forgotten.

The combination of clauses in Hebrews 6:4-6 provides the *finest brief definition of what is normally understood to be a Christian found anywhere in the New Testament!* The writer has *intentionally* sought to make his definition conform to almost every element of observable Christian experience. What are these elements? The persons were said, first, to have evidenced decisive enlightment. Such terminology in the first century normally was identified with a knowledgeable transformation or commitment to a religion. Second, these people were said to have tasted of the heavenly gift. Here *taste* must mean ingest or swallow because the other use of *taste* in Hebrews means that Jesus really died when he tasted death (see Heb. 2:9; see 1 Pet. 2:3 where taste is used of the Christian experience). The third element indicates that the persons were partakers (*metochoi*, by now this term should be familiar as a term for participant or member; see, for example, Heb. 3:1,14) of the Holy Spirit.[35] The fourth element indicates a tasting (ingesting) of the goodness of the Word of God; the fifth element, a tasting of the powers of the age to come. This last element obviously means that these persons had given every indication of being eschatologically (futuristically) oriented. They were apparently driven by an ultimate goal in life. Taken as a whole, these elements form a unique, composite picture of the major aspects of the Christian life.

If this combination statement had appeared in any other context, it probably would have been proclaimed throughout the world by preachers as a sign of Christian life—as the classic statement of Christian identity! Where can you find in the New Testament a better definition of the elements that seem to be basic necessities for being a Christian? On the surface, the case seems closed. To put the matter more bluntly, one might ask: What would you add to that list for identifying a Christian? Are there other elements? I can think of several things, such as the self-giving of resources and energies, but most are not as basic as the elements listed. The immediate implications of such a statement may not be readily welcomed by Christian readers who are fearfully concerned about the issue of security. But please remember, as I suggested above, that such a statement does not end the matter.

One more factor needs further reflection. The elements in the statement of Hebrews 6:4-6 all seem to be centered on the *self-confirmation* of the persons described. I have the distinct feeling that the persons described in this statement and their friends would have regarded the persons in these verses to be Christians before they experienced what in Hebrews 6:6 is said to be a "falling away" (*parapesontas*). Whether these persons were Christians, I submit, is not the issue! *The real issue is whether they seemed to themselves and to the readers of Hebrews to have given the appearance of being Christians!* I think the intention of the preacher was to make his definition so strong that the readers of Hebrews could hardly have missed the point that the warning was addressed to those who were regarded by others or judged themselves to be Christians.

Notice that our problem with this text is not really with the precision of the words. The words are far more precise than many other expressions in the Bible. The problem, then, is not one of the words which were used but with Christian interpretations of these words. Minds are often closed to the words of the Bible because of what people *think* the implications of the words might be. When Christians spend their energies arguing about the alternatives of apostasy or security in this text, they usually miss the great point of the text. Instead of arguing with Scripture, we should ask, What was the point of the warning in these words?

The text of Hebrews 6 is framed in verses 4-8 as a warning. There seems little doubt in the phraseology that it was definitely intended to be a strong warning. Indeed, it builds with such intensity that it must have produced a kind of shock! The point of Hebrews 6:4-6 is underlined by verses 7 and 8. The people described in verses 4-6 were like soil that had soaked up the marvelous blessings of God yet in the end had produced nothing but a thorn and thistle patch. It was ready (*eggus*), the preacher announced, to be cursed and burned (6:8). The warning is clear, eminently clear. Do church people ever need to be shocked out of their lethargy and non-Christian ways of life? The answer to that question must be a resounding yes! Remember Hebrews is a sermon! Its goal was motivational. Its purpose was not the development of a systematic statement of theology. Its purpose was to ensure consistency of living so that true sanctification and glorification—living with Christ here and hereafter—might be obtained.

Hebrews, however, does have a balance, but its balance is different than that of Paul or of John. One must not be too quick to get to the comfortable balance; otherwise, one may not hear its message. When the warning had been forcefully sounded, the preacher of Hebrews brought the other side of his message—the word of assurance. Lest the brothers and sisters in the church become insecure over the warning, the preacher shifted from warning to assurance when he added, "But with respect to you, beloved, we have been persuaded of better things which pertain to salvation" (6:9). Why was he able to make this assurance statement?

The preacher of Hebrews knew the cost of salvation, and he knew the cost of discipleship. He was not offering his readers an easy gospel. He knew that believing in Jesus might cost them their lives, and he wanted them to be secure in their commitments. Thus, he forced Christians to ask the uneasy question: At what point do we have assurance? But after shocking the readers with a warning which must have forced them all to reexamine their commitments, he assuringly added that he was confident that they had evidenced and would continue to the end to evidence the eager earnestness of pilgrims in the pursuit of their desired hope (6:9-12). Such was genuine assurance for the preacher.

The preacher of Hebrews was here not interested in a debate over apostasy or in discussing a hypothetical situation.[36] He sensed the incredible pressures which undoubtedly would come upon his Christian readers, and he wanted them to realize that entertaining the thought of abandoning Jesus would leave them totally devoid of hope. To spurn Jesus meant to spurn the only means of salvation that was available to them (6:6). The Christian life was not one of bouncing in and out of salvation, even when the pressures were intense. To deny the Lord or to repudiate Christ was for the preacher of Hebrews both unthinkable and intolerable!

The purpose of the warning, therefore, was to deal with the lazy or sluggish (*nōthroi*) among them and to encourage them to imitate those who were faithful and patient (6:12). In this respect Abraham's patient pilgrimage is cited as an important example of the Christian life of pilgrimage. It is because he endured faithful to the end that the preacher insisted that Abraham obtained the promise (6:15). Endurance, or perseverance, to the end is the focus of Hebrews.

The writer of Hebrews rested the next part of his argument not on Abraham but on God. God was the basis of Abraham's security and assurance, not Abraham's works. Thus, the preacher argued, it was *impossible* (*adunaton*) for God to be proven false in His word because of two reasons (6:18). The first reason is that God is absolutely consistent. Lying for God is an impossibility. The second reason for confidence is that God supports His promise with an oath which He swore by the most consistent factor in the universe—Himself![37] According to first-century Jewish perspectives, finality of argument was reached in an oath that was regarded as an indisputable surety of accuracy.[38]

Having, therefore, supported his rationale for confidence by reference to God, the preacher concluded this major warning and assurance passage by reminding Christians that in the midst of trial and persecution they should take refuge (escape, *kataphugō*) in Jesus, the Forerunner (*prodromos*), who has become their High Priest forever after the order of Melchizedek (6:18-20). But assurance is not something external and automatic. Both parties to this divine-human relationship are very important. God certainly does not prove false, but humans must flee for refuge and must grasp the hope that is set before them. In so doing, they are promised the secure and reliable anchor (*agkuran . . . asphalē . . . kai bebaian*) for their lives, even Jesus, the High Priest, who entered the inner sanctuary within the veil (6:19-20).

We have now come full circle back to Jesus, the High Priest. Assurance and security do not vest in human words or experience. Security vests only in Jesus, our divine-human priestly Mediator (go-between). In a day and age when we emphasize correctness of words, let us all remember that commitment to and following Jesus brings us the marvelous assurance of our faith. When I left home to go to seminary many years ago, my pastor told me, "Don't commit yourself to labels. Commit yourself to Jesus." I have learned since that time that labels are not really authentic representations of who we are. Whether we are called conservative or liberal, moderate or fundamentalist, we can lie and cheat. Labels are no test for authentic Christian living because words can easily be just words. But Jesus, our High Priest, knows our motives and knows whether we are relying on Him or on our own human constructions.

3. Jesus the Great High Priest: Part Two (Heb. 7:1-26)

The mention of Jesus as the High Priest according to the order of Melchizedek at Hebrews 6:20 reintroduces the theme of a Superior Priest from which the author had departed at Hebrews 5:10 when he began his extended exhortation. In what follows (Heb. 7), the writer pursued a very labored discussion to prove that Jesus was, indeed, the Priest of an order superior to the Levitical priesthood. Moreover, the preacher argued that Abraham had recognized the legitimacy of such a priesthood by paying tithes to Melchizedek and by receiving a blessing from him.

The focus of this long Midrashic argument, however, was not on Melchizedek. The argument, instead, pointed beyond Melchizedek to Jesus. Melchizedek is significant only in that certain aspects of his story are typologically illustrative of Jesus. Since the story in Genesis 14 does not mention Melchizedek's beginning or end (death) and gives no parents or genealogy for him, the writer of Hebrews used the omission of these details to suggest a likeness or a resemblance to the Son of God who he believed is a perpetual (*diēnekes*) priest. Even Melchizedek's name is suggestive because in Hebrew it is a construct that could mean "king of righteousness" (*melek* plus *zedek*). Moreover, his domain or territory *Salem* means "peace" (7:1-3). Abraham's payment of a tithe to Melchizedek suggested to the preacher that the Levitical priesthood through Abraham acknowledged the superiority of Melchizedek. But notice that the author avoided similar implications with respect to the fact that Judah was likewise in the loins of Abraham (7:14).

The argument is hardly one that excites modern minds. Yet it is extremely important because it moves with a sense of definiteness to the rejection of the Jewish priesthood and its legal prescriptions as the basis for assurance. It emphasizes, instead, the act of God in Jesus as the foundation (*egguos*, surety) for a superior covenant (7:22). The rationale is quite rabbinic in orientation. The preacher first claimed the oath of God in Psalm 110:4 for support (Heb. 7:20-21). Then argued that Jesus' superiority was evident for several reasons: Jesus' priesthood is continuous or eternal in contrast to the temporary and successive priesthoods of the descendents of Levi (7:23-25); Jesus' priesthood is holy, sinless, and once for all effective in contrast to the sinful, weak, and repetitive work of human priests (7:26-28). Thus, the power of God in His oath is evidence of perfection in Jesus and of providing for our salvation to the end ("completely," *eis to panteles*). The argument yielded a marvelous assuring balance (7:25,28) in the message of the Book of Hebrews.

D. Assurance and Warning:
"A Superior Covenant and Ministry" (Heb. 8:1 to 10:18)

In contrast to the previous sections of Hebrews, exhortations in this section were kept to a minimum by the writer. Instead, he seems to have given his attention primarily to making his assuring case that the covenant and ministry of Christ are superior in every aspect to the old covenant and ministry which came through Moses. The argument is rather complex but the balance nevertheless continues.

1. CHRIST'S COVENANT MINISTRY IN THE GREAT TABERNACLE (HEB. 8:1 TO 9:11)

The author began his transition of focus from Jesus as the superior Priest to Christ as the Inaugurator of the new and superior covenant and ministry by employing a familiar picture of Christ as a Regent seated at the right hand of God (see 1:3,13; 10:12; and 12:2). Christ is portrayed as a regal High Priest who is enthroned next to the transcendent, majestic God in heaven (Heb. 8:1; see Ps. 110:1).[39] The reason the Christian can have assurance, according to Hebrews, is because all other religious traditions (including the religion of the Jews through Moses) pale before the vision of Christ, the one who is the fulfillment and ideal of the Jewish hope. Christ is God's minister or servant (*leitourgos*) of sacred matters, including the authentic tabernacle pitched (established; *epēxen*) by divine act and not by mere human instrumentality (for example, Moses; Heb. 8:2).

The Mosaic tabernacle with its sacrifices was merely a copy (*hupodeigma*) and shadow (*skia*) of the great one in heaven (8:5). Whatever type of dualistic structure might be suggested by this text, it is not Platonic, as some scholars have thought. Rather it is a strange generalized mixture containing patterns similar to Jewish apocalyptic and Philonian thought, all integrated into the service of the preacher of the new way of life.[40] Because the Mosaic tabernacle was flawed by its human nature, the preacher argued, it pointed strongly toward the need for the superior covenant and ministry that were brought by Christ (8:6-7).

In support of the establishment of a new covenant in Christ, the preacher cited, in Hebrews 8:8-12, the longest single quotation of an Old Testament text found in the New Testament—the new covenant passage in Jeremiah 31:31-34 (LXX). That text from the weeping prophet is very significant because it seems to be a mirror image of the theology evidenced in Hebrews on the subject of assurance and warning. Indeed, if one were to look for an Old Testament text that may have served as the inspiration for Hebrews, it may well have been this combination judgment-promise text from Jeremiah. God had made a covenant with the people of Israel but, because the people were unfaithful, God declared through Jeremiah the coming of the new—a new covenant, a new mind or heart of commitment, a new personal way of knowing God, and a new merciful forgiveness of sins. This new-covenant way of being related to God, from the perspective of the preacher of Hebrews and based on Jeremiah, rendered the first covenant old (*gēraskon*), or obsolete (*palaioumenon*), and ready to disappear (*aphanismou*) from the scene (Heb. 8:13).

From the view of Hebrews, there are *not two covenants still in effect*. The coming of Jesus rendered the first covenant void, obsolete! Those to whom Hebrews was addressed may have thought that they could have one foot in each covenant or that both covenants would continue to be valid. The message of Hebrews is clearly positioned against any such theories, whether those theories were ancient or are of a more modern vintage![41] The New Testament recognizes only one covenant in effect and one way to God as valid.

Having concluded the general statements concerning the old and new covenants, the preacher turned next to discuss the pattern of ministry in both of the covenants. As the basis for understanding Christ's ministry, the preacher briefly introduced the tabernacle setting and the ministry of atonement according to the old covenant (9:1-10). While his description of the positioning of the furniture and the contents of the ark is complex and may raise issues for commentators on this text, there are other matters that particularly need to be noted here.[42] The preacher's main concerns were with the following ideas: (1) that the high priest entered the most holy place on the Day of Atonement, taking blood as an offering for the sins of the people (9:7);[43] (2) that the Holy Spirit showed that access to the divine was not open while the "first" or "outer" tent was standing (9:8);[44] and (3) that the offerings (gifts or sacrifices) of the old covenant could not make the conscience of the worshiper pure and wholesome (9:9).

According to the preacher of Hebrews, everything changed with the appearing of Christ, the true High Priest. Christ entered a greater and "more perfect" tabernacle, not constructed by humans and not part of this creation (9:11).[45] Christ's access was *directly* to God and was contrasted with access to a humanly constructed ark and mercy seat which merely *represented* the presence of God on earth.

2. Three Pictures of Ministry and Covenant Based on the Blood of Christ (Heb. 9:12-22)

Hebrews 9:11 is a transition verse. Its purpose is to focus the reader's attention in verse 12 on how Christ entered the great tabernacle. The preacher announced that Christ entered the presence of God on behalf of humanity not with the blood of animals but with *His own blood*. The preacher of Hebrews treated the death, resurrection, and exaltation of Jesus as a unit and focused attention on access to

God. Thus, in his first picture or sermonic illustration (9:12-14), he compared two priests. The old high priest entered the earthly presence of God *one day each year* with the substitute blood of animals which really did not change the consciences of the people. But Christ, the superior High Priest, entered the heavenly presence of God *once forever* (*ephapax*) with His own unblemished blood. Because of who He is, Christ's ministry is able to transform human consciences so that people will be turned from dead activity to serve the living God. The preacher was, thus, developing a powerful argument on assurance in Jesus Christ, the One who obtained (perhaps, "secured" or "provided"; *heuramenos;* the Attic use of the middle) for us eternal redemption (9:12).

In the second illustration (9:15-20), the preacher used the theme of Christ's blood to suggest the establishment of a new covenant, just as the sprinkled blood of animals related to the Mosaic covenant. While there is no exact parallel in the Old Testament for the description in Hebrews 9:19-21, these verses probably represent the preacher's combined thoughts about the inauguration of the Mosaic covenant. By using the twofold meaning of *diathēkē* as both *"covenant"* and *"will,"* he argued for the need of Christ's death as the basis for the new covenant. By His death Christ made His will (testimentary intention) valid (9:16-17). Thus, from the principles of probate law, the preacher was able to add support for assurance by indicating that Christ's unique work as Mediator provided those who have been called (*hoi keklēmenoi*) the marvelous promise of an "eternal *inheritance"* (9:15).

But the sprinkled blood also suggested to the preacher a third picture about blood—the important concern of forgiveness. By employing a thesis from Leviticus 17:11, he reminded his readers that without bloodshedding there would be no forgiveness, cleansing, or release from sin (Heb. 9:22).[46]

Today we hardly think of blood as a cleaning agent. We use water and detergents to get rid of blood stains. But the mind-set of the preacher of Hebrews was shaped by what he knew of sacrificial offerings. Substitutionary blood was said to cleanse humans from sin, and the sprinkled blood was supposed to make instruments of worship holy. If that were the case in the Old Testament, just imagine what the precious blood of Jesus could do. The implications are awesome! Christ's blood is the basis for our cleansing, for our covenant relationship to God, for our forgiveness from sin, and for all aspects of our holiness and life in God.

3. A FOURTH PICTURE: THE COMING FINALITY TO CHRIST'S MINISTRY (HEB. 9:23-28)

In the last part of this chapter (9:23-28), the author again turned to the ministry of Christ in the heavenly sanctuary. This time it provided an illustration for the assurance which comes from the eschatological aspect of Christ's ministry. As the high priest returned from the most holy place and appeared before the congregation of the people, so it will also be with Christ. In His sacrifice, Christ appeared once (*hapax*) on earth in this period called the end time (*epi sunteleia tōn aiōnōn*) for the purpose of dealing with sin once (*hapax*). So also He will appear a second time (*deuterou*), not for the purpose of dealing again with sin, but for the purpose of assuring final salvation (glorification) to all those who eagerly wait (*apekdechomenois*) for him (9:26-28).

4. CHRIST, THE MINISTER OF THE NEW TORAH (HEB. 10:1-18)

As the preacher moved to the conclusion of this major section of Hebrews, he used a reference to law (ch. 10). For those schooled in the epistles of Paul and the Pauline rejection of rabbinic prescriptions, the Book of Hebrews offers an interesting contrast. While law in Hebrews relates to rules, it is primarily oriented to the rules of priestly service—the rules of sacrifice rather than the legalistic prescriptions of the Jewish scribes and rabbis. This fact seems to confirm the suggestion of many commentators that the author of Hebrews was probably from a priestly or Levitical family. It is also suggestive of the reason, although the Lord sprang from the tribe of Judah (see Heb. 7:14), Jesus Christ is pictured most descriptively in Hebrews as the High Priest.

One fact that has become most evident to me through studies in the quest for the historical Jesus is how writers throughout the centuries have tended to paint Jesus in the garb of their *ideal person*. I think that such a phenomenon is not merely a late pattern but that it was evident even in the New Testament itself. One only needs to see how Jesus was pictured by Luke as the great humanitarian, by John as the universal inspiration of believing, and by Paul as the answer to the bondage from the Law to remind readers why we need all the books of the New Testament to provide us with the multidimensional nature of our Christian faith.

When moving to Hebrews 10:1-18, one finds a collection of Midrashic thinking, which expands and comments on texts of the Old Testament to prove a certain thesis.[47] In the first part of this subsection (10:1-10), the law of sacrifice is viewed as imperfect and in need of termination. Whatever the writer of Psalm 40:6-8 may have thought of sacrifices, in the hand of this Midrashic preacher, the will of God had been performed by Jesus Christ, who through the offering of His body once for all (*ephapax*) abolished the order of the Law pertaining to repeatable sacrifices. By His coming He offered a new way to sanctification or holiness (Heb. 10:9-10).

In the second part (10:11-14), the preacher used Psalm 110:1 as the basis for insisting that the single sacrifice of Christ is the assured means of dealing with human sins (*huper hamartiōn*). For the preacher, nothing more needed to be done. The act of Christ in sitting down at the right hand of God was an indication that the work of sacrifice had been completed once and for all.

In the third and final part of this subsection (Heb. 10:15-18), the assurance given to the believer reaches a high point. Employing verses 33 and 34 from his foundation text of Jeremiah 31, the author asserted that, by witness of the Holy Spirit (Heb. 10:15), the Christian can be absolutely confident in the forgiveness of God. When God forgives, *He remembers no longer* (10:17)! Where forgiveness is given, believers should be confident that the offering was for all time *absolutely sufficient* (10:18). No one should need more assurance than that. To use a theme from the Johannine picture of Jesus, Christians should confess with their Lord, "It is finished!" (John 19:30).

E. Assurance and Warning:
A Superior Faithfulness (Heb. 10:19 to 12:29)

The major expositional section of Hebrews, with its strong basis for Christian assurance, was concluded. The preacher turned with determined force to another major exhortation, as he began to discuss the subject of faith or, more precisely, faithfulness and perseverance.

1. WARNINGS AND EXHORTATIONS TO ENDURANCE (HEB. 10:19-39)

Beginning with the conviction that Christ had brought assurance to Christians, the preacher firmly charged them to exhibit boldness, or confidence, in living in this world in spite of persecution. After all, Christians had gained access to the holy presence of God by the blood of Jesus. Indeed, they had been inaugurated into the new and dynamic way of life, as God unmasked His veil of hiddenness in the flesh of Jesus (10:19-20).[48] Because the Great Priest of God's house continued to minister for their sakes, Christians were not to be separated or to remain distant from either God or the church assembly (10:22,25). Both worshiping God and church attendance were very important to the preacher of Hebrews![49] Furthermore, because Christians had been cleansed in conscience and washed in body (baptized), they were summoned to exhibit the three cardinal virtues: an assured faith, an unwavering hope, and a working love (Heb. 10:22-24; see, for example, the simple form in 1 Thess. 1:3; 1 Cor. 13:13; and the expanded patterns in Rom. 5:1-5; 1 Pet. 1:3-9).

Given that conclusion, the next words strike with the force of another unexpected lightening bolt. The power of the Greek words of Hebrews 10:26 is reduced in English translations. The preacher began the discussion with the powerful adverb "deliberately" (*ekousiōs*). He followed it by the participial phrase emphasizing sinning, and then used a precise prepositional phrase "after" (*meta*) "receiving" the "knowledge" (*epignōsin*, the emphatic form) "of the truth." Finally, he employed with the concluding statement that "there remains a sacrifice for sin" the extremely emphatic adverb "no longer" (*ouketi*). The result was a motivational shock of the first magnitude. If there were any chance that the Christian readership had been on the verge of falling back into a lethargic, satisfied sleep of assurance, it was gone completely. The jolt to an early Christian audience or readership must have been absolutely intense. It is not much different today!

But if one expected relief in what followed, one was badly mistaken because the preacher announced that if, after receiving the truth, one engaged in such sinning there was clearly "a terrifying expectation of judgment." Indeed, he spoke of "a zealous [or hungry] fire which is ready to eat the opponents" (10:27). There are few preachers of hell fire and brimstone who can do a better job in twelve Greek words than our preacher of Hebrews. He was talking about those who had sinned deliberately after having received the knowledge of the truth! Whatever he meant, stunned Christian audiences had better listen. This sermon was not an intellectual game because the expression "the knowledge of the truth" is a consistent New Testament description for saving knowledge (see, for example, 1 Tim. 2:4; 2 Tim. 2:25; Titus 1:1; and the verbal forms in John 8:32; 1 John 3:19; 2 John 1; see also Col. 1:6).

The reference to deliberate sin in Hebrews would be the equivalent of sinning "with the high hand" in Numbers 15:30. Such a person who nullified or rejected the law of Moses, the preacher reminded his readers, was put to death without mercy (Heb. 10:28). The logic for such a severe punishment was that the community could not tolerate the rejection of the major basis for the community's existence by any member of that community (see Deut. 17:2-6). The logic of the preacher in Hebrews seems to have been that, if such a pattern were true of the old covenant, how much more serious ought to be the contemptuous disregard of the Son of God, His sanctifying blood of the new covenant, and the Spirit of grace.

This sin was, indeed, of the most serious nature because it meant the rejection or nullification of everything that brought assurance to the Christian.[50] Therefore, the preacher punctuated his verdict with the major warning themes from the Old Testament: vengeance is God's; God judges His people; and to fall into God's hands can be a life-threatening experience (see Deut. 32:35-36; Gen. 28:17). Especially would meeting God be terrifying if God came in judgment because a theophany or angelophany (a meeting with God or an angel) was traumatic enough to unglue persons even when they heard the word of "peace" (see, for example, Gideon in Judg. 6:22 or Isaiah in Isa. 6:5). Such rejecters of Christ deserved the worst imaginable treatment, according to the preacher.

In spite of his sense of justified wrath at what he considered to be a serious sin, the preacher was more concerned about encouraging his flock than scalping the renegades. In this respect, he reflected the spirit of Jesus who openly condemned the self-righteous renegades and hypocrites but turned in gentle concern to the bruised and helpless sheep of God's fold (see Matt. 9:36; 23:13-39). The preacher of Hebrews had earlier condemned the enlightened ones (*phōtisthentas*) who had turned away from Christ (Heb. 6:4; see 10:26). Now he reached out to the enlightened ones who were struggling to be authentic Christians in the midst of suffering, insult, and persecution (10:32-34). This roll call of abuses, including the plundering of their property and the public mistreatment which they suffered as Christians, does not necessarily imply a formal imperial persecution; it is an indication of the rough experiences encountered by Christians at the instigation of both Jews and Gentiles in many of the Roman provinces throughout the empire.[51]

The Christians needed confident endurance in the midst of such suffering. Therefore, the preacher's exhortation to endurance was two-fold. First, on the basis of a Midrashic rewriting of the Septuagint of Habakkuk 2:3-4, he sternly warned his readers about God's displeasure against withdrawing or shrinking back (*huposteilētai*) because of fear from outside pressures (Heb. 10:37-38). Second, he spoke assuringly as he united himself with his readers, confident that "we are not those of the withdrawal [shrinking back; *hupostolēs*] unto destruction." Instead, he was sure that he and his readers belonged to the faithful and to those of the "preservation (*peripoiēsin*) of the soul" (10:39).

In the spirit of 6:9-12, the preacher showed that he believed that his readers would be faithful to the end. The preacher of Hebrews believed that it was unthinkable and intolerable that a believer would withdraw (shrink back) from Christ.

The preacher believed in perseverance and was very concerned that the Christians persevere. Therefore, he did all in his power to convince them not even to contemplate any other way. This clear sense of assurance is set in the context of a frightening warning. In this passage, the preacher again recognized both assurance and warning in the gospel and somehow sought to account for both the divine and the human dimensions in salvation. In the present context, the human setting was in the forefront of attention, and the preacher did everything authentically possible—whether by tactics of shock,

threat, or loving embrace—to motivate his readers to evidence faithfulness in the Christian life.

2. The Roll Call of the Faithful (Heb. 11:1-39)

Having introduced the goal of faithfulness, the preacher turned to
illustrate what he meant by lives of faith through examples from the
past in the roll call of the faithful (ch. 11). The Greek word *pistis*,
usually translated "faith," is one of those multifaceted words in the
New Testament that has various shades of meaning.[52] The context
is, therefore, extremely important in determining its sense. Hebrews
11:1 is not really a definition of *pistis*, though it may mark out certain
aspects of the life of faithfulness which the preacher considered important in his models from the past.

What one can say at the very least is that, for the preacher, *pistis*
(faith) included a sense of both "assurance" (*hupostasis*)[53] and "conviction" (*elegchos*) based upon some kind of inner awareness of evidence
or proof (Heb. 11:1; see RSV). This assured conviction of the *expected*
and the *unseen* aspects of life is a kind of fountainhead that is necessary
for consistency of living that was the preacher's goal of "faithfulness."
Assured conviction is basic to our understanding of creation and redemption, and it makes sense only if God is active in the world (Heb.
11:2-3). God is not dead, despite what some have thought. He has
been and is very much alive. Faithfulness to God makes a great deal
of sense.

Moreover, persons like Abel, Enoch, and Noah became models of
pleasing God for the preacher (11:6; see the warning in 10:38), not
because they were perfect (see 11:40), but because they possessed
certain qualities that enabled them to recognize that the patterns
and rewards of the visible world were not the ultimate tests of authentic
life (11:6). Their basis for security came from the unseen God (11:7).

The model of Abraham with his wife, Sarah, expands the perspective
by providing the preacher with a great example of pilgrimage, an
important theme in Hebrews. The significant work of John Elliot on
1 Peter, *A Home for the Homeless*, reminds us again that the idea of
stranger, exile, sojourner, refugee is crucially relevant for Christians![54]
God's earlier people, Israel, and God's later people, the early Christians experienced this reality. These Christians lived with the threat

of being persecuted and dispossessed. They were a homeless type of people on earth who needed to see beyond their painful circumstances to the assuring invisible God of their hope. Therefore, writers like Paul (Rom. 4; Gal. 3) and the preacher of Hebrews found Abraham to be such an attractive model of faith.

Abraham, and other patriarchs who succeeded him, accepted the call to pilgrimage (following God) even though he did not know the full implications of the journey beforehand (Heb. 11:8). All of them died without realizing the full expectations of their promised inheritance (11:13-14). Whether it was their expectation of inheritance through land or lineage, their faithful adherence to their unseen God made the Exodus (11:22-29) and the entrance into the Promised Land (11:30-31) seem inevitable. The preacher assured his readers that God is hardly ashamed to be called their God. The preacher proclaimed their inheritance to be unquestionably secure (11:16).

The preacher drew major illustrations from the premonarchy, pre-Temple period, in keeping with his perspective throughout this sermon.[55] He generalized quickly over the later period of Israel's history (11:33-38) in an effort to draw the entire scope of the faithful people of God into a single sweep of holy history (*Heilsgeschichte*). The preacher's goal was to make certain that his readers caught the vision that they were part of this magnificent history. Indeed, he wanted them to see that they were living in the concluding or perfected (*teleiōthōsin*) segment of this history of assured conviction (11:39-40).

The preacher was convinced that, because of the interrelation of the people of God from one era to the next, the way his readers reacted to the summons to faithful living would also affect the models of the past, who he believed were in some sense participating in the perfection of the saints (11:40). For Western Christians who have been raised on the "self-made" concepts of nineteenth-century individualism, the Jewish ideas of corporate personality are far removed from the mind.[56] But by contrast, the preacher of Hebrews seemingly believed that generations affected one another. One can almost sense that, in the mind of the writer, the faithful of the past were standing on tiptoe, waiting to see whether Christians would heed the warnings that were given and would follow the faithful models of the past.

3. Perseverance and Three Great Sermon Illustrations (Heb. 12:1-29)

Serving as a major transition, Hebrews 12:1-2 is a forceful call of assurance for Christians to accept the models of the past as witnesses to the integrity and viability of the way of faithfulness. It is also a warning to reject anything that bespeaks the way of sin and turning back. The first illustration the preacher used was that of a great marathon race of life where all of the extra training weights and the impediments of sin are laid aside and where the faithful of the past (as witnesses) watch the Christian runners from the seats of a holy stadium (cloud). The race is not pictured as a quick or easy one. It demands perseverance. But this race of life is not uncharted. Jesus, the lead runner (pioneer: *archēgon*) and the model finisher (perfecter: *teleiōtēn*) of the way of faith, has indelibly sealed the nature of the Christian's race (pattern of life) by accepting the cross and rejecting the categories of world achievement (note His view of joy and shame).[57] Jesus is Himself now seated majestically at the right hand of God (12:2); He is the One, knowing the course, to whom the Christian must look for guidance and assurance.

Jesus had endured the cross (12:2-3), and the preacher found in Jesus a model worthy of challenging Christians who were becoming weary (*kamēte*) and losing courage (*ekluomenoi*) in their struggle (12:3). Hebrews does not preach easy prosperity, which has become the badge of much of Western Christian television. The Christians had suffered persecutions and plundering (see 10:32-34), but the preacher's word of encouragement was that they had not yet suffered martyrdom ("resisted unto blood"; *mechris haimatos antikatestēte*) in their church (12:4).

We might wonder how such a message could provide encouragement. But the preacher reminded his readers of the nature of sonship.[58] Jesus had "learned" (*emathen*) obedience through suffering (5:7-8). He was the originator (pioneer) of salvation through suffering (2:10); He, indeed, is the Son of God (1:2-3). If, therefore, the preacher argued, God had used the discipline (*paideia*) of suffering with His own Son,[59] according to the pattern suggested in Proverbs 3:11-12, would not God do the same with His Christian children (Heb. 12:7)? The discipline of suffering was not to be understood as a judgment of God but rather as an assurance that Christians were truly children of God and were not illegitimate offspring (12:8)! How often today Christians speak of suffering merely as tragedy. But we need to understand the other side as well. Discipline is a mark of relationship, even in earthly families (12:9-11). Therefore, among Christians it is to be understood as a powerful sign of a Christian's assurance.

Having, thus, argued for the reality of suffering as an evidence of legitimate Christian sonship and daughterhood, the preacher of Hebrews summoned his readers back to the marathon of life (v. 12). In the words of Isaiah 35:3, he called drooping (*pareimenas*) hands—a sign of defeat—and weakened or disabled (*paralelumena*) knees—a sign of exhaustion or injury—back to their invigoration (*anorthōsate*). In addition, he used the words of Proverbs 4:26 (LXX) to exhort his readers to make ready the track for the race so that Christian athletes might not be unnecessarily injured (12:13). This latter picture could also suggest a community effort in track preparation, an emphasis which needs to be reasserted whenever a self-made philosophy infects Christian work.

With the athletic illustration in the background, the preacher quickly turned to the second illustration, which provided him with the warning side to his words of encouragement. His concern was that the readers might not measure up to the standards of Christian integrity in the pursuit of peace and holiness (12:14). The vision of Esau, the rejected one, thus, came to mind. As a result, the preacher addressed a stern threefold warning to his readers: against failing to deal appropriately with the grace of God, against bitterness, and against immorality and godlessness or profanity (Heb. 12:15-16; see Deut. 29:17-19, LXX). Whether Esau could be said to have been guilty of activity like immorality has been debated by scholars. But the point here is that Esau was a symbol of rejection and of one who was not given the opportunity to repent (12:17).[60] The preacher of Hebrews was, thus, holding out a big stick at his congregation and warning them about activities he considered to be extremely dangerous. Whether his readers had actually engaged in these activities is a matter for speculation. One thing is clear; the preacher of Hebrews had no problem calling sin "sin!"[61] And he was against it.

Moving the sermon to its climax with unusual skill, the preacher drew together the disparate elements of his sermon into a third illustration, which provided a unique combination of assurance and warning. Hebrews 12:18-29 is a magnificent picture. It stands as one of the truly great texts of imaginative thinking in the New Testament. The creative force in the preacher's contrast between the terrifying experience of Israel at Mount Sinai and the assuring assembly at Mount Zion provided the early Christian reader with a marvelous sense of the dynamics at work in the old and the new covenants. Terror and fear that were present at the inauguration of the Mosaic covenant (12:18-21) are sharply compared to the festival (*panēgurei*) experience which has resulted from the new covenant grace mediated by Jesus (12:22-24). The opening words of the climax (12:18) could not help but signal to the reader that the theme of access to God was once again in focus. In the old covenant distance was emphasized as the untouchable God demanded His sanctified space. Indeed, God commanded that any unauthorized violation of His space, even by a hapless animal touching His mountain, should result in death (Heb. 12:20; see Ex. 19:12-13). In the new covenant, however, access to Mount Zion and to the city of the living God was a basic assumption. Such was the assuring word of the preacher: The sprinkled blood of Jesus was the gracious sign of access to God for the faithful of the new covenant.

But the preacher did not want anyone to think of the gospel as a spineless message. Therefore, he warned his readers yet again. This time he set forth Jesus as the real Spokesman for the warning. He reminded his readers that, if there had been no fleeing or escaping from a warning (*chrēmatizonta*) delivered on earth, there could be little hope of escape for *us* (*hēmeis*) *who turn away* (*apostrephomenoi*) from the warning which comes from heaven (Heb. 12:25)! To punctuate this warning, the preacher reminded his readers that as God had shaken the earth at Sinai (Ex. 19:18) so He would fulfill His promise in Haggai 2:6 that He would yet shake not only earth once again but also heaven as well (Heb. 12:26).

The purpose of this shaking judgment or upheaval of both earth and heaven, from the preacher's point of view, however, was not ultimately to be seen as judgment. Instead, he viewed it as the basis for identifying and establishing those who belong to the unshakable kingdom (12:27-28). Thus, in his climax, the preacher's warning merged once again into assurance as the Christian's hope is expressed in the confidence of the unshakable kingdom.

The only appropriate response to such a great message is authentic worship that evidenced both godly reverence and awe in the presence of the holy and mysterious God who is a consuming fire (Heb. 12:28-29; see Deut. 4:24)![62]

F. Assurance and Warning, the Conclusion: A Superior Life (Heb. 13:1-25)

Chapter 12 of Hebrews ended on a high note. It is almost as though the sermon had reached its conclusion. Therefore, some commentators have concluded that chapter 13 is an appendix added by a later scribe to give it an epistolary form and to ensure that the book would be accepted as part of the Pauline corpus of letters. This line of reasoning has been effectively countered by Floyd Filson who, I believe, has made a strong case for the unity of the letter.[63] Such a conclusion, however, does not mean that I would argue that the ideas in the letter did not pass through a period of development in the mind and homiletical experience of the author. But I strongly maintain that Hebrews in its canonical form is a unit and that chapter 13 reveals something significant about the mind-set and concerns of the preacher who wrote this sermon.

This section is composed primarily of practical exhortations, but it is not devoid of theological reflection. While the instructions may seem to be very brief, they are important because they provide principles for the pilgrimage life of the community. Furthermore, these exhortations seem to enfold and enflesh the assurance and warning concerns of the preacher.

The opening exhortation to continue in brotherly or sisterly love (Heb. 13:1) is rooted in a confidence that the Lord is bonded to His people (13:5). Love and bonding is the theme of the first six verses. The Christian is instructed to show hospitality or loving concern for strangers because, as in the case of Abraham (Gen. 18), strangers may turn out to be messengers (angels) of God (Heb. 13:2). In the context of the early church where Christians traveled between communities and may not have had easy access to places of lodging, hospitality was a sign of community bonding. Similarly, concern for those in prison was a mark that the community was knit together as fellow prisoners (*sundedemenoi*). Likewise, persecuted or mistreated believers were to be regarded as part of the body (*sōma;* 13:3). Marriage relationships were to be held in honor (*timios*) because an immoral person (*pornos*) or an adulterer (*moichos*) destroyed bonding (v. 4). Furthermore, a style of life (*tropos*) that was motivated by the wrong kind of love, namely love of money (*aphilarguros*), was to be rejected because it did not advance community contentment (*arkoumenoi*) but was undoubtedly viewed as divisive in the fellowship (13:5).

The rationale for these life-oriented instructions was built upon the relationship that Christians have with their Lord. Employing the classic words from the farewell address of Moses, the preacher reminded his readers that the Lord will neither abandon (*anō*) nor forsake (*egkatalipō*) His people (Heb. 13:5; see Deut. 31:6-8; Josh. 1:5). This sense of divine nearness is the basis for Christian confidence or assurance (*tharrountas*). Such confidence led the preacher to express, in the spirit of the psalmist, his sense of fearlessness (*ou phobēthēsomai*) in the face of mere human opposition (Heb. 13:6; see Ps. 117:6, LXX; or Ps. 118:6).

This sense of confidence focused directly upon issues of church life (Heb. 13:7-17). The first exhortation of the preacher concerned pricking the memories (*mnēmoneuete*) of his readers so that they would recall their leaders. They were urged to reflect both on the message which their leaders delivered (namely, "the word of God") and on the consistency of the lives (or "the result of their behavior") which they lived (13:7). This is the incarnational model at work at the second level—the gospel enfleshed in Christian leaders whom the readers were exhorted to copy or imitate (*mimeisthe*). But these leaders were not ends in themselves; nor were they the foundation of Christian security. That foundational role belongs only to one Person, the subject of the early Christian confession: "Jesus Christ, the same yesterday and today and forever!" (13:8).

The second exhortation related to church life focused on the question of doctrine and practice. The preacher warned his readers not to be dragged off (*mē parapheresthe*) by the many strange doctrines that were circulating. They needed to concentrate on confirming or strengthening (*bebaiousthai*) their hearts by grace (*chariti*) rather than assuming that they could become strong by external matters which involved food (*brōmasin*) practices and the like (13:9). That was the way of the old covenant. But the heart or altar (*thusiastērion*) of the new covenant was not available to provide sustenance to those who continued to serve in the manner of the priests of the old covenant tabernacle (*skēnē;* 13:10). The old way was passé; the new had dawned. The two ways were not to be mixed. The new way of life for the Christians was superior to the old.

Indeed, the new way was seen as the reverse of the old. In the old way, the blood of animals offered for sin was brought into the sanctuary, but the bodies of those animals were burned outside the camp (13:11). By contrast, the preacher argued, Jesus "suffered" (*epathen*) outside (*exō*) the gate in order that through His blood He might make the people of God holy (*hagiasē;* 13:12).

At this point, it is important to note the intriguing contrast between the early tabernacle experience of the pilgrim people and the later experience of Jewish worship. The tabernacle in the Mosaic pattern was placed outside the camp (Ex. 33:7). However, the later worship experience in the city was inside the walls. The preacher here apparently was reflecting a city experience and, of course, the picture of Jesus "outside the gate" (*pulēs*) is definitely an urban reference.

In any event, the burning of the sin offering outside the camp in Leviticus 16:27-28 probably suggested the illustration to the preacher. The exhortation was for the Christians to join Jesus as outsiders who are willing to suffer insult (*oneidismon*) and persecution (Heb. 13:13; see 10:32). To be an outsider meant for the Christian to be an exile or a homeless person (see 1 Pet. 1:1).[64] But from the preacher's point of view, that should hardly be an unexpected way of life or indicate a lack of assurance.

In the Book of Hebrews, the way of the Christian was the way of pilgrimage. The goal of the Christian was not to receive an inheritance or a city *on earth* because the Christian sought "a city which is yet to come" (Heb. 13:14). Security for the Christian, then, did not lie in the privileges and things of the earth but in the acknowledgment of the name of Jesus, through whom praise to God was to be offered as a continual sacrifice (13:15). But the sacrifice of the Christian was not to be simply a matter of words. The preacher's balance comes through clearly again. Deeds must be added to words. The doing of good and the practice of sharing (*koinōnias*) are marks of authentic worship which must not be neglected by the Christian (13:16)!

To these aspects of church life, the preacher added two further areas. Because of his concern for the care (*agrupnousin*) of souls, he realized the necessity for orderly leadership and a sense of willing submission to those in charge (13:17). Furthermore, he exhorted them to pray for him in order that he might act authentically and might soon be restored to his role among them (13:18-19). Here then may be a capsule insight into the rationale for the writing of the letter—a preacher, perhaps in prison, very concerned about external pressure and persecution brought against his flock, yet confident in the power of God through Christ to bring them through the dangerous journey of life. To them he addressed his impassioned sermon of assurance and warning.

The preacher's benediction (13:20-21) is a classic concluding prayer of assurance that called upon the God of peace who in the death and resurrection of the great Shepherd signaled hope and the establishment of an eternal covenant.[65] But this prayer is not concerned only with privilege and status in Christ. It is equally a prayer for responsible Christian living in doing the will of God, to the end that the Christians in the flock may be well pleasing to God through Jesus Christ. For the preacher who wrote Hebrews, privilege in Christ implied responsible living.

Conclusion

The message of Hebrews is directed to both privilege and responsibility. It contains both a powerful sense of assurance and a stern sense of warning. The balance between assurance and warning in Hebrews is very delicate.[66] To consider one without the other is to misunderstand the preacher of Hebrews. He knew the history of Israel, and he understood the failure of the people of God in the wilderness and in the rejection of Jesus. He also knew the faithfulness of God and the reality of the faithful remnant whom he enshrined in his memorable roll call of the faithful.

Turning to consider the superior way of Christianity, the preacher could not forget the history of Israel, which is etched so deeply into the whole experience of God with His people. The Book of Hebrews continues to remind us of the crucial nature of understanding history. Jesus—whom the preacher confessed as the same yesterday, today, and forever (13:8)—is also the Son of the God who is likewise thoroughly consistent in dealing with His promises and with the frail responses of weak humanity. Thus, the preacher was forced, throughout this book, to ask his readers: If Israel (the people of God) rejected God's way and was punished, what did they think would happen to those who, knowing the way of Jesus, turned away from Him?

But as the preacher raised his haunting question, he consistently raised a partial answer. That answer was an assuring word of personal conviction that his readers were not rejecters of the faith. His conviction in the power of God to assist mere mortals in running the race with perseverance, as they looked to the lead runner (pioneer) and model finisher (perfecter) of their faith, provided his readers with a delicate answer to any fear which might arise from an academic question of apostasy.

The answer also pointed to a Christian journey. The preacher felt a pressing need for Christians to sense both the marvel of God's work in Christ and the reality of Christian frailty in living out the implications of the gospel. The emphasis in this sermon does not fall on justification or on the beginning of the Christian life. He had assumed the fact of a beginning with Christ because his readers would hardly be interested in reading his involved sermon if they were not Christians. His concern was for holy living or what the church has called sanctification.

In encouraging Christians to live holy lives the preacher was not a dreamer who lived with his whole life in the clouds. He was a thorough realist who understood the difficulty of living life in a world setting that cared very little about God or authentic Christian living. He knew what it meant to suffer for being a Christian, and he understood the pressure that made Christians ask questions like: "Why me, Lord?" or "Is it worth it, God?" He also knew that the only answer to those questions was to be found in persevering in the way of holiness.

The concept of perseverance is a theme that needs to be recaptured by the church. This theme has a great history in Christianity and has been found again and again when the church is struck by persecution. But it also needs to be found when church members begin to debate academic questions of security. Life is more than reasoned answers. It involves both the realities of the divine and the human, and it deals not only with the questions of the mind but also with the actual pains of the heart and the body. To the realities of life, the preacher of Hebrews addressed a message of both caring assurance and decisive warning. To the weak and fearful, the preacher counseled, "Move forward!" To the proud and self-centered, he cautioned, "Watch out!" The reaction he expected was an unreserved commitment to perseverance by all the people of God. Who can doubt that his message and his anticipated reaction are of incredible relevance for today?

Notes

1. G. Borchert, "A Superior Book: Hebrews," *Review and Expositor* 82 (1985): 319. I have cited all of the articles in this issue because I think they can be helpful to pastors, students, and laypeople alike.

2. See William G. Johnson, *Hebrews*, Knox Preaching Guides (Atlanta: John Knox Press, 1980).

3. W. G. Kümmel, *The New Testament: The History of the Investigation of Its Problems*, trans. S. Gilmore and H. Kee (Nashville: Abingdon Press, 1973), pp. 19-24.

4. W. G. Kümmel, *Introduction to the New Testament*, trans. H. Kee (Nashville: Abingdon Press, 1975), pp. 393-394. Roger Nicole, "Some Comments on Hebrews 6:4-6 and the Doctrine of the Perseverance of God with the Saints," in *Current Issues in Biblical and Patristic Interpretation* (Studies in Honor of Merril C. Tenney) ed. G. Hawthorne (Grand Rapids: Wm. B. Eerdmans, 1975), pp. 355-364. I. Howard Marshall, *Kept By the Power, A Study of Perseverance and Falling Away* (London: Epworth Press, 1969).

But see also my remarks at footnote 70 in this chapter which reflect some tendency toward more balance in his chapter on Hebrews.

5. See Borchert, pp. 319-332.

6. Donald Guthrie, *New Testament Introduction*, 3rd ed. (Downers Grove: Inter-Varsity Press, 1970), pp. 685-735 and W. G. Kümmel, *Introduction*, pp. 387-403.

7. Two important commentaries are those by F. F. Bruce, *The Epistle to the Hebrews*, New International Commentary on the New Testament (Grand Rapids: Wm. B. Eerdmans, 1964) and G. W. Buchanan, *To the Hebrews*, The Anchor Bible (Garden City: Doubleday, 1981). An older work which is dated in matters of introduction but very significant in matters of interpretation is B. F. Westcott, *The Epistle to the Hebrews* (Grand Rapids: Wm. B. Eerdmans, 1967 reprint of 1909). William Lane, *Call to Commitment* (Nashville: Thomas Nelson, 1985).

8. Origen wrote: *tis ho grapsas tēn epistolēn, to men glēthes theos oiden.* See Eusebius, *Historia Ecclesia*, 6.25.14.

9. For further discussion see Borchert, pp. 320-323 or the introductory discussions in Bruce, Buchanan, Guthrie, or Kümmel.

10. See Borchert, pp. 323-324. See J. A. T. Robinson, *Redating the New Testament* (Philadelphia: Westminster Press, 1976), pp. 200-210.

11. Borchert, pp. 323-324.

12. Ibid., p. 324.

13. *De Pudicita*, #20.

14. Borchert, pp. 325-327.

15. Ibid., p. 328.

16. F. V. Filson, *"Yesterday": A Study of Hebrews in the Light of Chapter 13*, Studies of Biblical Theology, 2nd series, vol. 4 (Naperville: A. Allenson, 1967).

17. See Buchanan, pp. xix-xxx. See discussion of Midrash at footnote 29 (below) of this chapter.

18. Donald A. Hagner, *Hebrews*, A Good News Commentary (Cambridge: Harper & Row, 1983), p. xxii.

19. Robert Jewett appropriately entitled his commentary on Hebrews *Letter to Pilgrims* (New York: Pilgrim Press, 1981).

20. The organization here is a mirror of my editorial division of the Hebrews issue of the *Review and Expositor* (1985) with one exception. In that issue the major part of chapter 12 was joined to chapter 13 for the purpose of equalizing commentary responsibilities.

21. For a discussion of the ideas related to character, image, and reflection in Hebrews see Thomas G. Smothers, "A Superior Model: Hebrews 1:1-4:13," *Review and Expositor* 82 (1985): 334-335.

22. See Bruce, p. 8.

23. The usual motif employed in Hebrews for victory is the exaltation picture of Jesus at the right hand of God because the emphasis being made is that of the reigning Jesus who is stronger than the rulers of the world. The preacher's concern is that Christian pilgrims need to understand that their Lord is superior to the powers and rulers who are persecuting them.

The only use of resurrection and shepherd here has been employed by some to argue for the disunity of chapter 13 from the rest of the Hebrews. For a discussion of the issues see Filson.

24. For Jewish styles of argument see Buchanan, pp. xix-xxx.

For a discussion of the use of Old Testament citations in Hebrews see F. Schröger, *Der Verfasser des Hebräerbriefes als Schriftauslegen* (Regensburg: Friedrich Pustet, 1968).

For the suggestion that early Christians may have employed lists of Old Testament passages which served as supporting documentation for their position concerning Jesus see D. M. Hay, *Glory at the Right Hand* (Nashville: Abingdon Press, 1973), pp. 37-39.

25. Buchanan, p. 26 indicates that only in Acts 2:1-41 is there such a strong four-part evidentiary argument made for divine support of the Son.

26. See Marshall, p. 140.

27. Midrash is a general term for the Jewish interpretive patterns which are usually divided into two primary categories. The first is called halakah and is concerned with Jewish legal perscriptions or the later Jewish interpretations of the law of Moses (*Torah*). The second is called Haggadah and is concerned with nonlegal interpretations which involve a vast variety of materials from traditional interpretations of passages to stylized linguistic arguments and ancient Jewish folklore. Both types of materials have been preserved in Jewish materials such as the Talmuds, the Targums, and the Writings of the rabbis. See also the references in footnote 26 (above) of this chapter.

28. See Schröger, pp. 112-113.

29. See the helpful discussion of Calvin R. Schoonhoven, "The 'Analogy of Faith' and the Intent of Hebrews," *Scripture, Tradition and Interpretation*, eds. W. Gasque and W. LaSor (Grand Rapids: Wm. B. Eerdmans, 1978), pp. 92-110.

30. Harold Songer, "A Superior Priesthood: Hebrews 4:14-7:28" *Review and Expositor* 82 (1985): 346 has argued that the expression "great priest" was the usual term used in the Old Testament and that "high priest" was the more typical Greek expression. The joining of "great" and "high" may be intended for emphasis by the preacher.

It is interesting to note that the more typical Old Testament expression "great priest" (*kōhēn gādol*) is found in Hebrews 10:21 (*hiera megan*). It is also significant to note that the expression "great high priest" (*archiereus megas*) is found in Philo (*On Dreams* 1:214,229; 2:183) with reference to the divine Logos and in 1 Maccabees 13:42 where an attempt is made to elevate Simon. See Bruce, p. 85. Contrast Hugh Montefiore, *The Epistle to the Hebrews*, Harper's New Testament Commentaries (New York: Harper & Row, 1964), p. 90.

31. This text forms part of the humility motif in Hebrews (see Heb. 2:7-9). But the text raises the question of whether the preacher might have had in mind a contrast of Jesus with some particular ambitious high priest(s) of his day.

32. See the discussion in John W. Bowman, *The Letter to the Hebrews*, The Layman's Bible Commentary (Richmond: John Knox Press, 1962), pp. 39-40. As I have argued below (see footnote 63), I do not see any hint of Käsemann's redeemed redeemer here.

33. Bruce, p. 111. See H. P. Owen, " 'The Stages of Ascent' in Hebrews v. 11-vi. 3," *New Testament Studies* 3 (1956-1957): 243-253. See also Marshall, p. 141.

34. See Bruce, pp. 112-118; Buchanan, pp. 103-105; Montefiore, pp. 104-105; Songer, pp. 350-351; Westcott, pp. 144-146.

35. It is a smoke screen to suggest, as some have, that the word *partaker* means these persons have merely been exposed to the Holy Spirit and have not been sharers of the Spirit. See Nicole, p. 360. Contrast Marshall, pp. 142-143.

36. Technically the word *apostasy* from the Greek *apostēnai* is not used in this context as it is in Hebrews 3:12. Here at Hebrews 6:6 the term used is *parapesontas* which means "falling away," but it can by implication also carry the meaning of "committing apostasy." See for example the translation of the RSV at this point.

37. For a discussion of oath see Montefiore, pp. 115-116.

38. See James Moffatt, *A Critical and Exegetical Commentary on the Epistle to the Hebrews*, International Critical Commentary (Edinburgh: T. & T. Clark, 1924), p. 87.

39. Realizing the distinctions that have been made by scholars such as Rudolf Bultmann between the Jesus of history and the Christ of faith, it is important to assert that such a distinction is hardly in the mind of the writer of Hebrews. For his existentialist distinction, see R. Bultmann, *Jesus and the Word*, trans. L. Smith and E. Huntress (New York: Charles Scribner's Sons, 1958) and R. Bultmann, "New Testament and Mythology," *Kerygma and Myth*, ed. H. Bartsch (New York: Harper & Brothers, 1961), pp. 37-42. See Morris Ashcraft, *Rudolf Bultmann* (Waco: Word Books, 1972), especially at pp. 35-41.

40. For some helpful thoughts on this subject see Aelred Cody, *Heavenly Sanctuary and Liturgy in the Epistle to the Hebrews* (St. Meinrad, Ind.:

Grail Publications, 1960); J. W. Thompson, *The Beginnings of Christian Philosophy: The Epistle to the Hebrews*, vol. 13, The Catholic Biblical Quarterly Monograph Series (Washington: Catholic Biblical Association of America, 1982); S. G. Sowers, *The Hermeutics of Philo and Hebrews: A Comparison of the Interpretation of the Old Testament in Philo Judaeus and the Epistle to the Hebrews* (Richmond: John Knox Press, 1965).

41. I am not here presenting a diatribe against modern Judaism although I am committed to the evangelism of the entire world. I believe that contemporary Christian exponents of two covenants or more than one way to God render the preaching of Jesus meaningless for Christians. I am firmly committed to the fact that the ethics of Jesus are applicable to contemporary Christians. See the perspective of George Ladd, "Historic Premillenialism," *The Meaning of the Millenium: Four Views*, ed. Robert Clouse (Downers Grove: Inter Varsity Press, 1977), pp. 25-26. See also the responses to Ladd following his article.

42. Roger Omanson has well summarized the issues in "A Superior Covenant: Hebrews 8:1-10:18," *Review and Expositor* 82 (1985): 363-364.

43. While Hebrews 9:7 indicates that the high priest entered the most holy place once a year, according to Leviticus 16:12-16, three specific cultic acts were administered, but all three acts would have been regarded as a combination event which marked the high point of the Jewish year known as the Day of Atonement (*Yom Kippur*).

44. Whatever "first" or "outer" meant for the preacher of Hebrews, it is clear that the block (the curtain) in access to the holy presence of God evident in the Old Covenant system was regarded by the preacher to have passed from the scene in its effectiveness of separating humanity from God through the coming of Jesus. Contemporary Christians, however, seem to have a different problem. They must take great care lest they trivialize the holiness of God in their proclamation of access. God remains holy and must be treated by sinful humanity as holy, pure, and undefiled. We have access to the holy God but that right of access is through Jesus and must be treated as a very precious gift which we dare not regard lightly.

45. Westcott's attempt to identify the church with this new tabernacle seems to be untenable. The thesis might work if the view of the church in Hebrews was a Platonic ideal. But for the preacher of Hebrews the church would have to be part of both the phenomenal (earthly) and heavenly realms. The thesis, I submit, will just not work in Hebrews. See Westcott, pp. 255-258.

46. There were some exceptions to the rule of Leviticus 17:11. See Lev. 5:11-13.

47. For information concerning Midrashic thinking and Jewish interpretive methods see footnotes 26 and 29 in this chapter.

48. The translation of the New English Bible—"The new, living way which he has opened for us through the curtain, the way of his flesh" (Heb. 10:20)—seems to catch the emphasis of the preacher here. See Westcott, pp. 319-320 and R. Alan Culpepper, "A Superior Faith: Hebrews 10:19-12:2," *Review and Expositor* 82 (1985): 376.

49. Johnson, p. 76, has summarized very tersely the preacher's view on church attendance: "The author has exposed in the passage four reasons in answer to the query, "Why go to Church?": because of what Christ has done, because of who we are, because of the opportunities for mutual encouragement and growth, and because of the times (God is Lord of history, and the time is moving according to his purposes)."

50. Marshall, p. 148, joins those who think the sin may be blasphemy.

51. For a discussion of this very complex matter see Borchert, pp. 324 and 327.

52. For a helpful discussion on the shades of meaning see Montefiore, p. 187.

53. Helmut Koester, *"Hupostasis," Theological Dictionary of the New Testament*, eds. G. Kittel and G. Friedrich, trans. G. Bromiley (Grand Rapids: Wm. B. Eerdmans, 1972) 8:586.

54. John Elliot, *A Home for the Homeless: A Sociological Exegesis of 1 Peter, Its Situation and Strategy* (Philadelphia: Fortress Press, 1981).

55. See the discussion in connection with footnote 14 in this chapter.

56. For a discussion of corporate personality see H. Wheeler Robinson, *Corporate Personality in Ancient Israel*, rev. ed. (Edinburgh: T. & T. Clark, 1981).

57. The clause in Hebrews 12:2 translated in the RSV as "who for the joy that was set before him" may instead be rendered by the prepositional phrase, "against the joy" (*anti charas*). The latter translation may be more consistent with the humility motif of the incarnation in Hebrews (as well as in Paul in Phil. 2) and certainly would conform much better to the following expression in Hebrews 12:2 of enduring the cross and despising the shame. See for example, Buchanan, pp. 207-208. Contrast, for example, Bruce, p. 353. Buchanan's additional theory that Jesus gave up an earthly life of wealth seems less likely. For a brief review of the situation see Culpepper, pp. 388-389. See also the less convincing argument of G. W. Buchanan, "Jesus and the Upper Class," *Novum Testamentum* 7 (1964-1965): 195-209.

58. See Gunther Bornkamm, "Sonschaft und Leiden, Hebräer 12, 5-11" *Geschichte und Glaube*, Beitrage zur evangelischen Theologie (München: Christian Kaiser Verlag, 1971) 53: 221-224. For a helpful review of the theme of sonship in Hebrews see Julius Kögel, *Der Sohn und die Sohne*, Beitrage zur Förderung Christlicher Theologie (Gütersloh: Bertelsmann Verlag, 1904).

59. There is from my perspective no hint of Ernst Käsemann's suggestion

that the redeemer needs to be redeemed. See Ernst Käsemann, *Wandering People of God: An Investigation of the Letter to the Hebrews*, trans. R. Harrisville and I. Sandberg (Minneapolis: Augsburg Publishing House, 1984), pp. 87-117.

60. For a balanced perspective of the problem of Esau see Peter Rhea Jones, "A Superior Life: Hebrews 12:3-13:25," *Review and Expositor* 82 (1985): 394-396. See Marshall, pp. 150-151, who suggests a model of apostate Christians.

61. See the interesting work of Karl Menninger, *Whatever Became of Sin?* (Ne York: Hawthorne Books, 1973).

62. Theologians since Rudolf Otto, *The Idea of the Holy*, rev. ed., trans. ,. Harvey (London: Oxford University Press, 1928) are fond of referring to the mysterious terrifying aspect of God as the *mysterium tremendum*. There is something present about God that makes mere humans sense their unworthiness. Without the blood of Jesus we would fall in utter terror. But even in and through the blood of Jesus we must bow in grateful wonder at the mercy of God. Christians must take care never to play fast and loose with the grace of God in Christ Jesus our Lord.

63. Filson.

64. Elliot.

65. See note 26.

66. Marshall, p. 152, moves part of the way in the direction which I have sought here.

5

A Conclusion Concerning
Assurance and Warning

A Brief Review

As you journeyed through the pages of this study with me, it should have been evident that the messages of the apostle, the evangelist, and the preacher were quite different in structure and perspective. Nevertheless, it should have been equally evident that there was a great compatibility of viewpoints when dealing with the interrelationship between our wonderfully consistent God and the frail ties of us who are inconsistent human beings.

While studying the Corinthian epistle, we have seen that Paul sustained a positive sense of the assurance of God, even with such a chaotic group of Christian windbags. Somehow the apostle must have seen the hand of God working in the midst of chaos. Perhaps Paul's vision can inspire tired Christian workers of today so that we will look beyond the divisive situations in our churches and remember that we may be called to warn our people that immorality and factionalism is not the way of Christ our Lord.

Or as we reflected on the great Johannine gospel with its picture of the rejection of Jesus, the hostility of His enemies, and the helpless lonely feeling of the disciples, we have gained the feeling that John understood very well the elements of discouragement that often plague Christian servants. But even as we identify these feelings, we need to recognize that the Johannine answer is not to be found by looking at the world and its confusing ways. Rather the answer is to be perceived in looking to King Jesus, who stands serene in the midst of every type of frustration.

If we have pondered sufficiently the magnificent sermon of the preacher who wrote Hebrews, perhaps we are in some measure able to identify with that fearful group of Christians who knew firsthand the pain and anguish of persecution and the looting of their property. Maybe we can even stretch our imaginations to feel with them the terror of an approaching dark cloud on the horizon that would demand the blood of the early Christians. If we can sense these feelings of fear, perhaps we can also understand the powerful force that was communicated by the images of the way of Christ as being superior to angels, Moses, the high priest, and the patterns of ancient worship. Indeed, we might even discover a message of strength and contemporary relevance in the preacher's call to remember the faithful of the past and join the company of those who, with reliance on God, are able to persevere in the face of torture and death itself.

Each of these inspired writers glimpsed a vision of God's amazing power in the world, and each understood where true security was to be found. Each reached a marvelous assurance in God, and each longed to communicate that confidence to others. Each of them also knew that the cost of such assurance was a genuine commitment of a person's life to the way of Christ Jesus, the Lord. All of them, therefore, warned their readers that halfhearted commitment, grasping self-interest, and playing games with the way of God had devastating consequences.

They knew that God was absolutely serious in sending His Son into the world. To treat God's Son casually, therefore, is tantamount to spitting in Jesus' face. So convinced were these writers in the righteous severity of God's judgment that they did not want *any Christian reader* to treat sin casually. They were appalled at the thought that any Christian might suffer judgment. Therefore, their warnings flash like lightning on the pages of Holy Scripture. "Flee immorality," thundered Paul (1 Cor. 6:18). "Dreadful" it is, responded the preacher, "to fall into the hands of the living God" (Heb. 10:31). "I have spoken these things," said Jesus, "in order that you might not be scandalized" is the awesome message in John (John 16:1).

These warnings are harsh in their intensity. The calls for repentance in the face of sin are absolutely clear. Positive response is expected because failure to treat the warnings seriously is regarded as the equivalent of placing one's life in jeopardy. The writers, however, were convinced that Christians would heed these warnings and not treat lightly the discipline of the Lord.

Now the concern of the New Testament writers was not the academic study of security or apostasy. That may be the concern of some Christians today. We may have free time and extra energy to debate these issues. Such was not the case with the apostle, the evangelist, and the preacher. These writers were convinced that the very existence of the church was at stake. They were writing in the face of hostile forces and de-energizing threats. To yield to the threats of persecution or to the temptations of syncretistically adopting the ways of culture would have meant the demise of the church. They were not going to let that happen. They had a mission from God to establish the church as God's outpost in their society, and they were about that business in earnest.

Our Great Questions

As we of today study these books, however, questions flood our minds. Particularly is that true of people who are heirs of both the Armenian and Calvinistic traditions. In their evangelistic zeal, they often vigorously proclaim that "whosoever will may come!" And in their deep concern for security, they equally preach "once saved, always saved!" In confidently affirming these slogans, they scarcely recognize the incredible theological tensions they bring on themselves.

There is tension in the books of the New Testament, and we have witnessed this tension throughout our study. But often our superficial practice and our slogans force our tensions into an intolerable position. Using another slogan, constructed from a misreading of John 1:12 "*even* to them that believe in his name" (KJV), we even fiercely proclaim that *all* you have to do is believe in the name of Jesus. The "*even*" in that text becomes for us a kind of minimal amount of belief necessary for salvation. But that "*even*" is not even in the Greek!

To believe in the name of Jesus for John was not a minimal statement of belief; it was a maximal statement since "the name" for him implied an understanding of the nature of Jesus. Moreover, believing for John was not an intellectual assent to a "belief" but the entrusting of one's self to a person. Remember that John avoided the noun for "belief" (*pistis*) and used only the verb "to believe" or "to entrust" oneself to Christ (*pisteuein*).[1] Remember also that a growing heretical tendency in John's day, later known as Gnosticism, focused on "beliefs." John wanted to make sure his readers understood clearly that it was not *what* you believed but *in whom* you entrusted yourself that brought about salvation.

I am committed to the evangelization of the world, but evangelism must not be superficial.[2] All preachers and evangelists need to look for better ways to ensure that the people who answer their invitations are concerned about genuine transformation. If we gave more attention to transformation, perhaps we would have less concern for the security of the people in our churches. In other words: If we guarded the front door better, perhaps we would have less concern about the back door!

It is absolutely tragic when anyone tries to phrase salvation in terms of a quick-fix treatment. Salvation is a life commitment of a person to the living God. The idea of a quick-fix treatment trivializes our Christ, our gospel, and our marvelous salvation. Such ideas are the result of poor theology by Christians who are trying to appeal to the rootlessness of the "now" generation in which all of eternity is pigeon-holed in the "now." The "now" can be very appealing; if one only sees the "now" of salvation, one can easily forget to deal with the implications of the gospel. I am absolutely convinced in the need for decision-making. Yet far too many decisions are being encouraged where people have little intention of living the Christian life. To the rootless and fruitless advocates of salvation, writers like the preacher of Hebrews and the teacher of James fling their fiery darts.

Those who define salvation merely in terms of justification—in the manner of the street evangelist who, as I mentioned earlier, asked the Scottish theologian, "Brother, are you saved?"—need to see the multidimensional nature of salvation. Justification or beginning the pilgrimage with Christ is not the only meaning of being saved in the New Testament. Being saved also refers to the process of becoming holy or to sanctification. In addition, being saved refers to the final experience of joining Christ in heaven. It is not all over when one joins Christ in justification. There is far more to salvation than an initial yes to Christ and a public profession of faith in Christ. That is the reason Paul the apostle, John the evangelist, and the preacher of Hebrews all warned Christians.

These inspired writers were fully aware of the tendency among members of the Christian community to take lightly their initial commitments. Therefore, they did not want anyone to misunderstand the nature of Christian commitment. They were not interested in debating "the apostasy issue," as we phrase it. They knew too much about human nature to get involved in such a debate. They seemed to understand better than we do the ingredients of salvation, and they knew God was continually working to bring the salvation relationship to its conclusion.

The New Testament writers were not boxed-in by our *"thingified" view of salvation.* We tend to "thingify" grace and faith, and we end up with a *thing called salvation* that is foreign to the Bible. We often think about salvation as an exchange of things. Accordingly we may imagine that God gives us some *thing* called grace, and we give to God some *thing* called faith. We seem to think that the exchange of things results in another *thing* called salvation, which we can lock in some safety deposit box because God will not take the *thing* (salvation) away from us. We are even more convinced that we have the thing (salvation) if we can obtain a baptismal certificate because we somehow think that it will guarantee to us that we have that *thing*.

But salvation is not a thing! It is the description of a relationship. God does not merely give us a thing called grace. He gives us Himself! And we do not simply give God a thing called faith. We give Him ourselves! We are, therefore, in a relationship with God that needs to be nurtured and needs to grow constantly. Some of us are growing, and some of us are not.

The New Testament writers took seriously the necessity for growth. As Christians, we need to remember that the New Testament books were not primarily written to non-Christians. They were written to Christians who needed to grow in Christ. Even the Synoptic Gospels were catechetical documents (written for the purpose of instructing new believers). The question then is, How much attention do we give in our churches to the issue of faithfulness and growth in Christ?

One of the big problems in many churches is a great lack in the understanding of faith development.[3] We have concentrated so much on the invitation and the issue of justification that when persons want to make a further commitment to God we sometimes think we need to baptize them again and again or that they need to go into the full-time ministry.

Perhaps someone's first baptism was understandably inadequate, given the way we often deal with children. But I doubt that such would be the basic problem with the second or third baptisms. I have met some people who have been baptized four times! I wonder if we really understand what growth and sanctification is all about.

With respect to the full-time ministry, I am fully convinced that we need continually to issue invitations to consider the ministry. My point, however, is that we also need a focus on the great middle ground between the initial commitment and a call to ministry. We need to deal more effectively with the life of holiness *in all believers*. That middle ground was the main interest of the writers of the New Testament.

These writers took seriously the reality of the church and expected the people of the church to live like transformed people. They also knew that living in the world would be an immensely difficult task because of the constant temptation to compromise with the ways of the world. Moreover, they were fully aware that new members in the infant churches were on the verge of experiencing imminent hostility in the form of various persecutions from both Jews and Gentiles. Therefore, their writings are laced with warnings.

The New Testament writers were concerned with holding the church together in the face of all sorts of threats. Their answer was rooted in a deep sense of the living reality of God in their midst. They lived in the confidence that if they trusted in God, God would preserve them. There was no need to fear because God was with them. Their only responsibility was to live authentically for God. But what a responsibility!

Out of this sense of threat and this deep reliance on God, the

New Testament writers forged one of Christianity's most compelling doctrines—*the belief in perseverance*. The two books which seem to trouble concerned readers the most in terms of warning passages are Hebrews and James. The warnings in Hebrews 2:1-3; 4:11-13; 6:1-8; 10:26-31 are matched by similar warnings to faithfulness in James 1:12-15 and to the task of saving our souls in 1:21 and saving a wandering brother's soul in 5:19-20. Yet these same works speak most eloquently of perseverance. In Hebrews 12:1-2 the call is to sense the resources of our great heritage and to run with perseverance the difficult marathon of the Christian life. In James the call is no less gripping. Christians, James argued in 1:25, are not merely superficial hearers of God's Word but are those who persevere in putting into action what they have heard. Real religion and real Christianity, therefore, are to be seen in people who do God's Word and not merely listen to it (Jas. 1:22-27).

But lest readers once again become involved in the intellectual questions of apostasy, let it be quickly noted that the writers of the New Testament had an almost incredible conviction that Christian readers would listen, understand, and obey the admonitions and warnings. The inspired authors did not write in the anticipation that they were making mere suggestions. They expected real Christians to live like Christians. Anyone not living up to the life-style expected of a Christian needed to be disciplined like Paul ordered concerning the man who was living with his father's wife (1 Cor. 5:1-5). Moreover, Paul expected the discipline to work to the man's ultimate salvation.

But what shall we conclude of our churches today? Is life-style actually important? Are we really interested in whether people have genuinely come to terms with the sin that is in their lives? Or are we primarily involved in *the words* of the gospel? Do we lie and cheat in the name of Jesus? Do we bless God and curse men as James suggests (3:9-10)? Are we at war and is there fighting among us (James 4:1)? Is our Christian life on the line? Or has our religion become as institutionalized as that of the Jews in the days of Jesus? Perhaps we need another visit from the God who will force us to cleanse our lives and our churches of the spreading evil of inconsistency that defiles the name of Christ (see 1 Cor. 5:8; Gal. 5:7-10).

Do we as Christians join battles in matters of words and let the weightier matters of our faith, like justice and integrity, pass us by with little notice. The prophets knew the nature of such superficial religion in Israel, and they told the people God was sick of their religious sacrifices (see Amos 5; Hosea 6-10; Mic. 6). What would the prophets say of our churches and denominations today? May we all pray that God will permit us to experience the cleansing power of repentance, and may we turn from our superficial proclamations of salvation to evidence the depth of authentic faith. May we hear not only the assurances of our salvation; may we, likewise, attend to the warnings of Scripture. Thus, may we truly understand the power of a persevering faith in the God who is with us.

A Needed Perspective

John, 1 Corinthians, and Hebrews were written to Christians. These writings were directed toward strengthening both the church and Christians. The Christians needed a word from God about their lives. We must never forget this fact as we read the New Testament. These writers knew the battle was not over when a person took the name Christian. It had barely begun! To become a Christian meant the beginning of a total transformation process in life. Such a transformation would not happen without a struggle. The devil would see to it.

God, however, is also involved in the struggle. He cares about His people. His Son died for them! He wants them to reach the eternal promised land. God, of course, could have made His people robots. He could have punched in a program on the computers of their lives. But he did not create Christians that way. If he had, His Son would not have needed to die. Yet Jesus Christ did die! But that death was not the end of the message because our Lord was raised from the dead. Jesus' resurrection has become the basis for the Christian hope (for example, 1 Cor. 15:20). Somehow our Lord understood human weakness and human sinfulness, as He understood the motivations of Judas Iscariot (John 6:70-71; 13:21-30)! God knows how to deal with humanity!

But we may not know how to deal with God. When human weakness touches divine strength, we humans confront the threshold of an almost intolerable tension. We cannot resolve this tension with simple defini- tions or pious verbal formulas. This tension is part of the mystery inherent in the divine-human relationship. While God graciously works with us, we do not become divine. We, like the writers of the New Testament, never become gods—not even mini-gods! As Christians we are still frail, imperfect human beings from whom God does not remove our personal wills. Even though we may struggle to become more like our Savior, we do not become perfect.

Perfection, as Paul indicated in his hymnic chapter on love, is not experienced in this world's order. Even for the best of us, the perfect or complete is only our hope, or goal. It is not our experience (1 Cor. 13:9-10). It is something about which we may talk, discuss, and theologize. But we do not understand perfection firsthand. We strive for it and fail. Therefore, we must confess our sinfulness and our willful straying from God's way. Sin is not something that is foreign to us as Christians. It is a reality with which we all struggle.

In writing to his Christian children in the faith, John reminded them that a holier-than-thou attitude was totally unacceptable. If we suppose for a moment that we are devoid of sin, he reminded us, we create a critical situation because we treat Jesus as a "liar" and we indicate that his redeeming "word is not resident in us" (1 John 1:10; see 1:8). John wrote those words particularly for Christians! He did not want the followers of Christ to live before others and pretend before God an inauthentic piety. He wanted Christians to be honest, and he wanted them to live continuously in a state of dependence upon God in which humble confession of sin was a way of life (1 John 1:9).

Dependence on God is one of the most pervading themes of the Bible. From the tree of life in the Garden (Gen. 3:22) to the tree of life with its monthly fruit in the great city of God (Rev. 22:2), the hope of humanity is found not in self-assertion (to be "like God," Gen. 3:5), but in dependence. From the guiding pillars of both smoke and fire and the traveling tabernacle of meeting in the Exodus to the tabernacling Holy Spirit, which substitutes as a companion for the earthly Jesus in the life of the believer (John 1:14; 14:16), dependence is an encompassing biblical theme.

As Christians we must admit openly that we are not perfect and that we are surely not gods. But in utter dependence and in reverent humility, we are to proclaim that "Emmanuel" has come ("God with us," Matt. 1:23). Moreover, we are fervently to desire that God's Spirit continually dwell in us and bring about the marvelous transforming work of "God in us" (John 14:17). The presence of God in our lives does *not* make us *superhuman*. It ought to make us *supersensitive to sin* in our own lives. What frequently happens, however, is that Christians become *superjudgmental* of others and fail to notice the sin that is in their own lives.

We as Christians need to be sensitive to the destructive nature of much of the criticism that is present in the church because it is frequently accompanied by a satanic hypocrisy. Jesus condemned forthrightly such hypocrisy among the Jewish pietists. The Pharisees prided themselves in their holiness and in their correct interpretations of Scripture. They even developed protective rules and interpretations around scriptural texts because they feared being slightly out of sync in one area of interpretation. Scholars refer to that ancient process of protecting Scripture with more rigid interpretations than enunciated by Scripture itself as "fencing the Torah." The Pharisees felt perfectly justified in complaining about the tiny splinters of what they considered improper faith patterns in the eyes of other people. Their big problem, Jesus said, was that they failed to see the huge logs of life-inconsistencies in their own eyes (cf. Matt. 7:3-5).

Hypocrisy is an ever present cancer that feeds among religious people. It is not something that was confined to the synagogue and Jewish pietists. It haunts the halls of the church as well. Our Lord knew how to condemn unrighteousness and warned us not to condemn others quickly or easily. Instead, He soberly promised us that the way we judge others would become the pattern for the way we would be judged (see Matt. 7:1-2).

But there is something else to consider. The life of the Christian ought to be marked by a spirit of forgiveness and reconciliation. Many Christians fail to recognize that every time we pray the Lord's Prayer we may in fact be *calling on God to send judgment* and condemnation upon us. We ask the Father to "forgive us . . . as we forgive" (Matt.

6:12)! In providing us with this Model Prayer, Jesus gave us a warning of the way we ought to live. Failure to recognize this warning can be devastating in its consequences.

Moreover, we must never suggest that the warning in our Model Prayer does not apply to us. Matthew knew it applied to Christians. And God knows it applies! As Christians we need to realize that no matter what positions we may hold in our churches, schools, or denominations, we will not move God by our places of authority.

When God warns us about our lives and we fail to heed His warning, we need to understand that that attitude is what the Old Testament calls sinning with the high hand. Only a direct confrontation with God, involving a humble confession of sin and a covenant to change one's life, can deal with such a problem. But thanks be to God that He sent Jesus and assured us in Christ that we might find His ever-needed forgiveness and strength to start our lives daily anew with our Savior.

Our concern, however, is not merely to deal with our sinfulness. Our task as Christians is also to prepare for Christ's coming. He has assured us that He will return. Our daily prayer, therefore, together with Paul ought to include some form of the early Christian prayer *marana tha*, "Come! our Lord!" (1 Cor. 16:22). Set in the context of a Greek letter, these Aramaic words were undoubtedly so well known in their meaning that they did not even need to be translated into Greek. Here was the early Christian hope wrapped into a very few words. Christian assurance is ultimately packaged, not in ourselves, but in the coming of our Lord. That prayer ought to tingle the spine of every Christian because that prayer summarizes who we are.

We, as the preacher of Hebrews viewed us, are a people on pilgrimage. We await the great day of the coming of our Lord (see, Phil. 1:6; 2:16; 4:5). In the meantime, we have the responsibility to prepare ourselves for that wonderful day. Our prayer, therefore, is also a warning to pay attention to what kind of people we are. To look forward to the coming of the Lord means to take seriously the warnings of Holy Scripture and to join the people of God in their journey to holiness.

Christians who fervently look for the coming of Jesus and seek authentically to prepare themselves in purity with lives that consistently represent the self-giving love of Christ will persevere to the end! God will see to it because they have set their sense of security in God who will not fail them. They are, indeed, *the people of God.*

These people take seriously the divine warnings and know that their security is not found in themselves or in simplistic verbal formulas. Their security is found in their Savior to whom they owe their absolute allegiance and whose life of self-giving love they have taken as the model for their own lives. They are the genuine people of God because as frail human beings they have found their security in God alone! They can live with the tension of assurance *and* warning! They can live with this tension because in Christ they know they will persevere to the end!

Notes

1. Not only did John not use the noun for belief (*pistis*) but he also did not use the noun for knowledge (*gnōsis*). He used only the verbs "to believe" (*ginōskō* and *oida*). See also my remarks in Chapter 3 in relation to John the Baptist.

2. See Gerald L. Borchert, *Dynamics of Evangelism* (Waco: Word Books, 1976).

3. See my faculty address "Romans, Pastoral Counseling and the Introspective Conscience of the West," *Review and Expositor* 83 (1986), pp. 81-91.